Interactions with Japanese Buddhism

Eastern Buddhist Voices

Series Editor: Michael Pye

Shin Buddhist Comprehensive Research Institute, Ōtani University, Kyōto, Japan

Volume 1
Beyond Meditation: Expressions of Japanese Shin Buddhist Spirituality

Volume 2
Listening to Shin Buddhism: Starting Points of Modern Dialogue

Volume 3
*Interactions with Japanese Buddhism:
Explorations and Viewpoints in Twentieth-Century Kyōto*

Volume 4
Buddhist Temples of Kyōto and Kamakura
Beatrice Lane Suzuki
Edited by Michael Pye

Volume 5
Lay Buddhism and Spirituality: From Vimalakīrti to the Nenbutsu Masters

Volume 6
*A Taiwanese Mahhyamaka?
The Monk Yinshun (1906-2005) and his Study on Da Zhidu Lun*

Interactions with Japanese Buddhism

Explorations and Viewpoints in Twentieth-Century Kyōto

Edited by Michael Pye
with the assistance of
The Eastern Buddhist Society

Eastern Buddhist Voices, Volume 3

SHEFFIELD UK   BRISTOL CT

Published by Equinox Publishing Ltd.

UK: Unit S3, Kelham House, 3 Lancaster Street, Sheffield, S3 8AF
USA: ISD, 70 Enterprise Drive, Bristol, CT 06010

www.equinoxpub.com

Paperback edition published 2013.

© Michael Pye and contributors 2012

© Editorial matter and selection, 2012 Michael Pye.
Individual essays, *The Eastern Buddhist*.

All rights reserved. No part of this publication may be reproduced or transmitted in any form or by any means, electronic or mechanical, including photocopying, recording or any information storage or retrieval system, without prior permission in writing from the publishers.

ISBN: 978-1-908049-18-6 (hardback)
978-1-908049-19-3 (paperback)

British Library Cataloguing-in-Publication Data

A catalogue record for this book is available from the British Library.

Library of Congress Cataloging-in-Publication Data

Interactions with Japanese Buddhism : explorations and viewpoints in twentieth-century Kyoto / edited by Michael Pye, with the assistance of The Eastern Buddhist Society.
    pages cm -- (Eastern Buddhist voices ; v. 3)
Includes bibliographical references and index.
ISBN 978-1-908049-18-6 (hardcover)
  1. Buddhism--Doctrines. 2. Philosophy, Japanese--20th century. I. Pye, Michael, editor of compilation. II. Eastern Buddhist.
BQ4165.I58 2012
294.30952'0904--dc23

2012010764

Printed and bound in Great Britain by Lightning Source UK, Milton Keynes

This book is dedicated to the memory of
Minoura Eryō 箕浦恵了 (1935–2011)
who through his life and work did so much to promote
interaction between the thought of East and West

Contents

Preface with Acknowledgements   ix
Conventions on Names, Titles and Scripts   xi

Introduction   1

PART I: FLASHBACK TO SOME EARLY EXCHANGES   9

1   Buddhism and Moral World Order   11
    Kiba Ryōhon

2   On Zen Buddhism   17
    Rudolf Otto

3   Dengyō Daishi and German Theology   24
    Bruno Petzold

4   The Unity of Buddhism   32
    James Bissett Pratt

5   Shinran's Concept of Buddhist History   47
    Soga Ryōjin

PART II: THINKING ABOUT ZEN BUDDHISM IN THE 1960s   61

6   Zen: Its Meaning for Modern Civilization   63
    Hisamatsu Shin'ichi

7   The Awakening of Self in Buddhism   82
    Nishitani Keiji

CONTENTS

8	Introducing Martin Heidegger *Nishitani Keiji*	91
9	Home: The Seven-Hundredth Anniversary of the Town of Messkirch *Martin Heidegger*	102
10	Zen and Compassion *Abe Masao*	109

PART III: RESPONSES TO SUZUKI DAISETSU — 123

11	The Stone Bridge of Jōshū *Kondō Akihisa*	125
12	The Enlightened Thought *Kobori Sōhaku*	132
13	The "Mind-less" Scholar *Alan Watts*	141
14	Memories of Dr. D.T. Suzuki *Erich Fromm*	145
15	A Personal Tribute *Edward Conze*	149
16	Zen and Philology: On Ui Hakuju and Suzuki Daisetsu *Ueda Yoshifumi*	151
17	D.T. Suzuki and Pure Land Buddhism *Bandō Shōjun*	165

PART IV: THINKING ABOUT THE PURE LAND — 171

18	The Concept of the Pure Land *Kaneko Daiei*	173
19	The Pure Land of Beauty *Yanagi Sōetsu*	183

Appendix 1: Synoptic List of Text Titles	207
Appendix 2: Character List for Historical Persons	229
Appendix 3: Original Publication Details	234
Appendix 4: A Note on The Eastern Buddhist	236
Index	239

Preface with Acknowledgements

This book, like its two predecessors in the series Eastern Buddhist Voices, is the result of collaboration between its editor and the staff of the Eastern Buddhist Society which, among its various activities, publishes the journal *The Eastern Buddhist*. This is the historic journal from which the essays below are drawn. The offices of the society are located within Ōtani University in Kyōto. In addition, the editor's work was facilitated by the research resources of the Shin Buddhist Comprehensive Research Institute, which is also housed in Ōtani University. Moreover, support was given in various respects by the head temple of the Shinshū Ōtani-ha branch of Shin Buddhism, the Higashi Honganji 東本願寺, also in Kyōto. To each of these institutions, my gratitude is hereby most warmly expressed.

The support of staff members of the Eastern Buddhist Society was most important in dealing with the resolution of various linguistic and other problems. Here I mention with warm gratitude Dr Michael Conway, Sanskrit specialist Dr Miyako Mao, and Ms Kisa Ito.[1] Overall guidance and advice was given by Professor Inoue Takami and Professor Yasutomi Shin'ya of Ōtani University and the Eastern Buddhist Society. Advice on Chinese derivations and transcriptions was kindly given by Dr Peiying Lin. Professor Thomas Sheehan's permission to use his copyrighted English translation of a piece by Martin Heidegger (details below) is gratefully acknowledged. Finally, thanks are recorded to those who translated or edited some of the articles at the time of their original publication in *The Eastern Buddhist*: Bandō Shōjun, Bernard Leach, Richard de Martino, Tokiwa Gishin, Dennis Hirota and Wayne

---

1. Japanese names are given in the Japanese order, family name first (as here Miyako), except in Americanized cases (as here Ito).

S. Yokoyama. Responsibility for editorial decisions relating to the re-use of materials from the journal lies with the editor of this volume. The opportunity and permission to present such valuable and interesting materials once again to a wider world are gratefully acknowledged.

Michael Pye

Conventions on Names, Titles and Scripts

In principle, all words from Asian languages are shown in italics with diacritical marks as appropriate. The exceptions are as follows:

Buddha	for "the Buddha" or in names of buddhas
buddha/s	for any buddha or buddhas in the plural
Bodhisattva	in names of bodhisattvas
bodhisattva/s	for any bodhisattva or bodhisattvas in the plural
Dharma	meaning the Teaching of the Buddha
dharma/s	meaning elements or factors of existence
karma	
Nembutsu	capitalized and with an "m" if the author so used it, otherwise *nenbutsu*
nirvana	when so used in a general context by an author, otherwise *nirvāṇa*
Nirvana	may also be shown capitalized, if the author so used it
Samgha	only when capitalized in English as a proper noun for the Buddhist order, otherwise *saṃgha*

The same exceptions apply for Pāli forms: bodhisatta/s, Dhamma, dhamma/s, kamma, nibbana, Nibbana, Sangha. In the earlier decades of the twentieth century it was still quite common, in English, to capitalize all kinds of words deemed to be important, and this practice was imitated by non-native users with some enthusiasm. Here, capital letters have usually been edited out, but insofar as they remain, the intention is to maintain the flavour of the original publications.

Policy on the presentation of personal names, the titles of Buddhist works and the scripts used have been guided by three considerations. First, we have tried to be fair to the authors, maintaining the flavour of their writing while not leaving correctable errors. Second, we have sought to be of service to readers, who may be coming to these writings for the first time. Third, while alternatives provided by authors were in many cases helpful, this also led to considerable unevenness; in this regard we have aimed for greater consistency throughout the volume.

Transliteration systems used here follow modern standards, that is by using the *pīnyīn* system for Chinese and Sanskrit transliteration with diacritical marks as used by Indologists today. This is good practice for Buddhist Studies in general. For Japanese, the Hepburn system is used with slight modifications. The main modifications are the use of "n" instead of the phonetically closer "m" in words such as *nenbutsu* (except when Nembutsu is maintained because of the flavour of the period) and the use of an apostrophe to separate potentially confused syllables when the letter "n" is followed by a vowel (e.g. *den'e*). While there is wide agreement over preference for the Hepburn system there is no completely authoritative guide to its modifications.[1] When it comes to Chinese characters as used in Japan (*kanji*, or Sino-Japanese characters) we generally follow the typographical reform undertaken in the postwar years. Alternatives may also be shown, especially in some historical China-related contexts. Some use is made of spaces and hyphens, although they do not occur in the original languages. Thus endings in Japanese such as –*shū* (meaning denomination) are shown with a hyphen. Endings of Chinese text names such as *jīng* (*sūtra*) and *lùn* (treatise) are shown separated, but not in Japanese where they have become fully integrated. In general, the tendency to break text titles up into their components has been resisted. Shinran's famous work is shown as *Kyōgyōshinshō* rather than *Kyō Gyō Shin Shō*. Special details of policy will be found in the reference lists of text titles and personal names at the end of the volume.

Japanese Buddhists typically use canonical texts in their Chinese form, even though many of them are presumed to have originated in India. When our authors were writing, the Sanskrit originals of such Chinese texts were still being identified for the first time, while in some cases it was becoming clear that no Sanskrit original could be found at all. There are two reasons why there may be no Sanskrit original for a Chinese Buddhist text. First, it may have been irretrievably lost. This can never be finally determined, as the

---

1. This is explained in detail in the first volume of this series, *Beyond Meditation*.

very recent discovery of a Sanskrit manuscript of *The Teaching of Vimalakīrti* has shown. Second, however, a text may never have existed in Sanskrit to begin with, even though it was named as "a *sūtra*" of the Buddha or was a treatise ascribed to a famous Indian Buddhist personality. Reluctance to recognize such fictions led to the retrospective invention and use of Sanskrit titles to create an aura of authenticity, even though this misled students and other readers. In a number of cases the *non*-existence of a Sanskrit original has now become clear for very good reasons of language and content. Important examples of this are the *Sūtra on the Visualization of Amitābha* (観無量寿経 *Guānwúliàngshòu jīng*, Japanese: *Kanmuryōjukyō*), which is one of the three basic sūtras of Pure Land Buddhism, and *The Awakening of Faith in the Mahāyāna* (大乗起信論 *Dàshèngqǐxìn lùn*,[2] Japanese: *Daijōkishinron*), a very popular text in East Asia which was piously ascribed to Aśvaghoṣa.

To some extent it is the notion of "authenticity" and the very respect in which Sanskrit is held which has led to unnecessary difficulties. As a matter of historical fact there are many *sūtras* in Sanskrit itself which are piously ascribed to the Buddha but do not in fact go back directly to him at all. The Sanskrit of the *sūtras* was in any case not the Buddha's own personal language. Given this, the mere fact that a *sūtra* developed or was composed in Chinese does not necessarily make it less "authentic" than one which first appeared in Sanskrit. Fortunately, in the pages of *The Eastern Buddhist*, while the assumptions of traditional piety continue to be evident to some extent, we also find a clear respect for the findings of modern scholarship. This is itself part of the voice of modern Buddhism.

---

2. Also pronounced *Dà chéng qǐxìn lùn*.

Introduction

From the very beginning of the publication of *The Eastern Buddhist* in the 1920s much interest was directed towards the underlying ideas of the Buddhism of the Great Vehicle – Mahāyāna Buddhism. It was within this perspective that the Pure Land Buddhism of Hōnen, Shinran and others was explored in *Beyond Meditation*, the first volume in the present book series. In the second volume, *Listening to Shin Buddhism, Starting Points of Modern Dialogue*, a stronger emphasis was placed on Shin Buddhism, as defined by Shinran and Rennyo, and on how the voice of Shin Buddhism came to be heard increasingly by the world outside Japan. The present volume, the third in the series, is subtitled *Explorations and Viewpoints in Twentieth-Century Kyōto*. Here a greater complexity is brought into view. In view of the postwar resurgence of interest in Zen, it is not surprising that much interest came to be focused on what is generally known as the "Kyōto school" which was mainly Zen-oriented. Yet we should also recognize that there were considerable interactions between Zen and Shin Buddhist thinkers, and that it was in fact this wider complex which developed such a strong base in Kyōto. Thanks to *The Eastern Buddhist* the interactions between Shin Buddhism and Zen Buddhism, and between both of these and Western intellectual and religious orientations, were developing rapidly in various ways. This process is reflected in the present volume.

To maintain the historical perspective we introduce first some contributions from the prewar period in Part I, "Flashback to Some Early Exchanges." These refer to Zen, Tendai and Shin Buddhism. The first interaction arose out of the global activities of Rudolf Otto, who while holding a position as professor of systematic theology at the University of Marburg in Germany (i.e. Christian theology in the Protestant tradition) did so much to push forward the historical and systematic study of religions in general. He was particularly interested in the devotional and mystical traditions of India and, within the multifaceted religious scene of Japan, in Zen Buddhism. At that juncture the "study of religions" was itself in large part a religiously motivated activity, and Otto founded not only a religiously neutral museum of religions (Religionskundliche Sammlung) in Marburg but also, in 1921, an interreligious organization known as the Religiöser Menschheitsbund ("Association of Religious Humanity"). It was at a gathering of this association that Kiba Ryōhon 木場了本 contributed the paper "Buddhism and Moral World Order" with which we begin. This is followed by Rudolf Otto's "On Zen Buddhism" which, while deeply indebted to D.T. Suzuki, documents the former's own perceptions of Zen.

At that time, however, German observers of the Buddhist scene were not at all fixated on Zen alone. Indeed the earlier engagement with Buddhism within Germany had been more focused on the Theravāda transmission, then widely presumed to be the most ancient and hence authentic tradition derived from the Buddha himself. However, in the remarkable case of Bruno Petzold we meet a fascination with the complex system of Tendai Buddhism, out of which so much of later Japanese Buddhism developed, including both the Zen and Pure Land schools. Like Otto, Petzold was not interested in philological research for its own sake, but in posing comparative challenges, and this he did in his article "Dengyō Daishi and German Theology." Dengyō Daishi (or Saichō 最澄, 767–822) was the systematic introducer to Japan of the Chinese Tiāntái school founded by Zhíyǐ 智顗 (538–97). By "German Theology" Petzold means, not the theology of his day, which at the time was still engrossed in dealing with the impact of historical criticism, but the mediaeval mystical writing known as *Theologia Germanica* which had been picked up with enthusiasm long before by Martin Luther. This was an early example of those Buddhist–Christian encounters which have focused on the mystical strand within Christianity as the most promising point of contact for exploration. We see from this that a new form of interreligious globalization was already bursting into being.

But what is "Buddhism"? This question is one which cannot be avoided, as James Bissett Pratt most plausibly explains. His title "The Unity of Buddhism" may certainly be taken as a challenge, even though it does not bear a question mark, for Western observers and interlocutors were increasingly aware of "Buddhism's" diversity. Today we sometimes meet impatience both with such questions and proposed answers, which are very quickly stamped on as "essentialism" – by which is meant an unwarranted search for an "essence" where there is none. In fact "essence" is not a word which Pratt used. But he addresses head-on the inevitable questions of coherence and consistency which arise within any religious tradition which displays striking diversity. These questions are as pertinent today as they were then. While Pratt's main work was about Indian religions, mainly in the Hindu mould, he was well aware of the varieties of Buddhism in East Asia. His essay is therefore extremely instructive, whether or not we now follow the specific details of his attempt to summarize the "character" of Buddhism.

What such Western and Eastern thinkers shared was a profound consciousness of the historicity of religious traditions. It is striking that while the Western authors were taking cognizance of the Eastern faiths as part of a newly emerging "history of religions" this very aspect of historicity was being taken up as a challenge to the religious consciousness itself in the context of Shin Buddhism. The subtle essay by Soga Ryōjin 曾我量深 (1875–1971) was not translated into English until 1995, and yet it was first published in Japanese in 1935.[1] By raising the question of "Buddhist history" in the mind of Shinran, the mediaeval founder-figure of Shin Buddhism, it challenges readers to regard all these developments as legitimate parts of "Buddhist history" while at the same time insisting on historicist presuppositions. It therefore illustrates one of the ways in which Shin Buddhist thinkers were coming to terms with modernity at that time, just as were their early twentieth-century counterparts in the field of Christian theology.

In Part II, "Thinking about Zen Buddhism in the 1960s," we move forward to a time when Zen Buddhism was becoming more prominent in the Western mind. Some important figures are introduced here: Hisamatsu Shin'ichi 久松真一 (1889–1980), Nishitani Keiji 西谷啓治 (1900–90) and Abe Masao 阿部正雄 (1915–2006). We begin with Hisamatsu's "Zen: Its Meaning for Modern Civilization," relatively brief and in some ways idiosyncratic. Nishitani Keiji was the successor of the philosopher Nishida Kitarō 西田幾多郎 (1870–1945) at Kyōto University, and shared his general orientation in relation to Zen Buddhism, thus leading to the popular designation "the Kyōto School." But his approach to Buddhism was based on considerations which go beyond the denominational characteristics of Japanese Zen, as may be seen here in "The Awakening of Self in Buddhism."

Nishitani had a significant interaction with the Western world in the context of which he met Martin Heidegger in Germany. As a result *The Eastern Buddhist* was able to publish two early writings by Martin Heidegger in German with an introduction by Nishitani in English. Though incidental in character, the pieces by Heidegger are quite characteristic of his thought. The first, "Home: The Seven Hundredth Anniversary of the Town of Messkirch," has been translated into English by Thomas Sheehan.[2] Space does not permit the inclusion of Heidegger's rather longer second piece, entitled "Über Abraham a Santa Clara," which leads into directions which are not quite so relevant

---

1. For a more detailed introduction see also Wayne S. Yokoyama's, "Two Thinkers on Shin: Selections from the Writings of Soga Ryōjin and Kaneko Daiei," *The Eastern Buddhist* New Series 28.1 (1995), 123–6.
2. His translation was first published in an earlier form as "Messkirch's Seventh Centennial," *Listening* 8.1–3 (1973), 40–57.

here. However, Nishitani's introduction is sufficiently informative about the contents of both articles for his interaction with Heidegger's thought to be easily comprehensible. It is fascinating to see how Heidegger's existential positioning is taken up by Nishitani. More explanations about these texts will be found in an editorial note from the time (1966) which will also be found below.

Following this exchange we place "Zen and Compassion" by Abe Masao, an influential presenter of Zen Buddhism to the Western world and informally a kind of successor to Suzuki Daisetsu. Many of his essays are collected in *Zen and Western Thought*[3] where he shows how Zen might be correlated with a whole string of Western thinkers, Christian or otherwise, such as Nietzsche, Whitehead and Tillich. The present piece is very characteristic of Abe's style and intellectual approach. In general his understanding of Zen somehow fed on his interaction with the West, and in this inverse orientalism he was similar to Suzuki Daisetsu. As he writes himself,

> "If the Greeks," says Dr Suzuki, "taught us how to reason and Christianity what to believe, it is Zen that teaches us to go beyond logic and not to tarry even when we come up against 'the things which are not seen.' For the Zen point of view is to find an absolute point where no dualism in whatever form resides. Logic starts from the division of subject and object, and belief distinguishes between what is seen and what is not seen. The Western mode of thinking can never do away with this eternal dilemma, this or that, reason or faith, man and God, etc. With Zen all these are swept aside as something veiling our insight into the nature of life and reality."

This particular article by Abe was at the same time part of a memorial collection for Suzuki Daisetsu, whose life work was being celebrated in *The Eastern Buddhist* at that time. It leads us to Part III, "Responses to Suzuki Daisetsu," in which we have selected just a few of the many appreciative responses to the influential master. Kondō Akihisa 近藤章久 (1911–99) like Abe, compares Suzuki himself to the stone bridge of Jōshū (Zhàozhōu), an image which was apparently in the air at the time. Kobori Sōhaku 小堀宗柏 (1918–92) explores the relationship between "scholarship" and central features of Zen experience associated with *prajñā* (insight, or "great Wisdom"), *satori* (enlightenment) and compassion. Like Abe, both Kondō and Kobori reflect on presumed differences to Western ways of thinking. Yet there were so many Westerners who seemed to feel an affinity to Suzuki-style Zen. The language inevitably becomes hard to organize consistently. While Kobori refers to "the enlight-

---

3. Edited by William R. LaFleur (Basingstoke: Macmillan, 1985).

ened thought," Alan Watts, the indefatigable promulgator of Zen in North America, writes of Suzuki as a "mind-less" scholar, that is one who overcame the restrictions of ratiocination. Kondō's foray into comparisons with Western psychology are complemented by the valuable reminiscences of psychoanalyst Erich Fromm, with whom the mature Suzuki enjoyed creative collaboration. These statements all tell us not only about the impact of Suzuki Daisetsu in person, but illustrate many of the interactions focused on Zen Buddhism which were taking place between Japan, North America and Europe during the 1960s. We include also a personal tribute by Edward Conze who, in the context of a difficult life experience, found emotional inspiration in the underlying themes of Mahāyāna Buddhism (rather than Zen in particular).[4] Here the question of the role of "scholarship" arises again, for Conze himself worked in the borderlands of Indology to present the important Prajñāpāramitā ("perfection of wisdom") literature to the world. But how does Suzuki's contribution fit into the wider world of scholarly Buddhist studies? Two articles explore this most instructively. On the one hand, the piece by Ueda Yoshifumi 上田義文 (1904–93), first published in Japanese in 1982, brings out a most interesting counterpoint between the motivation of philologically oriented specialists in the Buddhist tradition, represented by the influential figure of Ui Hakuju, and Suzuki's own more existentialist or spiritual interest. Modern Japanese scholarship on the whole corpus of Buddhist literature was beginning to achieve world status, though it was still insufficiently recognized. Suzuki, however, was concerned with the general matrix of Zen Buddhism and Zen-related experience, and it was for this reason, and not as a philologist, that he went to the trouble of working on well-known Mahāyāna texts such as the *Laṅkāvatāra Sūtra* and the *Awakening of Faith in the Mahāyāna* (*Daijōkishinron*). The range, even tension, between philological or "Indological" studies and the philosophico-religious exploration of Buddhist thought, can still be observed in "Buddhist Studies" today. This is also influenced by geographical and institutional location. Being resident in Kyōto as well as in Kamakura, Suzuki's attention was being steadily drawn to the Pure Land tradition, especially Shin Buddhism. While Pure Land Buddhism in general was scorned by the likes of Conze, it was clear for both Suzuki and his commentator Bandō Shōjun that faith centred on the "Original Vow" of Amida Buddha was a significant trend within the more complex tradition of Mahāyāna Buddhism as a whole. For them, it is in this shared matrix that the correlation of Shin and Zen Buddhism is able to take place.

This leads us to the influential concept of the Pure Land of Amida Buddha. In Part IV, "Thinking about the Pure Land," therefore, we conclude this

---

4. Conze also makes awed if relatively slight reference to Suzuki in his privately circulated autobiographical writing *The Memoirs of a Modern Gnostic* (Sherborne: SAMIZDAT Publishing Company, 1978), Part I, 1–100 and Part II, 101–204.

volume with two articles about the Pure Land, the first by Kaneko Daiei 金子大栄 (1881–1976) and the second by Yanagi Sōetsu 柳宗悦 (1889–1961). Both of these, though so different, display distinctly modern orientations. For Kaneko, writing earlier, in 1925 (in Japanese), it is the question of the relation between myth and consciousness which is central, given the abandonment of religious naïvety. With Yanagi, who was a driving force in the folk art (*mingei* 民芸) movement, we find a perception of the Pure Land in this very life, not just in consciousness, but in the objects of ordinary daily use such as pots and cloths which by their very ordinariness take on an irresistible beauty. Kaneko's underlying historico-critical questions in a certain sense go with those of Soga Ryōjin.[5] For him, therefore, the Pure Land is something to be grasped, if at all, here and now through demythologization and interiorization. It is in some respect an intellectual matter, at least in the approach if not in the resolution, even if he did not think of it as being exclusively so. For this reason his essay makes a most interesting companion to that of Yanagi, for whom the intellectual process is hardly necessary. The latter's perceptions are aesthetic, and yet because the objects of his interest are existent here and now, while partaking of the qualities of the Pure Land, they are more than aesthetic. In the end he is talking about the aesthetic appropriation of "suchness," in which inequalities disappear, thus re-balancing the apparently ordinary. And all the while, "suchness" is a theme which runs through all the schools of Mahāyāna Buddhism.

To understand the full import of this we need to recall that there is an exceedingly complex question about the relations between religion and culture, in the sense of aesthetic activities, not only for Zen but also for Shin Buddhism. In the earlier schools of Japanese Buddhism, that is those of Nara Buddhism, of Tendai and of Shingon, artistic activities have been largely geared to the needs of didactic and presentational iconography, and to some extent this continues into Shin Buddhism as well. As time went on, the patronage of the imperial family and the aristocracy, as well as the various warlords who ruled Japan such as the Ashikaga shōguns, led to the promotion of varied forms of art which were more tangentially influenced by Buddhist ways of thinking: ink paintings, gardens, implements of the tea ceremony and so on. Much will be found about this in Suzuki Daisetsu's book *Zen Buddhism and Its Influence on Japanese Culture* which was first published in Kyōto in 1938 by the Eastern Buddhist Society. This included, for example, material on the relations between Zen and swordsmanship, samurai or the tea cult. Others such as Hisamatsu Shin'ichi have emphasized the influence of Zen on fine arts such as painting and ceramics. Because of such publications it has been widely

---

5. Again, see Yokoyama's "Two Thinkers on Shin" (1995) mentioned in note 1 above. The selections to which he refers are the articles by Kaneko and Soga in this volume.

assumed in the West that artistic creativity has been specifically pushed forward by Zen Buddhism, and because of the relative freedom of movement in the Zen way of thinking there is some truth in that. However, both Zen and Shin Buddhism developed subtle relations with aspects of Japanese culture in the broader sense.[6] It is significant that the folk art movement is only conceivable as a *modern* process, while Yanagi himself was also very interested in the traditional development of Pure Land Buddhist religiosity, particularly that of Ippen 一遍 (1239–89).[7] He combined these two interests as follows, in his own words: "Thankfully, the Pure Land seems to be so made that humble objects, just as they are, are allowed to become bound to great beauty." He also argued that in the "Heaven of Beauty" or, that is, the Pure Land, three great oppositions disappear, namely that between intelligence and stupidity, that between skill and a lack thereof, and even that between beauty and ugliness. This corresponds to the Pure Land and Shin Buddhist idea that the most humble or indeed the most morally inadequate of persons can be reborn in the Pure Land through reliance on the Original Vow of Amida Buddha. Thus, transposed to aesthetics, this means that, just as paradoxically it is the most inadequate of persons who will most surely be born in the Pure Land, so it is the most ordinary of objects which are the most beautiful. They display nothing but their own true nature. We owe a particular debt to the English potter Bernard Leach (1887–1979) for his share in making Yanagi's ideas known in the wider world.

In sum, we see that the fascinating tapestry of Mahāyāna Buddhism includes various spiritual options, some of which may seem to be in competition. Yet the wiser interpreters view the options as mutually regulating or in some other sense complementary.[8] The contributions of Shin Buddhist thinkers such as Kaneko Daiei and Soga Ryōjin (reminiscent of their dialogue with Suzuki Daisetsu and Nishitani Keiji in the "Dialogue of Shin Buddhism and Zen Buddhism" in *Listening to Shin Buddhism*) should help to set the Western fascination with Zen Buddhism into a more complex and a more appropriate perspective. The writers whom we meet here were all exposed to "modernity" and pioneered responses to its challenge. Yet, and also precisely so, they were inheritors of a living, socially grounded Buddhist tradition, which is still of great importance in Japan today.

---

6. The balance has recently been righted in a fine study by Elisabetta Porcu, who emphasizes the impact of Shin Buddhist thought and spirituality on art and literature: *Pure Land Buddhism in Modern Japanese Culture* (Leiden and Boston: Brill, 2008). Cf. also her discussion of the work of Yanagi Sōetsu including the article reproduced here.
7. Cf. his article "Ippen Shōnin," *The Eastern Buddhist* New Series 6.2 (1973), 33–57, which unfortunately cannot be included on this occasion.
8. Cf. the interesting exploration by Mark Blum, "Pure Land Buddhism as an Alternative Mārga," *The Eastern Buddhist* New Series 27.1 (1994), 30–77.

Part I
Flashback to Some Early Exchanges

1

Buddhism and Moral World Order

Kiba Ryōhon

This address was given by Kiba Ryōhon, professor of philosophy at Ōtani University, Kyōto, at a meeting of the Religiöser Menschheitsbund which took place near Berlin in August 1922. This Religiöser Menschheitsbund ("Association of Religious Humanity") was founded in 1921 by Rudolf Otto. The article was translated for *The Eastern Buddhist* from a German text which appeared in the second Report of the association.[1]

We, the various peoples, have fostered among ourselves not only material but also cultural exchange to a fairly large extent, yet we still lack inner understanding and confidence in each other as men. The difference of nationality and creed as well as of rank and class within a nation still hinders common thinking and feeling. The affirmation and accentuation of individuality and idiosyncrasies should not be permitted to obscure the consciousness of our common origin. Unfortunately, nearly every nation fears others, and every creed distrusts the others. It is tragic to see how this fear of one nation for another renders both unhappy. Neither of them is able to recognize that their mutual anxiety is based on one and the same reason. In like manner, he who has reached something high and beautiful through the unfolding of his personality strives more to obtain rulership and power over others than to develop that which he has attained. He forgets that in this way he cheats himself out of that which he has already won and at the same time hinders the voluntary participation of others. The mistaking of culture itself for its bearers is the cause of the tragedy of the modern civilized world. He who would serve the higher and more beautiful must for its sake be modest. In Buddhism it is a difficult yet important virtue to rejoice at the property of another as at your own, without envy, as well as to divide your own with others without a thought of ownership. There are naturally differences in capabilities and progress among individuals. But if one turns his glance to such a relative difference, he loses his capacity for the Highest. The consciousness of one's own nothingness before the Highest is ever lacking among men. It is often

---

1. Ed. This is an edited version of a footnote that was originally appended to the title.

believed that one may identify oneself with the Highest, that one may take possession of it for oneself. But it is rather the Absolute which is able to influence man and to make itself known to him. One often divides the one God by appropriating him for oneself and one's own affairs. General reflection and sympathy can spring only from a selfless negative common consciousness of oneself before the Highest. The "Cosmic Consciousness" must also be rooted in this negative consciousness. It is the great task of our growing Union [i.e. the Religiöser Menschheitsbund – "Association of Religious Humanity"] to contribute to the development of this consciousness.

At the instance of our esteemed Prof. Otto, I decided to speak on this theme. I confine myself to a brief exposition of the Buddhist view of the problem on the basis of the Canonical Writings. I hope that you will understand the basic view from which we Japanese Buddhists build and are to build still further the idea of world order, and that I may in this manner contribute my quota to the success of the future work of the Association.

I shall explain then: (1) How Buddhism conceives this world and the reason of its existence, and how it judges the world; (2) Which world it recognizes as the ideal, the Real World, and by what conduct it believes it possible to reach this world; (3) What attitude we should assume with regard to the two worlds.

First: The world from which Buddhism starts is naturally that in which we daily live, wishing, feeling, suffering. The well-known doctrine of the Twelve Causal Links of Gautama Buddha proclaims his insight into the origin and continued existence of this world. This causal chain of twelve links is traceable in its essentials to three chief motives, namely: nescience, wrongdoing, and suffering. Whenever we do evil in consequence of our original ignorance, misery and sorrow follow us as inevitable retribution. Ensnared by misery and sorrow, nescience becomes ever deeper and more involved. In this endless circle we are drawn ever deeper into the maelstrom.

Corresponding to this process of our life, the unhappy world develops before us. It is true that a common karma runs through these giddy paths, but it is modified in diverse ways by various conditions of the individual. Then the world which we perceive differs as the individual karma differs. Blinded by this individual karma, one cannot recognize at all that which we have in common. In reality, this earthly world consists of "worlds of different births." Every one lives in a parcelled-off world of his own, and suffers and rejoices quite differently from his fellow-beings. There is "no common accord either in fortune or misfortune." Either someone envies another, or he arraigns him. Who is then to blame for this unhappy fate? "No one but thyself; thou who art the author of thine own world." And if someone who performs now only good and righteous deeds should be maltreated by others, even then he is not to consider the others really wrong or evil. For, according to the Buddhistic point of view, the moral law of causation is absolute and without exception, and he who finds others arrayed against him should seek definite causes therefor in his own past. The idea that one can undergo evil without housing a reason for it within himself is rejected in Buddhism as a pagan delusion which denies the moral law of causation. Every man has himself to blame if evil befalls him. According to the Buddhist view, one can never judge another his antagonist or enemy, or betrayer and feel himself more upright than the other. It is a noteworthy fact that Gautama Buddha called Devadatta (who had tried by several plans to murder him) his good teacher and believed that he would at some time in the future become Buddha, and that they would work together for the enlightenment and salvation of the world. Yes, it should be quite immaterial to us whether others treat us well or ill. "For the venomous serpent transforms the purest water into poison by drinking; the cow, on the other hand, converts even the impure water which she drinks into nourishing milk." This recognition of absolute individual responsibility is the fundamental principle of Buddhism, through which Buddhistic conversion is effected.

This doctrine is sometimes confounded with solipsism, but it is in reality its opposite, and rests on the Buddha's experience of omni-unity. Through the recognition of individual responsibility, one can see within himself all that he formerly saw outside, and can recognize the common karma. When one has once recognized the common karma, he can no longer accuse others and set himself in opposition to them. According to Buddhism, the relation between Good and Evil is not an outer opposition which gives rise to a struggle between the two. He who posits the Good as the polar opposite of Evil is still in error, and is not yet free from egoism. True Good should comprehend Evil within itself. The allegory of the relation between light and darkness, water and ice is ubiquitous in Buddhist scriptures. For this reason, Buddhism teaches first instead of the struggle for Good the calm endurance of Evil. An unerring endurance of Evil is only possible, however, where something positive exists. And he who possesses this is thereby liberated from Evil. What is this positive? Are we to create it ourselves?

In order to answer this question, I go naturally to the second point, that is to the positive idea of the Real World of Buddhism. The Buddhist Real World is the so-called Jōdo, the "World of Purity." It was constituted by the Buddha in eternity. Man can in no manner create this world, not even with the aid of the Buddha. The Bodhisattva who has clearly grasped the previously mentioned first element of Buddhist conversion finds, through the wisdom of omni-unity, this Real World everywhere before him.

Then: What is the nature of this Real World? I should like to give you a descriptive sketch of it according to the *Commentary on the Amitāyus Sūtra* by Vasubandhu (third century).[2] It consists in the absolutely pure virtue of

---

2. Ed. The author refers to *Amitayussutropadesa*, "short commentary on the *Amitāyus-sūtra*," i.e. on the *Amidakyō*, but there is no known text of precisely this name. He may be referring to Vasubandhu's *Jōdoron* ("Treatise on the Pure Land").

Amida Buddha which is fundamentally different from human virtue. His Enlightenment and Teaching which cannot be locked up rule and penetrate all, so that one is instructed also by trees and grasses, wind and water. Their denizens are "of one birth from the Wisdom of the Buddha." "They nourish themselves on thoughtfulness (*dhyāna*),[3] free from suffering and passion." This world receives "all beings without distinction of their capabilities and nature, as all streams empty into one sea" (for further details, see *Amitāyus sūtra*, Volume II).[4] How can one attain this world then? And what does one do in this world? This question leads me to the third point, namely, our position with regard to the two worlds.

So when the mature Bodhisattva once sees this Real World before him, he directs all his efforts to "being born in this blissful Land with all his fellow-beings, inasmuch as he gives himself and his fellow-beings without reserve to the Buddha of Infinite Light." In this pure devotion his wish for the Land of Bliss becomes wholly free from self-interest. He wants it only for purity's sake. His deed has no longer anything to do with the erring world directly. The earthly world, however much it may be improved, remains afterwards, as before, earthly. And even the wish to improve this world is at bottom somehow tainted with self-interest. As long as one cannot entirely renounce the earthly world as a field of endeavour, just so long is one bound to it. This striving for the amelioration of the world often gives rise to hatred and contention. Man has a tendency to use this idea as a protection and a weapon for himself rather than to follow it selflessly. According to my point of view, there can be no way to realize the Real World unless all forsake the erring world to be born in the World of Reality. So,

> When the Bodhisattva recognizes the truth, he understands true sacrifice and the passing to that world. Through this knowledge he perceives clearly the condition of the suffering beings in the three impure worlds, and in consequence of the perception of their false condition, he is filled with genuine compassion and pity.

Now he cannot enter the Real World unless he saves the suffering beings in the erring world. Until he has made all beings identical with himself, he cannot cross over. Therefore he enters the erring world unconditionally in order that he may lead it with him into the Real World. But if you long for the Pure Land for the sake of mere happiness, you cannot follow him. He must show them the pure will from the Supreme Bodhi (discernment or insight into Truth). For this purpose, he supplements his charity with immovable resolve,

---

3. Ed. The translation of *dhyāna* as "thoughtfulness" is unusual.
4. Ed. I.e. the *Amidakyō*.

and enters the three erring worlds. Now what are his deeds? No contention, no opposition, no abuse, no reproach, for he knows at the beginning that the others are a part of himself, and at the same time that such deeds tarnish the wish for the real Good – but he practises only the four comprehensive deeds, namely: unselfish sharing with others of one's own material and intellectual treasures; second, meekness which is free from adulation as it is from disdain; third, beneficent deeds which he will perform in various ways in order that his fellow-beings may have leisure to contemplate the Good; and, fourth, to become like men in order that he may become intimate with them. With these deeds he strives to imbue them with pure endeavour for the Real World. When he has perfected these deeds, all beings of the impure worlds will be born in the Real World as a matter of course. If they do not grasp true will, he feels it as his own fault. So he remains always in this troubled world in order to perform the four deeds mentioned above. But these deeds are only the consequence and development of the one, pure, self-sacrificing, praising deed of the Real World, as Vasubandhu and Donran (Tánluán 曇鸞, 476–542) have established it. According to Shinran, our own reformer,[5] it should be "purpose-less purpose."

To sum up as clearly as possible, in Buddhism there is no moral world order attained by man, but only through the Eternal Buddha. Man is to enter, and can enter only the world constituted by the Buddha. We must have a universally valid idea clearly before us as an inexhaustible source from which we cause all our deeds and labours to proceed. But wherever the most important is lacking, there all is lacking. We can only realize that with which our soul is already filled. We should first live in the Real World and participate in its bliss. All deeds should flow spontaneously from this bliss. Nearly all are suffering from spiritual aridity these days. They long for the fruit-bringing spiritual rain. I close my talk with the resigned words of Shinran:

> I am constrained, unfortunately, to differentiate the good deed of the way of the Pure World, that is of the man who feels himself to be nothing, from the good deed of the saints, that is of those who consider themselves towering above their fellows. The latter deed is performed when one has compassion for others of his own will, and saves them. But to my great regret, I am hardly capable of doing this. The good deed of the former, on the other hand, consists in saving one's fellow-beings fundamentally through the absolute Excellence of the Buddha by attaining Buddhahood through exclusive devotion to the Eternal Buddha. However great may be the kindness and love which a man

---

5. Ed. For "our own reformer" the original had "our inner reformer," presumably meaning the reformer within "our own" tradition of Shin Buddhism.

such as I may feel toward his fellow-beings, yet it does not extend as far as it should, and will eventually fail to reach the goal. So I believe that absolute devotion to the Buddha is the only lasting salvation for others as for me.[6]

---

6. Ed. This passage is reminiscent of *Tannishō* 4, of which it may be a free paraphrase.

2

On Zen Buddhism

Rudolf Otto

Preface by Prajñā[1]

Professor Rudolf Otto, of Marburg, is the author of *Das Heilige*, whose English translation entitled *The Idea of the Holy* appeared recently. Not satisfied with scholarly achievements he is one of the active workers in the movement of a world religious union.[2] His view on Zen as a special form of Japanese Buddhism was published in the second report of the said movement. The article is more or less a recapitulation of Professor Suzuki's paper on Zen in one of the previous numbers of the *Eastern Buddhist*, but as it comes filtered through the brains of such a scholarly author, it is reproduced here in an English translation for the perusal of the readers of the present magazine.

Zen, Sanskrit Dhyāna, is the name of a great school of Chinese-Japanese Buddhism whose foremost saint is Bodhidharma. Its peculiar form, which is still living in Japan, was given to it by the Chinese master Hyakujō, circa 800 CE.[3] The ground of the teaching upon which it rests is Mahāyāna. And so are its ceremonies, its myth, its pantheon (if it is permitted at all to apply such a distorted expression to the Mahāyāna). The solemnity of the Numinous that in general lies over Buddhist ceremonies and over the conduct of the better monk is also in keeping with their wonderful temples, halls, religious paintings, acts of worship and personal conduct. In distinction from the great principle school of Japanese Buddhism, the Shin-shū, which is essentially personal in nature and which seeks salvation in personal faith in the saving grace of the personal Amida Buddha, the Zen followers are mystics. They are at the same

---

1. Ed. The identity of "Prajñā" can no longer be ascertained. Contrary to speculation it is unlikely to be a pseudonym for D.T. Suzuki, who is himself referred to respectfully in this editorial note.
2. Ed. This is the Religiöser Menschheitsbund ("Association of Religious Humanity") referred to by Kiba Ryōhon. *Das Heilige* appeared in 1917 and the English translation in 1923. Rudolf Otto is also known as the founder of The Museum of Religions (Religionskundliche Sammlung) at the University of Marburg, Germany.
3. Ed. Hyakujō: Hyakujō Ekai 百丈懐海 (Bǎizhàng Huáihǎi 749–814).

time practical mystics; for like Benedict they couple *ora* and *labora*, like the Benedictines they are tillers of the soil, men of practical labour, or, according to talent, men of creative art in sublime works of painting or sculpture. "He who does not work shall not eat" was the motto of Hyakujō. Yet all that is not their essential characteristic. I asked a venerable abbot in a fine quiet abbey in Tokyo the question, "What is the basic idea of Zen?" Since he was wedged in by this question, he was obliged to answer with an idea. He said, "We believe that *saṃsāra* and nirvana do not differ, but that they are same. And that everyone should find the Buddha-heart in his own heart." But in truth this is also not the chief thing; for it is still "said," still "doctrine," still transmitted. The main point in Zen, however, is not a basic idea, but an experience, which shuns not only concepts, but even the idea itself. Zen reveals its nature in the following instances in which its artists have drawn without words before our eyes in an incomparably impressive manner by mien, gesture, bearing, facial and bodily expression.

1. One must form here first of all a picture of Bodhidharma himself, the prodigiously heavy man who "sits before a wall ten years in silence," in concentrated, nay, in conglobate force of inner tension like a highly charged Leyden jar, the large eyes almost pushed out of his head by the inner compression, boring their way into the problem, eyes of an exorcist who wishes to conjure up a demon, or a God to stand before him in order that he shall reveal and deliver up his secret. What he is gazing at, what he wishes to compel, who could say? But that it is something monstrous, that it is the monstrous itself, that is revealed in his features. And the great pictures of Bodhidharma are therefore quite monstrous in every nuance of the term as I suggested in my book, *Das Heilige*.[4] That this seated person seeks a something, which matters above everything, compared with which all things are viewed with unconcern, a something in [a] word such as only the Numinous itself has, springs directly to the mind. And whoever loses himself entirely in this picture, to him must come the light terror in the presence of the thing which is mirrored in these eyes, in this collectedness.

2. At the same time this collectedness is nothing less than a self-scrutinizing, a self-marking[5] or the willingness to find the self. And the final discovery is, God knows, not the product of one's own cleverness, or of one's own doing. And the emancipation which is connected with the discovery is the farthest conceivable from so-called self-emancipation. The assurances of many expounders of Buddhism who consider that the superiority of Buddhism lies in its

---

4. Ed. Otto refers to page 51 of *Das Heilige*, presumably referring to the first German edition.
5. Ed. The original is obscure.

teaching of self-emancipation are miles astray. This discovery is a final cracking, a final breaking which comes to one simply as an altogether mystical fact, a fact which, however, cannot be made by anything. It either gives itself, or withholds itself. No man can make, produce or find it himself. One can hardly characterize it as "Grace," for to "Grace" belongs a "Gracious One." But it is related to grace, in so far as by grace and the experience of grace the utterly wonderful mystery is meant. It is the using of the "celestial eye" and is more fittingly comparable to an entering charm than to an emancipation of self.

3. What is the content of the discovery? The lips of those experiencing it are firmly sealed. And so it must be, for if this school has a dogma, it is that of the inconceivability and complete ineffability of the "thing itself." It is the Truth which has a bearing upon all things, which transmutes life in a trice, and which gives a hitherto unseen, misunderstood sense to the existence of oneself and of the world, it is accompanied by the most intense heightening of the emotions, and boundless joy. It is linked with a continuous "study of the Inconceivable." This study, however, is nothing intellectual, but an indescribable, ever deeper penetration into the discovered truth of Zen. It streams out into the daily conduct, and illumines the faces of those experiencing it. It engenders readiness to serve, for the meaning of life is service for salvation of all feeling creatures. It is revealed in an oft-repeated fourfold vow:

> How innumerable sentient beings are, I vow to save them all.
> How inexhaustible our evil passions are, I vow to exterminate them all.
> How immeasurable the Holy Doctrines are, I vow to study them.
> How inaccessible the path of Buddha is, I vow to attain it.

It stretches the mind to the highest ideal, but it enjoins renunciation of all personal fame, and inculcates willing humility: "Let one's ideal rise as high as the crown of Vairocana (the highest of the *buddhas*), while his life may be so full of humility as to make him prostrate before a baby's feet."

All self-discipline, however, and all actions for others are without compulsion, and "without recompense," unconscious of oneself, without emphasizing things and without merit for oneself.

> The bamboo shadows are sweeping the stars,
> But no dust is stirred:
> The moonlight penetrates deep into the bottom of the pool,
> But no trace is left in the water.

Saṃsāra itself is now nirvana. The feverish quest for a goal of salvation beyond being comes to an end. For the object of the quest is found in being itself and in union with it. This world of migration, otherwise a heap of sorrow and evil, is itself the blissful Buddha-sphere; it scintillates in transparent mystical beauty and depth, just as the inspired brush of this artist reproduces it with unparalleled impressiveness. It treats with equal disdain all book-learning and scholastic erudition. But it is a rare, deep, inner wisdom which finds expression in a laconic word, in a prompt maxim, in a concise verse, which only suggests. It is a truth which is not at all that of everyday and which expresses itself best in its own peculiar way in contrast to everyday truth, namely, in its apparent loutishness when judged from the outside, by which, as in the case of Socrates, the deep spiritual import becomes doubly visible in its victory over an ugly or bizarre form or face. Such constantly depicted, painted figures are especially Hánshān 寒山 and Shídé 拾得 whose representation by Shūbun[6] seems to me to be the greatest physiognomical masterpiece of the world.

In no other place has any one succeeded in making the perfectly ridiculous, grotesque of a given external appearance disappear so entirely into nothing, and to make one forget it before the outbursting depth, and in this manner to make felt the utter non-importance of all material or outer things compared to the Inner. And this quite in the laconic manner of Zen itself, with a few strokes and blurs of the most marvellous India-ink. And it is at the same time like "the bamboo shadow which plays without stirring up the dust," that is so indifferent to all outer effects and without ambiguity. Some have wished to explain the Mahāyāna in their favourite way as "a penetration of the Vedānta mysticism into Buddhism." One can learn, however, from the forms of Hánshān and Shídé, or also from the form of the big-bellied one, of Bùdài 布袋, how wary one must be of these assertions of smuggling. Such figures were simply unthinkable among the pupils of Śaṅkara. And their experience, however ineffable it is, is in tone utterly different from the Brahman-nirvana of the Vedānta. It is far more naïve, more blissful, more thoroughly illumined, far richer in potentialities; it is not world-rejecting, but world-transfiguring. It is mysticism. But it shows that mysticism is not all one and the same thing, that mysticism is not a separate, self-existent category of being, but something formal, namely the coming to preponderance of the Irrational, which may take place in various ways and with widely differing content. If one wishes analogies for figures like those named, they are offered most readily among disciples of St Francis such as Saint Egidio and Ginepro. The statement "nirvana and *saṃsāra* are the same" would constitute for Śaṅkara an enormous abomination.

---

6. Ed. Presumably Shūbun 周文, associated with the Kyōto Rinzai Zen temple Shōkokuji. Not to be confused with the approximately contemporary Shūbun 秀文, a Chinese painter who arrived in Japan in 1424.

4. In a sudden flaring-up the new viewpoint enters. The content of the experience is utterly ineffable. For that reason it simply cannot be transmitted. It must arise in all its originality in each and every person. Instantaneity and especially intransmissibility are the real dogmas of this peculiar school. It is for this reason that painters ever and again represent Bodhidharma tearing up and throwing away the *sūtras*, the sacred texts and the writings of the school. And yet there are masters and pupils. And this relationship is of the utmost importance. The pupil is not to be instructed in that which is incapable of being taught, but he is to be led as it were, or better, shoved, until intuition breaks in. That which helps him thereto is manifestly first of all the witnessing of the effects of experience which are listed in (3) (above). In their union vividly experienced they must awaken a preparatory conception in the *a priori* of the receptive person, and in that way prepare the breaking through. There are in addition drastic actions of an unusual pedagogy which must appear to us as mad, but which evidently attain their end with the summoning of the disciple.[7] Suzuki relates the seemingly very little enlightening story of the enlightenment of Hakuin by his master Shōju. Hakuin considers himself already deeply versed in the Wisdom of Buddha and parades his wisdom in front of his master. "Stuff and nonsense" answers the master when he has finished. Hakuin vindicates himself. Thereupon the master boxes him many a time, throws him out of the house, "so that he falls into the mud, and scolds him: 'O you denizen of the dark cavern!'" Hakuin comes another time firmly resolved to bring his master to speech. This time the master throws him over the veranda, and he falls to the bottom of the stone wall. And while he is lying half-senseless below, the master laughs scornfully down at him. Hakuin now wants to leave "the master." Then as he is going about begging in the village, the miraculous happens: a trivial occurrence – as the glittering of the can in the case of Böhme – gives the impulse which suddenly opens his eye to the truth of Zen. Boundless joy overcomes him, and half beside himself he returns to his old master. Even before he has crossed the front gate, his master recognizes him and beckons to him, saying, "What good news do you bring? Quick, quick! Come right in." Hakuin tells what "he went through," and the old master tenderly strokes him: "Now you have it; you have it now." Lectures serve as other aids, the strangest lectures, I suppose, which were ever delivered to salvation-thirsting souls. Their laconic, sometimes literally monosyllabic, statements are not instructions. They are seemingly often quite nonsensical, but in reality they conceal a point which is only not wasted on such as have become accustomed to this enigma-solving through previous training. They are rather a kind of edifying cuffs (knocks) for the soul in order to box it ideogrammatically in a given direction. Imagine "conversations"

---

7. Ed. Originally "with the disciple summoned."

like this one between Unmon[8] and his pupil: What is the (mental) sword of Unmon? – Hung! – What is the one straight passage to Unmon? – Most intimate! – Which one of the three *kāya*s of the Buddha is it that will sermonize? – To the point! – What is the eye of the true Law? – Everywhere! – What is the way? – Forward! – How is it that without the parents' consent one cannot be ordained? – Shallow! – I do not understand that. – Deep! – How do you have a seeing eye in a question! – Blind. Or a sermon like the following: Unmon is sitting on the master's seat. A monk comes and asks for an answer to questions. Unmon calls out aloud: "O monks!" The monks all turned towards him. Then he arose and left the pulpit without a word.

5. In quite paradoxical utterances, acts or gestures the utter Irrational and even the quite paradoxical are presented. It shows in an especially remarkable feature its paradoxical and at the same time its completely inner nature, which in the end is contrary to all outer appearance and ostentation. The experiencing of it should be and should remain entirely inner, which withdraws from the realm of the conscious, discursive, uttered into the deepest Inwardness. One should have the matter as completely within oneself as one has one's health, of which one only becomes conscious when it has fled, and as one has one's life within oneself, of which one knows the least and says the least when it is the strongest and most lively. From this spring the seemingly offensive statements of the masters. They do not want to hear anything of the Buddha or of Zen even. When these two have first come into consciousness, they are no longer possessed in their originality and genuineness. When one reasons about them, they are no longer there.

"When the Soul speaks, then – alas! – it is no longer the Soul which speaks." Just as nobility which is conscious of its being noble is no longer nobility, so is Zen, when it speaks of itself, no longer Zen. Goso[9] says to his disciple Engo,[10] "You are all light, but you have a trifling fault." Engo asks repeatedly what that fault is. Finally the master says, "You have altogether too much of Zen." Another monk asks him, "Why do you especially hate talking about Zen?" – "Because it turns one's stomach," says the master. He is annoyed when one wishes to speak of that which cannot be spoken of, which can only be lived and possessed in the soundless depths. And from this attitude spring apparently impious actions, as when a master warms himself on a cold day by burning Buddha-images, or when conceptual objectifications of religion are spoken of contemptuously. As Rinzai[11] says, "O you followers of Truth, if you encounter the Buddha, slay him; if you encounter the Patriarch, slay him." And one day Unmon draws a line in the sand with his staff, and says, "All

---

8. Ed. Unmon: 雲門 Yúnmén 864–949.
9. Ed. *Goso* = Goso Hōen 五祖法演 Wǔzǔ Fǎyǎn (+1104).
10. Ed. *Engo* = Engo Kokugon 圜悟克勤 Yuánwù Kèqín (1063–1135).
11. Ed. Rinzai = Rinzai Gigen 臨濟義玄 Línjì Yìxuán (+867).

the Buddhas as numberless as sands are here talking all kinds of nonsense.'" Or another time, "Outside in the courtyard stand the Lord of Heaven and the Buddha discoursing on Buddhism. What a noise they are making!" But then the talk may on occasion swing completely around and proceed in quite another tone. The discourse may gently point out the still speech of the things about us, waiting until it becomes intelligible to the disciple himself. Just as one day Unmon is going to the lecture hall when he hears all at once the deep tone of the temple bell. He says, "in such a wide, wide world, why do we put our monkish robes on when the bell goes like this?" And Buddhist painting, especially, has taken up such methods of instruction. For example, the last words of Unmon return directly painted in the picture, *Temple Bell at Evening*. There is the wide, wide world. One sees, half disappearing, the cloister. The accompanying strokes suggest the ringing of the bell, which one thinks one hears. That is not nature-sentiment; that is Zen. And Zen is also the paradoxical [element] of so many pictures which people today would like to class as immature Oriental expressionism – those peculiar impressive landscapes on which a few flaws, at first glance almost completely undecipherable, like a Zen laconism, comprise an entire microcosm and spiritualize them into ideograms of the Ineffable-Intransmissible. Here nirvana becomes in fact visible in *saṃsāra*, and the One Buddha-heart as the depth of things pulsates with such plainly audible beat that respiration halts. But both are too much "said."

3

Dengyō Daishi and German Theology

Bruno Petzold

Dengyō Daishi 伝教大師, the great Reformer of the Heian Era, who carried the Chinese school of Tendai to Japan and gave it a home on Mt. Hiei; Dengyō Daishi, the protégé of the emperor Kanmu and friend of Kōbō Daishi; Dengyō Daishi who opposed the Nara Priests, fought the principles of the Hossō sect, and taught the identity of Śākyamuni, Yakushi Nyorai and Amida – what has this Dengyō, the eleven hundredth anniversary of whose death we have just celebrated, to do with German theology?

Their association seems arbitrary and paradoxical, yet it may not be so forced as it appears at first glance.

When we speak here of German theology, we think immediately of the *Theologia Germanica* of the anonymous Frankfort Knight of the Teutonic Order, the famous work which constituted a landmark in the Christian theology of the dying fourteenth century, and which was brought out in modern form in 1907 under the title *Das Büchlein vom vollkommenen Leben* (*The Book of Perfect Life*).[1] But those theologians also, Master Eckhart, Tauler and Suso, who were intellectually akin to the Frankforter, are understood here to be representative of German theology. We must also include Martin Luther, who published the *Theologia Germanica* in 1516 under the title *Ein deutsch Theologia*, and who wrote in the preface to this Frankforter's work,

---

1. Ed. Frankfort is an archaic spelling for Frankfurt, residence of the author of this tract, and so the author is known as the Frankforter or Franckforter. Although this mystical writing was republished in printed form by Martin Luther in 1516 (full text in 1518), as *Theologia Deutsch* (or *Theologia Germanica*), for its spiritual qualities, it remains within the thought-world of mediaeval Catholicism rather than being reformatory.

This noble book, poor and, rude though it be in words and human wisdom, is so much the more precious in its art and divine wisdom. And I will say, though it be boasting of myself and "I speak as a fool," that next to the Bible and St. Augustine, no book hath ever come into my hands, whence I have learnt, or would wish to learn more of what God, and Christ, and man and all things are.

We may also reckon Jakob Böhme in with them, as well as every other German theologian who understood Christianity in a form apart from the formalistic church doctrines, and who understood it in the deeper manner which was peculiar to the men mentioned above.

All these divines – and Luther was surely one of them before he lost himself again in a net of dogmas – have this in common with Dengyō Daishi: they are mystics. They all believed in the comprehension of the supersensible, the divine, the transcendental, not through the senses, nor through reason, but through their own inner experience, through direct intellectual intuition, contemplation and perceptual experience in a state of ecstasy. They all believed that they were able to partake of the union with the Divine Being – the "unio mystica" – in an inconceivable, mystical manner by means of absorption in the depths of their own soul. As for that which especially concerns the founder of the Tendai sect, his teaching, so far as its practical side is taken into consideration, is built upon the most profound mystic system that Buddhism has ever called forth, the *Makashikan* 摩訶止観, or the "Great Meditation," of Chisha Daishi 智者大師, the founder of the Chinese Tendai sect. Dengyō Daishi, however, made his foundation still broader by including the mysticism of the Shingon and Zen schools, so that one might well say that the mystical element was never so strongly emphasized by the founder of any sect of Mahāyāna Buddhism as it was by Dengyō Daishi.

There are a great number of very eminent and deserving scholars – we refer here to the Western scholars only – who have not been able to see the slightest trace of mysticism in Buddhism. Some define Buddhism as a "rationalistic atheism"; others as a "practical system of morals"; while those of the third group see in the teachings of the Buddha an astronomy in pictures. These scholars cannot see the forest for the trees; they are so thoroughly philologists that they cannot grasp theological problems. It is only recently that a few isolated Western scholars have been aware of the mystical base of Buddhism. But scarcely does the road to an unbiased conception of Buddhist principles seem clear when another turnpike is raised, for these scholars conclude: Buddhism may be mysticism, but it is absolutely different from Christian mysticism; for Buddhism postulates (as all Oriental mysticism does) the total annihilation, the consummate absorption of the individual soul in the Infinite, whilst the European mystics seek instead of the suppression of the individual soul-life a greater intensity of it. According to these theoreticians, the foundation of Christian mysticism is positive and active, whilst that of Oriental (especially Buddhist) mysticism is negative and passive.

If this characterization does not prove entirely true even for Hīnayāna, in so far as it categorically denies the existence of an individual soul, the *ātman*, how much less does it apply to Mahāyāna Buddhism. How little negative and passive Mahāyāna is, is conclusively shown by Tendai Buddhism which was represented by Dengyō Daishi.

The Tendai philosophy is built upon the teachings of Nāgārjuna, whose "Eight Noes" are sufficiently known. They are

Without origin, also without end;
Not eternal, nor yet cut short;
Not one, and not many;
Without coming, as without going.

Such a definition of the Absolute seems to be purest nihilism, but it is not more nihilism than when Jakob Böhme says of Eternal Love,

It cannot, therefore, be compared with anything, for it is deeper than the I; it is, therefore, in all things a Nothing, because it is not conceivable. And since it is Nothing, it is free from, all things, and is the sole Good, so that one may not declare what it is.

That the Perfect is Nothing is clearly expressed in the *Theologia Germanica* also. There we read,

The things which are in part can be apprehended, known, and expressed; but the Perfect cannot be apprehended, known, or expressed by any creature as creature. Therefore; the Perfect is called Nothing: not being of the same kind, the creature as creature cannot know nor apprehend it, name nor conceive it.

If one, nevertheless, sees only nihilism in the negative formulation of Nāgārjuna's *Chūron* 中論, or *Madhyamikaśāstra*, which begins with the "Eight Noes,"[2] point out to him that Dengyō Daishi's Tendai philosophy depends not so much upon the *Madhyamikaśāstra* as upon the *Daichidoron* 大智度論, or *Mahāprajñāpāramitāśāstra*,[3] which also is ascribed to Nāgārjuna and states

---

2. Ed. I.e. the eight negations quoted in the stanza above.
3. Ed. *Chūron*: in Chinese (the original language of this treatise) *Zhōng lùn* 中論. This is in fact a commentary on the "Middle Stanzas," verses by Nāgārjuna, referred to in Sanskrit as *Madhyamakakārikā*. The title *Madhyamika-śāstra* for the *Zhōng lùn* is fictive. *Daichidoron*: in

clearly that back of the negative formulation of the Absolute, the Positive in its highest power is hidden.

This second *śāstra* is of all the writings the most characteristic of the philosophical content of the Tendai doctrine. Its religious content is best expressed in the *Hokekyō* 法華経,[4] or *Saddharmapuṇḍarīka-sūtra*, which teaches that all living creatures without distinction possess the Buddha-nature (*busshō* 仏性). The use which the *Hokekyō* makes of the word "Buddha" is not less free than the use which the *Theologia Germanica* and kindred mysticism makes of the word "God " or "Christ." Both books understand by these words the "Perfect," the "One," the "Truth," the "Highest Good." "Good," says the Frankforter, "need not first come into the soul; it is already there as yet unrecognized" – and he expresses a conviction there which may be considered the fundamental principle of the *Hokekyō*.

Dengyō Daishi defended most energetically this central truth of the *Hokekyō*, that all creatures without distinction possess the Buddha-nature, against the Hossō 法相 priests who clung to the doctrine of Five Natures (*goshō* 五性) and who asserted that only the creatures who had the bodhisattva-nature and the so-called undetermined nature (*fujōshō* 不定性) could become Buddha, whilst those endowed with human and *deva* nature, with *śrāvaka*-nature, and *pratyekabuddha*-nature were excluded from Buddhahood for eternity.

This is not the place to go into this controversy, so rich in dialectical snares, between Dengyō Daishi and the Nara priests – at the bottom of it on one side lies the belief in the absolute dissimilarity of human talents and the moral forces which fill the universe; on the other side the belief in the fundamental Unity of the universe and the nature of all creatures.[5]

In this latter comprehension Dengyō Daishi is at one with Christian mysticism, which proceeds from the hypothesis, "God reposes in all things, since He gave Himself to all," and which gives rise to the Claim, "Man must redeem Him – God – by creating!"

There is a great deal in the *Theologia Germanica* about the "Godlike man." It says among other things,

> Love in a Godlike man is pure, untinged, and of good will. Therefore, all things, animate and inanimate, human and infra-human, must be loved there, and only good wished and done to all: Let one do to a Godlike man whatever one will, good or evil, to please or to aggrieve; nay, if someone

---

Chinese (also the original language of this treatise) *Dàzhìdù lùn* 大智度論 or "Treatise on the Perfection of Great Insight." This has also been provided with the fictive Sanskrit title referred to by the author. See further in Synoptic List of Text Titles.

4. Ed. The author wrote Hokkekyō, which is in a sense to be expected, but the title is regularly pronounced and transcribed without a reduplication of the letter "k."
5. Ed. Possibly the "Buddha-nature" of all creatures was intended.

should kill him a hundred times and he should return to life, he would be obliged to love the person who had killed him and who had done him so much injustice and evil; he should be intent upon his welfare only and do for him the very best he can provided only that the other party will accept such kindness. Behold, where such a Godlike man is, here is the best, the most noble, and to God the most appropriate life that there can be...and should the same man die a thousand deaths, every misfortune fall upon him which may befall a creature, yet would he rather suffer all that than to be deprived of this noble life. And if he could exchange his life for that of an angel, not even then would he trade!

Now this conception of the Godlike man corresponds, word for word, to the conception of the Bosatsu (Bodhisattva) which Dengyō Daishi, relying upon the *Hokekyō* and the *Bonmōkyō* 梵網経 (*Brahmajāla Sūtra*), represented. It is the duty of the Bosatsu to release the God in man through works. And everyone who dedicates himself to the task, is, according to Dengyō Daishi, a Bosatsu, even if the talents of the individuals – he distinguishes 52 different stages of Bodhisattva-hood – differ according to their rank. If the Mahāyāna doctrine, as it existed in Japan before Dengyō Daishi – the so-called elementary or provisional Mahāyāna Buddhism – had recognized the existence of priestly *bosatsus* only, Dengyō Daishi went a step further and added the lay *bosatsus* to those who made up the priesthood. "Every one [that is every true Mahāyāna believer] is a Bosatsu"[6] is the basic principle of Dengyō. This principle may be compared with the conception of general priesthood entertained by Martin Luther. And according to the Frankforter, the possession of Perfect Life and not sacerdotalism or monasticism makes one an "Imitator" and "Servant" of Christ.

Dengyō's disciples, the Tendai priests, in particular were supposed to regard themselves as *bosatsus*, and to labour as *bosatsus* by placing their whole strength in the service of the State, which was understood to be the moral community based on the family, and as such, an incorporation of Universal and Eternal Truth. In accordance herewith, Dengyō divided the students of Tendai into three groups: (1) Those who distinguished themselves by singular virtue and eloquence should remain living on Mt. Hiei at the conclusion of their twelve years of study, become leaders of all the others, and be titled "Kokuhō" 国宝, or "Treasure of the State"; (2) Those who were possessed of great eloquence, but who had not distinguished themselves by any unusual virtues, should be "Kokushi" 国師, or "Teachers of the State"; (3) Whilst those who had distinguished themselves by their virtues, but who had not the gift of eloquence, should be called "Kokuyō" 国用, or "Assets of the State." The Kokushi and Kokuyō were made "Denpō" 伝法 and provincial "Kōshi" 講師

---

6. Ed. Square brackets here were added by the author.

by governmental charter. The Denpō, or the "Deliverers of Religion," had their residence for the most part in the large temples of Nara and Kyōto; the Kōshi, on the other hand, were lecturers who were on duty from four to six years in the various State Temples (*kokubunji* 国分寺) of the provinces. Here in the annual rest-period (*ango* 安居) of ninety days which corresponds to the Indian "Vassa," or rainy season, and which lasted from the sixteenth day of the fourth month to the fifteenth day of the seventh month, they recited and explained the *sūtras* and *śāstras* before the congregation, according to the ancient custom. The laymen would prove their appreciation of this work by giving all kinds of presents.

In the regulations which contain the foregoing provisions, Dengyō recommends the collection of the gifts to lecturers in the warehouses of the provincial governors, their careful auditing and their use for the public welfare [for purposes such as]: the improvement of pools and ditches to irrigate the rice-fields, the cultivation of unproductive fields (which had either been laid waste through flooding, or which had never yet been made arable), the re-terracing of worn-down terrain, the building of bridges and ships, the setting-out of trees (especially fruit-trees), the cultivation of hemp and useful grasses, the deepening of springs, and for all other things which conduce to the well-being of the province and of the individual, including the reciting of sūtras and the "edification of the human mind." Yet these gifts of the congregation were never to be used for agricultural or other commercial enterprises, that is the collective capital was not to be lent out at interest for purposes of gain.[7]

The tendency to be of service to the State, that is to the group, was emphasized in this regulation of the Tendai sect by Dengyō in a manner which is without precedent in ancient Indian, or even Chinese Buddhism. So strongly did Dengyō Daishi consider "care for the State" as the chief task of the Tendai priests that he wished to see his whole religion made the state religion. "O make this the state religion!" he prayed at the grave of Shōtoku Taishi, he who was looked upon as Shōtoku Taishi reincarnated. What is, then, this concern for the State (that is for the good of his compatriots), if not the fundamental principle of *"viriliter agite!"* – of "manly conduct" – which we find so much stressed in the *Theologia Germanica*? Is it not the affirmation of life in the highest sense? – even though Ignorance has said of the German mystics and the Buddhists without distinction that they fled into the deserts to escape life.

The founder of the Tendai sect as well as the *German Theology* demand activity in the most forcible manner for the good of all. They are both, nevertheless, as one in rejecting outward piety (piety of works); both believe in a sudden and complete conversion without the accumulation of merit; both repudiate the ceremonial law which had formerly been deemed binding

---

7. Ed. This paragraph has been edited for clarity.

by the representatives of their religion. Luther exclaims, "Your cowl, your shaven head, your celibacy, your obedience, your poverty, your works, and your merit, of what use shall they be to you? Of what avail is the Mosaic Law?" – and in the third month of the year 818, Dengyō Daishi makes a declaration which is not less memorable: "Henceforth I will never accept the merits of a Shōmon (śrāvaka), and will always turn my back upon the Hīnayāna ceremonies. I swear that I will repudiate the two hundred and fifty precepts."

Even Chisha Daishi, the great Founder of the Chinese Tendai, whom a later age will learn to honour as the Chinese Plotinus, adhered at least formally to the Hīnayānistic Moral Law (vinaya) of 250 articles, and represented a combined Hīnayāna-Mahāyāna Code. The great service of Dengyō in the field of ethics was that he threw completely overboard the Hīnayāna Law as obligatory for all Buddhist priests, and recognized only the pure Mahāyāna Law, namely the Ten Greater and the Forty-eight Lesser Precepts of the Bonmōkyō. It was not that man should merit salvation through the keeping of these precepts; the keeping of the precepts had rather the psychological meaning of preparing the soul for the highest life by annihilating the opposition of the flesh, by breaking self-will, and by bringing about that state of "willingness" and "resignation" which is a prerequisite for the *unio mystica*. The remainder of the moral actions which Dengyō Daishi retained in his ethical system, by obliging his disciples to keep the 58 commandments of the *Bonmō Sūtra* [i.e. the *Bonmōkyō*], should serve solely for purification, which must be accomplished before the spirit can be disclosed for meeting and union with the Divine. When this union had been consummated, the keeping of the precepts followed naturally. For the Godlike man is necessarily a moral man. Morality (called *kai* 戒 or *śīla*) was, then, not something which existed as a thing in itself, but which stood in the closest relationship, with contemplation (*jō* 定 or *dhyāna*) and the transcendental wisdom (*e* 慧 or *prajñā*) which resulted from it. As a matter of fact, the keeping of the precepts was considered to follow the mystical absorption and the enlightenment connected therewith. The "inner" man united with the Tathāgata kept all precepts necessarily and spontaneously, in Dengyō's opinion. We see once more that there was the closest agreement between the Founder of the Tendai sect and the author of the *Theologia Germanica*, who says,

> One must never forget, however, that God's commandments, counsels, and all His teachings refer only to the Inner Man, as he is united with God. Where this occurs, the outer man will be sufficiently directed and taught by the Inner Man, so that one does not need any outer commandments and teachings.

"All that is sound and good," we read in another place, "even the Good which is God Himself, will never make man virtuous, good or blissful so long as it is something extrinsic to the soul, and likewise with sin and evil." And in a third place we read, "Eternal Bliss does not rest with the Many nor with Diversity, but with the One and with Unity." That sounds as if Dengyō himself had said it, just as the words which the Frankforter quotes from St Paul are congenial to him: "Those who are directed, penetrated and guided by God's spirit, are children of God and do not stand under the Law."

The intellectual kinship of Martin Luther, the Founder of German Protestantism, and Shinran Shōnin, the Founder of Japanese Protestantism, has been pointed out many times. Here lies the parallelism in the clear light of day. Perhaps these lines may tend to make clear the less widely known connection which exists between the German mystics as the precursors of the German Reformation, and Dengyō Daishi, who, on his side, constituted the bridge which led to Shinran Shōnin and the Japanese Reformation of the thirteenth century.

4

The Unity of Buddhism

James Bissett Pratt

The visitor to Buddhist lands finds few things so striking as the varied and contrasting forms which Buddhism presents as one passes from the southwest to the north-east. Particularly notable, of course, is the difference between the Hīnayāna and the Mahāyāna. One familiar with the Buddhism of Burma and Siam, when suddenly set down in China, feels himself in the midst of an utterly new and unknown religion. In the smoke of incense and paper money, before Fos and Pusas,[1] among the artificial flowers and votive vegetables, he gropes around, at first in vain, for something familiar. And if he has the unusual good luck to find some monk or layman who can explain to him the Mahāyāna philosophy, he is the more mystified, and is tempted to exclaim, By what right is all this – or any of this – called Buddhism? How, indeed, can the religions of these various lands justly be subsumed under one heading, and be called by one name?

Most fundamental, perhaps, among the contrasts between South and North is the difference in the scriptures used by the two great schools. In theory the Tripiṭaka (in a Chinese rather than a Pāli version, to be sure) is recognized by the Buddhists of China and Japan. But it is practically never read, and the explicit teaching of the Mahāyāna is to the effect that these Southern Scriptures form merely a provisional statement of the truth, and have been entirely transcended by the fuller truth of the Northern School. The Southern School, in its part, refuses to recognize the Northern Scriptures as having any authority whatever: in fact, it quite ignores them. Following from this divergence in canonical scripture, an almost equally fundamental contrast is to be found in the attitude of the two schools on metaphysical questions.

---

1. Ed. I.e. before buddhas (fó 佛) and bodhisattvas (púsà 菩薩)

The Hīnayāna, in obedience to the warnings of the Founder, refrains almost entirely from metaphysical speculation; the Mahāyāna is interested in little else. Its emphasis upon morality is relatively slight, whereas the Hīnayāna teaching might almost be said to begin and end with moral matters. The moral ideals of the two schools have often been contrasted: Southern Buddhism holding up as the supreme norm for admiration and imitation the self-contained and enlightened Arhat while Northern Buddhism looks upon his attainment as but a little thing and points the learner instead to the unselfish example of the Bodhisattva. The moral teaching of the Southern School still makes a good deal of the Four Noble Truths and the Noble Eightfold Path. It is rare that one finds a Northern Buddhist who has so much as heard of these things. The Hīnayāna is emphatically realistic; the Mahāyāna as emphatically idealistic in its philosophy. In Hīnayāna lands, while there is a recognition of a long series of Buddhas, Śākyamuni alone plays any vital part in either theoretical or practical religion. In China and Korea he is associated with two or more other Buddhas who stand quite on an equality with him, and he is compassed about by a host of Pusas [bodhisattvas], Daoist deities, and Chinese generals who often seem to form a thoroughly polytheistic pantheon, while some of them frequently take from the Buddhas four-fifths of the offerings and adoration of the worshipers. In Japan the Daoist and Chinese additions to the Buddhist cycle merely give way to the innumerable deities drawn from Shintō; and Śākyamuni, far from coming back to his own, is in three of the most important sects explicitly put on a level greatly inferior to that of some of the other Buddhas. The interest of the Southern School is fixed almost exclusively on the teachings of the Buddha; the Northern School is principally interested in the teachings of philosophy *about* the Buddha. On Southern principles there seems logically nothing for the fully enlightened Buddhist at death but annihilation, and the Founder taught that the ultimate fate of the enlightened was one of the questions which ought not to be raised. The Northern School discusses the matter at length and usually teaches something very like a personal immortality for the enlightened soul. Southern and Northern teaching are usually alike in their insistence that salvation can be attained only through the individual's own efforts and his intellectual enlightenment; but many Chinese Buddhists and two of the largest and most forward-looking of the Japanese sects deny this, and in Christian fashion offer salvation purely through faith and grace, and by an act of will. Can religions having these enormous divergences be still called, in any significant sense, one religion? That is our question.

Before attempting to answer this question directly it may be well to remind ourselves that at any rate Buddhism is not alone in possessing wide varieties of belief. Of the four great religions of the world, Mohammedanism is unique in being capable of formulation within the compass of relatively narrow and exact theological definition; and even here, if one contrasts

Sunnis with Shias, or better still, orthodox with liberals, one will find very considerable divergences. Hinduism contains within itself ever greater contrasts than Buddhism. And what shall we say of the use of a single name to designate the religion of the Spanish peasant and the German philosopher, of the South American half-breed, the Russian ikon-worshiper, the English high-churchman, and the New England Unitarian? In fact, it would not be difficult to point out within Christianity rather interesting parallels to many of the Buddhist variations of beliefs and practice discussed in the last paragraph.

If Northern and Southern Buddhists do not agree on their authoritative books, Catholic and Protestant Christians agree no better on the question whether the source of authority lies in a book, in a man, in a Council, or in "the whole body of believers"; or in fact whether there is any such thing as authority at all. There is, indeed, within Christianity no such diversion as to the propriety of metaphysical discussion and the importance of metaphysical doctrines, as we found in contrasting the Hīnayāna with Mahāyāna. All forms of Christianity are more or less interested in problems of this nature. But the answers which different Christian bodies give to these problems vary almost as greatly as those furnished by the various schools of Buddhist thought. Wellnigh innumerable are the philosophical positions carefully expounded by distinguished Christian theologians, varying all the way from a simple realistic anthropomorphic scheme like that of the Old Testament to the most abstruse systems of Absolute Idealism. Particularly noticeable is this divergence when the discussion ranges about the person of the Founder. If Buddhists cannot agree on the nature and position of the Buddha; no more can Christians on the nature and position of the Christ. In Christianity as in Buddhism we find again the perennial disagreement whether the religion consists in the teachings of the Founder or in the teachings of the Church *about* the Founder. And as to his nature, there is an almost continuous gradation of beliefs, running all the way from the conception of him as God himself down to the picture of him as a deluded zealot and even to the denial of his existence altogether. To match the contrast between the Hīnayāna unitary worship and the popular polytheism of China and Japan, we have the contrast between Unitarianism and the saint worship of various Catholic and "Orthodox" countries. If the Goddess of Mercy has supplanted the Buddha in the shrines and worship of many Buddhists, have we not a striking parallel to this in the way in which the Madonna has taken the place of both God and Christ in the hearts of many a simple Christian? And if the Pure Land sects differ from the rest of Buddhism on the method of salvation, is not this identical disagreement to be found again within the Christian fold?

The truth is that if we try to define any of the great religions (except perhaps Mohammedanism) by means of creeds and doctrines, we shall find it altogether impossible to discover any unity in them. We shall be forced to split each of them into at least four or five quite distinct and even antithetical religions. As a matter of credal agreement there is no such thing as Buddhism, Hinduism or Christianity.

And yet learned writers and ignorant people, literature, history and common speech alike, continue to speak of Christianity, Hinduism and Buddhism, and everyone understands in a general way what they mean and (except in hypercritical moments) everyone knows perfectly well that this use of the words is justified. What, then, shall we make of these things, and how shall we come at any defensible definition of the world's great religions? What do we mean when we speak of Christianity, Hinduism and Buddhism?

As I have already pointed out, one thing is plain: namely, that all credal definitions are hopeless. For the truth is, the great religions of the world are not primarily schools of philosophic thought. They are something very much bigger, very much more living than any creed can be. They are, in fact, living things, organic beings, in a sense, and they can no more be identified with some form of teaching than can you or I. If we take the historical rather than the theological point of view, and consider what as a matter of fact Christianity and Buddhism have been in history and actually are in the world today, we shall see that neither of them is or ever has been a creed, but that each of them is a stream of spiritual life, one of the spiritual life of the race, taking its source back thousands of years and flowing steadily and continuously down through the ages. Each of these religions is, as I have said, an organic thing, and as such it has the same kind of unity and of self-identity that other organic things possess; not the unity of unchanging creed but the unity of a constantly yet continuously changing life.

If now we ask what constitutes the unity and self-identity of living organisms, we shall get the clue to the problem of this paper. You are the same person that you were twenty years ago, not because your body has remained unchanged, not because your mind has remained unchanged: change, in fact, has been the very condition of your being alive at all. You are the same person that you were for two reasons. In the first place, your life has been a continuous and unbroken stream from then to now, your self of today has grown out of your self of yesterday, and that grew out of your self of the day before, and so back to the beginning of your conscious existence. And second, you are the same with your self of twenty years ago because, in spite of innumerable changes, small and great, there are certain fundamental characteristics which were yours then and which are yours still. These principles hold of every organism and give it what self-identity it possesses. A material thing may be identified by the identity of its constituent atoms; a creed may be identified by its unchanging propositions; but a living, and therefore changing, organic being is identical with its own past self because of the continuity of its life, and because of the persistence of some of its more fundamental characters. A complex organism, moreover, possesses various organs of varied functions, developed out of and necessitated by the demands of its life and the exigencies of its environment. The eye *is* not the hand; it is very different from the hand; yet the two are one in the sense that they belong to the same organism and serve the same life. Through the unbroken continuity of growth both trace back their origin to the same parent cells, and both are informed by the same spirit and characterized by one dominating purpose, or innate tendency.

We may, I think, properly compare the great religions to living organisms. I do not mean, of course, that they are organisms in the full and biological sense of the word. It would be as appropriate, perhaps, to compare them to rivers. For rivers, too, have the self-identity of continuity and some of them the additional identity of persistent character. But the comparison of the religions to living things seems to me rather better; for religions struggle for existence and adapt themselves to new environments and to changing environments in almost biological fashion.

But whatever figure we use, it is, I trust, now clear that we have a right to speak of "Christianity" and of "Buddhism" and to attribute to each of them a certain unity and self-identity. For each of them is connected with its own past and its own origin by the unbroken transition of a continuous growth, and each of them can be shown to possess certain persistent characters in spite of an enormous amount of constant change. In short, it may be said that each of the great religions has its own controlling genius, which remains fairly constant underneath the almost endless branchings of its variations.

It is, of course, no part of our task here to deal further with the other great religions;[2] but if I am to sustain my thesis that in a real sense there is such a thing as Buddhism I must treat in somewhat greater detail those characteristics on which its unity and self-identity depend. The continuity of Buddhism must be patent to all readers of this paper. To me at any rate there are few phases of the spiritual life of man more interesting or more impressive than the growth and development and migration of Buddhism. Buddhism has been a pilgrim, beginning its career in a little town among the foothills of the Himalayas, wandering down the river valleys and over the great plains and across the mountains; a pilgrim, and after many years an exile, driven from its motherland and making its way through many a hardship and many a danger into strange countries and among strange peoples. Much of its early possessions it has carried with it, much it has left aside, much it has found in the new lands which it valued and which it has made its own. But throughout its long course there has been no break. Each phase of its career can be traced to the

---

2. I have made some suggestions toward this in the case of Hinduism in chapter 6 of *India and Its Faiths* (Boston: Houghton, Mifflin and Co., 1915); and more specifically on the question of Christianity in a paper entitled "Again What Is Christianity?" published in the *Hibbert Journal* and in an address on "The Nature of Christianity" printed by the Peking Union Medical College in 1924.

preceding phase, or to the reception by it of some tributary stream. Its course has been like that of a great river which with its tributaries drains an entire continent and, with many a bend, pushes its irresistible, majestic way to the sea. It has had the continuity of an individual life, the continuity of an organic species, the continuity (from another point of view) of the Hegelian dialectic.

All this I trust, is plain enough. Not so obvious, perhaps, are those persistent characteristics which help to make it, in all its ramifications and in all its history, still one religion. I shall not, of course, maintain that all those who burn incense in Buddhist temples or employ Buddhist monks at funerals are Buddhists, any more than I should hold that every ikon-worshiper is necessarily a Christian. What I mean is that there are certain qualities of character and feeling, of point of view, conduct and belief, which may properly be called Buddhist, and that these are not confined to any one school of Buddhism, whether Hīnayāna or Mahāyāna, but are to be found in all those who by common consent would be considered typically Buddhist, from southern Ceylon to northern Japan. These qualities, I hold, transcend not only nations but countries, and unite the earnest follower of the most up-to-date Japanese sect with the earliest disciples of the Founder. Taken together they constitute what, in a rough and general way, might be called the Spirit of Buddhism.

As fundamental among these qualities I would point out first of all a certain attitude, a certain feeling, a certain way of looking at things, a certain point of view, which is hardly to be described and for which I can think of no better word than the German *Innerlichkeit*. Our English *inwardness* perhaps suggests it, but not so well. Buddhism constantly lays its emphasis upon the subjective as having more importance than the objective. It is interested primarily in psychology and seeks in psychology for the solution to all important questions. Its glance is ever turned inward, and the events that go on within the soul it regards as immensely more significant than anything in the outer or material world can possibly be. Only in the inner life does it feel at grips with reality. This has been its point of view from the beginning; and with this fact in mind one sees that the development of the Mahāyāna idealistic metaphysics is not so out of keeping with the simple teaching of the Founder as at first it seems to be.

With such a view of relative values it is natural that Buddhism in all its forms should regard as of primary importance the cultivation of the inner life. Self-discipline and self-control are the first aims of its earnest adherents in every land. It is for this reason, I suppose, that whatever else of the teachings of the Founder it may have forgotten, Buddhism has never ceased to inculcate the Five Precepts – the five great rules of self-control. These are the primary requisites for reaching the supreme goal, which, whether it be that of the Arhat in this life or of the Buddhas and Bodhisattvas in the spaceless worlds, or of the simple Shin-shū believer sitting upon his lotus in the Western Paradise, consists in the attainment of a spiritual freedom and an inner Peace that the external world can neither give nor take away. Other religions have taught the value of an independent spiritual cairn, but no others have given it such repeated and almost exclusive emphasis. Once this is gained, the Buddhist feels, nothing else counts. He who through strenuous culture of the inner life has attained to this spiritual freedom, who has won the Great Peace, may snap his fingers at whatever comes.

The inner nature of this supreme goal has determined inevitably the characteristic form which the Buddhist moral teaching and moral training have assumed. The destruction of desire, as the chief enemy of inner peace, was the burden of the Founder's most significant and original sermons, and for long years this aim, embodied in the Four Noble Truths, seems to have constituted a large part of Buddhist teaching. The Four Noble Truths, as I have pointed out, form no real part of Northern Buddhism today, and there is no general attack upon desire as such. But the essence of the matter has been retained in the persistent attack which Buddhism the world over constantly makes upon Lust and Worry. In the insatiable nature of sexual desire and in the steady sapping of our inner strength that comes from anxiety, Buddhism sees the two great dangers to our Freedom and our Peace, and against these it launches its attacks, in every Buddhist land, with something of the same vehemence and systematic earnestness that the early Brothers and Sisters put into the practice of the Noble Eight-fold Path. In all these things the Northern Buddhists are at one.

As a reinforcement to these two great attacks upon Lust and upon Worry, or rather, as the principal offensive of the entire campaign, Buddhism when in earnest, in every part of the world, brings all its forces to bear against self-centredness and self-interest, against that common preoccupation with one's own possessions and schemes and wishes and rights which is so notoriously incompatible with the calm life of the spirit. I do not mean that all "Buddhists" do this: but all these in every land who would be singled out as notably and characteristically Buddhist are distinguished for this effort. The attack launched by the Founder upon self-centredness has never ceased to have its influence upon Buddhism in all the lands to which it has been carried. Sometimes, the Buddhist emphasis on the inner life has resulted in a sophisticated sort of spiritual selfishness, quite as ugly as the more brutal and naïve form which it has displaced; but there can be no doubt of the fact that the Buddhist point of view and the Buddhist training have resulted in great efforts, both North and South, to get rid of the more aggressive and obvious forms of selfishness. This has been reflected in the *anatta* or non-ego doctrine of both Hīnayāna and Mahāyāna, and in the readiness and eagerness of many Buddhists to merge the individual in the Absolute. It is seen more persistently in a trait which I think everyone must feel who has much to do with Buddhists who are steeped in the thought and training of their religion, namely a kind of "negative self-feeling" (to use McDougall's term), a kind of humility, an unwillingness to put themselves forward, a dislike for the aggressive attitude which seeks to emphasize Number Ones. This lack of aggressiveness is one of the most marked of Buddhist traits. It stands out in strong contrast to the large-footed, self-advertising, red-blooded, self-gratulatory efficiency of the West. For that matter, it is of course a characteristic not only of Buddhism but of the East in general; but in the East itself it belongs peculiarly to Buddhism. It is at the heart of much of Buddhist pacifism. Your typical Buddhist would rather give up his rights than fight for them. "Positive self-feeling" and the instinct of pugnacity have been as nearly eradicated by the Buddhist training as perhaps they ever are or can be in human nature. There is little longing in the Buddhist for a fight as such, or for that positing of the self, that assertion of one's own will, which is at the bottom of so many an altercation. Moreover, nothing that one can fight for is worth so much as that inner peace which a fight is certain to destroy. There is a kind of gentleness in the Buddhist nature which I think everyone must feel.

But this is not the gentleness and non-aggressiveness of weakness. It is not fear that prompts it. Behind it there is a spiritual strength of a quiet sort, a power of passive resistance that might well astonish a Western prize-fighter, forever feeling of his biceps. The non-aggressiveness of the typical Buddhist is a kind of strength in reserve; it is the gentleness of the strong man who refuses to push his own way in a crowd, or of the reflective man who is convinced the game is not worth the candle. Partly as an outgrowth of this gentleness of spirit, partly in obedience to the never-forgotten exhortations of the Founder, partly out of contagion from the example and influence of his mesmeric personality, Buddhism in all the lands to which it has gone has never ceased to preach and to practise universal pity and sympathy for all sentient life. *Ahiṃsā*, harmlessness, is the first law. No other religion, except perhaps Jainism, carries so far this fellow-feeling for all living things, enfolding in its merciful arms even the lowest forms of animal life. As everyone knows, it influences even the details of the monks' diet, and is not infrequently seen in what seem to us phantastic forms, as in the refusal of conscientious Buddhists to kill snakes or mosquitoes. Not only so. This feeling of pity sometimes defeats its own end, as in the refusal of Buddhists to put a suffering animal out of its misery. For the roots of it are emotional rather than reasoned. The unwillingness of Buddhists to kill animals is often explained in the West as due to the belief in transmigration and the consequent fear of destroying in the animal some deceased friend or relative. There is no doubt that the transmigration theory has something to do with it, setting the whole animal kingdom, as it does, on something like an ultimate equality with man and thus inducing a respect for our brute relatives which in the West is difficult to grasp. But I am sure there is more in the attitude of the Buddhist than this. It is by no means purely as a matter of reasoned theory that he feels for the lower forms of life and dislikes to kill them. The feeling of pity is quite as fundamental and original as the theory.

Naturally, not all Buddhists obey the law of *ahiṃsā*. Buddhist laymen often eat meat and nearly all of them eat fish. But this exception to the law is recognized as an exception, and he who practises it knows that in so doing he is not acting wholly as a Buddhist should. The necessities of this present evil world make it very difficult for all save the monks to follow completely the counsels of perfection. Nor would I assert that pity for all sentient things and harmlessness toward all human beings are displayed by every Buddhist, any more than efficient love for one's neighbour is seen in every Christian; but I believe it is true that whoever in the lands of the East is conspicuously devoid of these traits is by common consent regarded as a very poor Buddhist, no matter how many candles he may burn to the Fos and Pusas, to the *butsus* and *bosatsus*.[3] It is not without significance that the only members of the Buddhist cycle who are real rivals in popularity of the Buddhas are the Goddess of Mercy and Jizō. These are loved, I am very sure, not only because they may prove helpful to the worshiper, but because the Buddhist consciousness the world over holds in most reverend esteem and most enthusiastic admiration the qualities of sympathy and helpfulness which they embody. In China they will tell you that the Chinese learned reverence from Confucius and pity from the Buddha. Much the same thing seems to be true of Japan. Whatever be the sins of Buddhist monks, and they are frequently many and serious, they usually have the reputation, in all lands, for real feeling of sympathy; and if they teach anything to the layman it is likely to be the law of harmlessness. In the more earnest and consistent Buddhists, lay or cleric, South or North, this sympathy often blossoms into genuine love and a real desire for positive helpfulness.

Another outgrowth of the inwardness, gentleness and lack of aggressiveness which are so basic in the Buddhist character is an unusual degree of intellectual tolerance and liberality of thought. This tolerance for the opinions of others has an intellectual or theoretical root as well. It is in part the natural result of the lack of any absolutely authoritative book, Church or Pope. Buddhism has never had a theory of literal and plenary inspiration. The Founder seems regularly to have based his teachings upon his own experience or the common reason of the race. Hence, in Buddhism it is extremely rare to find any trace of that bigotry which has been all too common in religions which, like Judaism, Christianity and Mohammedanism, claim to possess a uniquely inspired and infallible book. In the case of the Mahāyāna, moreover, this natural tolerance has been reinforced by a theory of different grades or degrees of truth, and the possession of a worldview wide enough to make room for most scientific hypotheses and most non-Buddhist philosophies as approximate pictures of certain aspects of Reality. The universal Buddhist

---

3. Ed. Buddhas (Chinese *fó* 佛, Japanese *butsu*) and bodhisattvas (Chinese *púsà* 菩薩, Japanese *bosatsu*).

belief, moreover, that there is no absolute division between the sheep and the goats, but that most of us are both goats and sheep at the same time, the conception of many heavens and many hells and many conditions of rebirth in this world, with the refusal to shut the door of effort in the face of any sinner, however vile, or to believe that anywhere in the universe there is a gate bearing the inscription "Who enter here leave hope behind" – all these considerations make it natural for the Buddhist to recognize many ways of salvation besides just his own. In an oft-quoted parable in the *Lotus of the Good Law*, the Buddha shows not only that in the Eternal Heavens there are many mansions, but that there are many "vehicles" by which one may reach them. Over and over again have I asked monks in both Hīnayāna and Mahāyāna lands whether sincere Christians who lived according to their best light could be saved. In only one case, so far as I remember, have I received a negative answer; and frequently I have been assured not only that Christianity if followed out conscientiously leads to the same ultimate goal as Buddhism, but that a good Christian is really a good Buddhist, without knowing it.

I have dealt thus far with the fruits of what I have called Buddhist *Innerlichkeit* on their positive side. There are also negative results which are quite as characteristic and which must not be passed over. Like other things, Buddhism possesses *les défauts de ses qualités*.[4] The constant preoccupation with the inner and the great emphasis laid upon it naturally works a corresponding neglect of the outer. The typical Buddhist usually pays relatively slight attention to the external world. The consequence of this is seen in the lack of practical efficiency and of serious practical effort so often pointed out in the great majority of consistent Buddhists. A good Buddhist is likely to be "an ineffectual angel." Buddhists are not greatly interested in the regeneration of this evil world, and though they may wish for it in a mild way they are too busy cultivating their own inner lives to do much toward it. The morality which they preach and practise is mostly of a personal sort. It is in danger, in fact, of being largely of a negative sort. It is not insignificant that the Five Precepts – the one set of moral laws taught with emphasis over the entire Buddhist world – are all phrased in negative form. Earnest and efficient effort for social morality, for the reform of society, for cooperation with others in making this a better world, for positive and effectual helpfulness toward one's neighbour – these things are by no means incompatible with Buddhism, in a sense they may even be the natural outflow of Buddhist pity, but there is much in Buddhism that makes them difficult; and, as a fact, except among the modern sects that have been prodded into activity through Christian competition, they are rare. In all these ways of practical and efficient helpfulness and positive as well as loving service, Buddhism is far behind Christianity.

---

4. Ed. "The faults of its qualities," i.e. the faults which go with its qualities.

There are, of course, other causes for this contrast between Buddhism and Christianity besides the fundamental contrast in the genius of the two religions which I have been discussing. Foremost among these are the racial and economic factors. No one will question the obvious fact that the Western races, on the whole, are more practically efficient than the Eastern races. The reason for this may be what you like, but the fact is undeniable. The Western races are also more aggressive, they have a larger share of the sporting, combative spirit than have most Orientals. Now it is quite thinkable – I should say quite probable – that if, by some chance of history, Buddhism had gone west and Christianity east, Buddhism would have been the aggressive, practically efficient religion and Christianity the inactive one. The economic situation has reinforced the contrast of tendency within the two religions so largely brought about by racial characteristics. The charitable institutions and the missionary activities of Christendom have been made possible by the surplus wealth of Christian lands. In the West the population has never caught up with the food supply in the way it did ages ago in the East. It is perhaps more than a coincidence that Protestant missions date exactly from the period at which Protestant countries, as a result of the industrial revolution, began to have an excess of wealth. And it is, of course, perfectly plain that the possession of political and military power, as well as wealth, has done much to make possible the actual development of Christian missions. I do not think these racial and economic factors when combined are enough to explain the contrast in outer activity and efficient helpfulness exhibited by the two religions. I think the original teachings of the Founders and the ideas developed by their successors must be taken as co-causes in developing the differences we find. All these factors have doubtless had their influence.

Whatever the causes may be, however, there is no doubt that most Buddhist morality and goodwill are tinged with a certain passivity that is unfortunately almost as characteristic of Buddhism as that morality and that goodwill themselves. It did not, indeed, characterize the Founder; and innumerable cases of thoroughly consistent Buddhists probably might be cited who did not share it. It is perfectly thinkable and (as the Shin-shū in Japan demonstrate) it is practically possible that Buddhism may come to possess the active virtues of positive efficient achievement in the external world. But thus far it has done so only in exceptional cases; and its passivity and disregard of social, political, economic and material conditions are a natural if not a necessary corollary of Buddhist *Innerlichkeit* which is even more unfortunate than its passivity and which must be pointed out. The inner life is necessarily a private life. As William James expressed it, "the breaches between thoughts belonging to different personal minds...are the most absolute breaches in nature." It follows that one can do relatively little of a direct sort for the inner life of others. One may, indeed, teach morality and give instructions in *zazen*. But most of the work of self-cultivation must be done by one's self: by one's self and, consequently for one's self. When the chief business of life is the culture of one's spirit, the constant preoccupation with one's own inner life and one's advance in virtue naturally tends to breed much of the self-centredness which Buddhism is so deeply concerned to destroy. Only, as I have indicated above, it is a peculiar form of self-centredness, a kind of sophisticated spiritual priggishness and selfishness, which is indeed far removed from the brutal aggressive self-love which Buddhism constantly attacks, but which is hardly more attractive though it may be much less harmful. The belief in karma and in the acquisition of merit, with all that this means for future lives, also contributes to this most undesirable result. With the baser sort of Buddhist, the whole thing frequently boils down to a kind of spiritual materialism in which the merit to be acquired by each good deed is nicely calculated, and the cash value of virtue in this or another life is ever present to the mind's eye.

Fortunately, Buddhism possesses still a further characteristic which may in time, and possibly at no distant time, to a considerable extent counteract the unfortunate consequences of its inveterate inwardness. I refer to its remarkable elasticity and its ability to respond to new needs. Of this I shall have something more to say before the close of this paper. Already, in fact, in both Siam and Japan the needs of the times are bringing out in Buddhism qualities of practical and efficient activity in the external world which show that passivity and selfishness are by no means inevitable and inescapable consequences of its inward nature. And it is possible that these new movements within Buddhism may be only a foretaste of what is yet to develop.

In addition to the qualities I have discussed there are certain fundamental beliefs which all schools of Buddhism hold in common, the more important of which should be mentioned in this connection. Perhaps the most basic of these is the universal confidence of all Buddhists in the ultimate dominance of the universe by spiritual forces. Southern Buddhism is atheistic in a sense, and neither Southern nor Northern Buddhism has anything to say about creation or a creator. But both schools believe emphatically that the universe itself is supernaturally moral. The fundamental law of Reality, dominating all laws of the material world, is the law of karma, that whatsoever a sentient being sows, that he shall reap: that virtue and vice have their never-failing recompense. This faith Buddhism of course shares with Hinduism, from which, in fact, it borrowed it. Following naturally from this basal doctrine is the correlative belief in the unimportance of physical death. The laws of matter being so subordinate to the laws of spirit, it is unthinkable on Buddhist presuppositions that the accident of bodily death should put an end to the life of the spirit. It is conceivable, think some members of the Southern school, that absolute enlightenment may bring so full a completion that consciousness as we know it will cease at the expiration of bodily life; but mere bodily death by itself cannot possibly have any such momentous influence upon a member of the spiritual world. What form the future life may take is a matter of detail upon which different schools and different individuals disagree, though all accept transmigration as a partial solution. This common acceptance of the doctrine of transmigration, indeed, deserves more emphasis than I have space here to give it, as one of the great credal bonds that hold the entire Buddhist world together. But more important still is the spiritual and moral conception of the universe which I have been discussing, the basal faith that nothing on the physical plane can destroy the life of the spirit, and that not only the spiritual but the material world is ultimately governed by moral laws. On these great doctrines all Buddhists are firmly agreed.

One other common belief, moreover, should be mentioned, namely, the recognition by all Buddhists that their religion in its present form owes its reintroduction upon this earth to the great Indian Teacher, Śākyamuni. Together with this historical belief and this recognition of indebtedness goes the sense of gratitude and loyalty to him which loses in intensity, to be sure, as one gets farther away from the scenes of his earthly life, yet which has still a certain strength even in distant Japan. Connected with this item of the common Buddhist creed there is the further belief, accepted by all, in a series of supernaturally enlightened beings; the Buddhas, of whom Śākyamuni was one, who out of pity for all sentient things from time to time appear upon the earth to reinstate a knowledge of the way to salvation.

Before concluding this paper I must say one further word about a final quality in Buddhism which I have already mentioned and which has been and must of necessity be of great importance in the life of the religion. I refer to its remarkable elasticity and adaptability. Wherever Buddhism has gone, it has manifested this characteristic and manifested it in a superlative and unique degree. I do not think there is another religion that possesses so much of it. Buddhism has been emphatically a missionary religion. Its transplanting to new lands has been accomplished never through conquest or through migration but solely by the spread of ideas. Yet almost everywhere it has gone it has so completely adapted itself to the new people and the new land as to become practically a national religion. This has been partly due to the tolerance and liberality of its thought, to which I have already referred, a tolerance which it has exhibited both within and without. With the most extremely rare exceptions Buddhism has held no heresy trials and has carried on no persecutions. With daring catholicity that approaches foolhardiness it has recognized every form of rival as a possessor of some degree of truth. Its confidence in the inclusiveness of truth, and of its own truth, has been so great that it has taken up into itself all sorts of foreign cults and superstitions and seemingly incongruous and inconsistent beliefs. The doctrine or policy of *hōben* as the Japanese call it,[5] or "accommodation," has been applied to

---

5. Ed. The term *hōben* 方便 is the standard Japanese term for "skilful means" or *upāya*.

an extent that astonishes every Western student who reads of it for the first time. The conception that the beliefs and the gods of other religions may be true and real in their way, that they may be symbolic expressions of the truth which we possess in its fullness, hardly dawned upon the Western world prior to our grandfathers' time, and before that was guessed only by an occasional Lessing or *Nathan der Weise*.[6] But from the earliest introduction of Buddhism into Japan and even into China, when our Christian predecessors were anathematizing each other over an iota subscript, the Buddhist missionaries and thinkers were accepting into their religion all sorts of native beliefs as dim and symbolic expressions of the Eternal Dharma.

That Buddhism has carried this tolerance and liberality too far for its own good is beyond question, and is recognized today by all Buddhist leaders. The adoption of the innumerable deities of the Shintō pantheon as merely Bodhisattvas under new (and extremely long) names helped indeed to win over the Japanese people, but it brought into Buddhism a mass of primitive and superstitious cults which did much to put the religion into the degenerate condition from which it suffered for so many of the mediaeval centuries. Fortunately, its rival came to its rescue and through the effort of Shintō scholars who despised Buddhism a reform within Buddhism was initiated which has been carried on with increasing success to our own day. In China the situation has been and is much more serious. The welcoming of Daoist deities into Buddhist temples has been carried on with so liberal a hospitality that not infrequently the guests have deprived their host of all the best rooms and in some cases have turned him out of doors altogether. The deplorable condition of Buddhism in some of the more distant provinces of China is in part due to an excess of tolerance and an extreme extension of the doctrine of symbolic interpretation.

Yet when not carried too far this liberality, this elasticity and adaptability of which I speak, are undoubted elements of strength. Change is a necessity of life, a sign of life: in its readiness to change its outward forms, and to adapt itself to all sorts of new conditions, Buddhism has shown itself very much alive. When transplanted to a new land it has acted exactly as a virile biological species acts under similar circumstances. It has made the adaptations necessary to the new conditions, it has responded to the new stimuli with an inventiveness and a youthful energy that betoken an almost inexhaustible store of life, and strength. Never troubled by an excessive love of consistency, that "vice of little minds," never bound to an absolutely authoritative Past, never committed to an unchangeable loyalty, to that which has been believed *semper, ubique et ab omnibus*,[7] it has been able to develop its philoso-

---

6. Ed. Nathan "the wise" is the main character in the play with that title by Gotthold Ephraim Lessing (1729–81).
7. Ed. Always, everywhere and by all.

phy and its cult according to the fresh and changing needs of the peoples it has sought to feed. Prejudice and hostility have not stood in its way. Its rivals it has regularly sought to make into friends and allies; and when they refused this relationship and declared open war upon it, it has not been too proud to learn from them and adopt such of their methods as seemed adaptable to its needs. Christian missionaries frequently ridicule the Japanese Buddhists for their adoption of Christian hymn tunes and their imitation of the Y.M.C.A., the Sunday School, the Salvation Army and other Christian methods and institutions. As a matter of fact this action on the part of Buddhism is a token of its life and its wisdom. If it were the dead thing some missionaries depict, it could not thus adapt itself to the new needs of the new day. This unique ability to adapt itself to new conditions, to develop new organs and functions, is inherent in the fundamental nature of Buddhism. As I have more than once pointed out, the inclusiveness of its philosophy puts it in a better position to make room for new scientific discoveries and new philosophic hypotheses than can either Christianity or Islam. It can also deal with its own outgrown beliefs in a symbolic fashion which must be the envy of religions more explicitly bound to definite and authoritative creeds. The unity that it possesses, the spirit that holds it together, as I have tried to show, are not of the credal sort and not endangered by the new developments which a new age may demand of it.

The results arrived at in this essay are, therefore, not without their bearing on the question of the prospects of Buddhism. In particular, the peculiar elasticity of Buddhism puts the whole matter in a different light from that in which it would appear were we considering only the actual conditions from what might be called a quantitative point of view. A religion with the kind of self-identity and unity I have described and with the power of adaptation to changing conditions which Buddhism possesses is far from moribund. Such a religion has still a mission to perform in this world: and provided it has wise and awakened leadership it may face the future with head erect and with a growing confidence.

5

Shinran's Concept of Buddhist History

Soga Ryōjin

Owing to my own karmic contingencies as well as the blessings of the Buddhas and patriarchs, this year I enter my sixtieth year, an event so wondrous I find it hard to believe.[1] All of you have gathered from far and near, taking time from your busy schedules to celebrate this event with me. As you can see, thanks to you all, I am in the best of health, and even to be able to say this leaves me truly at a loss as to how to express my gratitude to you for honouring me in this way. I am most grateful to my good friend Kaneko Daiei for his salutary message, but I must admit I was not a little bit embarrassed by his words of praise. Though at present I do not intend to explain my reasons why, in the past year or so I have felt it imperative to stress the fact that I have never had any special penchant for "learning" or "research," those very words having little bearing on my career to date. And so when I announced the theme of my talk, "Shinran's Concept of Buddhist History," it was not intended to be a presentation of my research findings – certainly not – but

---

1. This is an adapted translation of the first lecture of Soga Ryōjin (1875–1971), *Shinran no bukkyō shikan* 親鸞の仏教史観 ("Shinran's Concept of Buddhist History," 1935), in the author's twelve-volume *Selected Works* (1970), vol. 5, 385–471. It was originally presented as a series of five lectures on 10–12 May 1935, in Kyōto, in celebration of the author's sixtieth birthday. Edited and supplemented by Soga, the lectures were published as a book of that title in December of the same year. In 1949 it was compiled with other works by Soga in a five-volume series, and in 1983 reissued as a single book by the Shinshū Ōtani-ha, Kyōto. Information on the circumstances surrounding this work, including the salutational address by Soga's close colleague Kaneko Daiei (1881–1976) mentioned in the opening paragraph, can be found in the afterword contributed by *Selected Works*' series editor Matsubara Yūzen, appended to the same volume. Portions of the original work have been condensed; notes have been provided by the translator (W.S. Yokoyama). Ed. In a few places square brackets have been removed for ease of reading.

rather to share some thoughts that have come to mind from time to time, fragments of which I may have presented elsewhere, but which I wish to review on this occasion; this, at least, is what I propose to do.

As for the theme of today's talk, "Shinran's Concept of Buddhist History," since many of you are followers of the Shōnin,[2] I suppose it may strike you as rather commonplace to hear a talk in which "Shinran" forms a central element. But, when I contemplate this element, it takes me back years, to May 1st, 1917, the place: the Main Lecture Hall of Ōtani University, then known as Shinshū Ōtani Daigaku, where a commemorative ceremony for the founder Shinran's birth was being held under the sponsorship of a university fellowship group. I had first heard of this function about a month earlier when travelling in Kyūshū with a friend who invited me to be a speaker. I cannot quite recall what the theme of my talk was, but when I assumed the platform this is what I said: "As of today I shall not say 'Shōnin' when I speak of Shinran, nor shall I say 'Shinran' when I speak of the Shōnin." In other words, I declared it my policy never to use the words "Shinran Shōnin" together. There have been times when I have strayed from this policy, but generally speaking I have stuck to my decision to use either one or the other term. As to when to say "Shinran" and when "Shōnin," I think you can generally infer its usage, and so I will not go into it here.

It is customary for people to refer to the religious figures of their own tradition as saints and teachers; these are terms of respect we all employ, calling them Great Teacher, Saint, or Zen Master So-and-so. However, when referring to the religious figures of traditions outside their own, these same people will drop the honorific language and call them merely by name, saying "Nichiren said..." or "Hōnen said..." My position on this matter is diametrically opposed to theirs. As an ordained Shin minister, I will refer to the religious teachers outside of Shin as Nichiren Shōnin, Hōnen Shōnin, Zen Master Dōgen and so on. The patriarchal teacher who has truly guided me, who constantly presents himself before me preaching the Dharma here and now, I refer to simply as "Shinran." This in a nutshell is my policy. As to how I apply this policy, I think it requires no special explanation.

Seventeen years have passed since then, and although I cannot expect all people to approve of my policy, I would assert that it is correct as far as etiquette goes and is one all people can follow naturally, and in this regard it is generally the line of action I take today. And so when deciding today's theme, I did not want people to think it was just another priest from some sect who was saying all this; I wanted people to know that here was a person who truly revered Shinran and held him in the highest regard; that here was a person

---

2. *Shōnin*. A term commonly used when referring to a Buddhist master.

who, if he can be credited with just one thing, was able to put into practice his resolve, his feeling this was the right thing to do.

My proposing the theme "Shinran's Concept of Buddhist History" may be seen in light of the common knowledge that Shinran is the patriarchal teacher who established the Jōdo Shinshū. But, in this world there are various strains of thought, and there may well be those who take issue with the assertion that Shinran indeed sought to establish the Jōdo Shinshū, who will ask where Shinran makes such a statement of intent. To get around this, some will argue that Shinran revered his teacher Hōnen Shōnin so deeply that when Hōnen told him to establish the Jōdo Shinshū he did so without question, and so it was in this way that Shinran came to do what he did. While it is difficult to refute such views, whenever I hear such arguments somehow they all sound so plausible that I do not find them to be very convincing.

It doesn't take much to argue intelligently about whether the Jōdo Shinshū was intentionally established or not; this is to inquire as to what went into the establishing of the Jōdo Shinshū [as a religious institution]. But, more than that, what exactly is this Jōdo Shinshū [as a religious teaching] – this so-called True Teaching of the Pure Land – what is it all about?[3] Concrete answers to what comprises the contents of that teaching are what we should seek. Left unresolved, the question of whether the Jōdo Shinshū [institution] was founded intentionally or not remains at the level of asking whether one has left the gate open or not; we know where the gate is, and so it is an easy matter to verify whether it is open or not. But what the Jōdo Shinshū [teaching] comprises is not something we can resolve so easily, for when we do not know what the teaching comprises, we can only respond uncritically when asked whether or not we know what it reveals. In broad outline, then, these are some of the thoughts that have occurred to me.

Recently, while earnestly reading the *Kyōgyōshinshō*, I ran straight into that very problem: What is this Jōdo Shinshū [teaching]? And suddenly, from out of nowhere, the thought came to my mind that the Jōdo Shinshū so called was the innovative concept of Buddhist history experienced by Shinran.[4] Shinran had gleaned insight into the true form of Buddhist history, that is the tradition and revelation of Buddhist history, to clarify the true spirit of the Buddha-*mārga*.[5] And so, what goes by the rubric of Jōdo Shinshū represents Shinran's insight into Buddhist history. Shinran received the teaching of the *nenbutsu* of the Original Vow from his teacher Hōnen Shōnin, and, of course, from that time on this select Original Vow, as the principle of his

---

3. Here Soga makes a play on words with *Jōdo Shinshū wo hiraku*, placing emphasis on Jōdo Shinshū as a teaching that unfolds (*hiraku*) in history, rather than on the Jōdo Shinshū institution as a historical development (*hiraku*).
4. We may see this as an instance of Soga's intuitive approach.
5. Buddha-*mārga*. The path leading to spiritual awakening.

concept of Buddhist history, was perceived by Shinran, however vaguely, as the fundamental spirit underlying Buddhist history. From the spring of his ninth year when he rapped on the gate of the Tendai prelate Jichin's abode, Shinran could find no resolution to the problem of how to free himself from the cycle of birth and death that plagued him first and last. Through the help of Hōnen Shōnin, however, aided by the teaching of the *nenbutsu* of the Tathāgata's Original Vow he was able to resolve this problem. Led by the tradition of the Buddha-*mārga* that flowed from the saintly personality of Hōnen Shōnin, moreover, Shinran was able to travel steadily upstream to the source that lay behind his teacher's religious instructions. Tracing back some two thousand years, Shinran searched for the core of Buddhist history in its panoramic sweep of two millennia from its origins to the present day. There he saw Buddhist history in its myriad forms, its hundred flowerings, each vying with the rest in beauty, woven together into a rich brocade – this was the history of the Buddha-*mārga*, magnificently outfitted with the treasures of eighty thousand Dharma repositories. What, then, lies at the core of these two thousand years in which Buddhism developed historically? Through the eternal interplay of factors by which the Dharma participates to benefit life, Shinran, for one, was by this means finally allowed an ancient insight into history, that is he was able to have his spiritual eye opened inwardly to the root cause of Buddhist history. This insight into history is, itself, none other than Jōdo Shinshū so called.

In recent times, the Pure Land teaching seems to be beset by a multitude of problems of various kinds. Further, as a topic of research, the intellectual world being what it is today, criticism of the Pure Land teaching is of course being voiced, this especially yielding newfound significance [for the teaching]. But criticism of the Pure Land teaching has been with us for quite some time. The Pure Land teaching has been the object of criticism and ridicule ever since its early origins in India and China, and in the past these instances, instead of abating, have increased in number. For the more the Pure Land teaching flourished, the more it was subject to tremendous criticism and censure. In other words, when I say that the doubts and criticism of the Pure Land teaching were rife, this is direct testimony to the viability of the Pure Land teaching.

There is a saying of Shinran's, "When you abide in the cause of faith and propriety, you make neighbours with the condition of doubt and deceit."[6]... What exactly is meant by the original terms for faith and propriety (*shinjun* 信順) and doubt and deceit (*gihō* 疑謗) is unclear, but here in this saying

---

6. Adapted here is a passage from the closing pages of the final, sixth chapter of the *Kyōgyōshinshō*. For a recent translation, see *The True Teaching, Practice and Realization of the Pure Land Way: A Translation of Shinran's Kyōgyōshinshō: Volume IV*, trans. Dennis Hirota (Shin Buddhism Translation Series; Kyōto: Honganji International Center, 1990), 617.

they are juxtaposed to show the necessary relationship they maintain; that is doubt does not appear where there is no faith, nor is there a life of faith where there is no voicing of doubt. There is of course no arising of faith in the doubting mind; when presently faith arises, doubt is allayed. Yet in spite of this, where there are those of earnest faith, there will always be those with deeply entrenched doubt. An uncomplicated, detached faith is established in response to the fierce doubter, and it is among those believers who exhibit an air of detachment that there throng the doubting multitudes. And so we might say that the history of the Pure Land as our true and sincere pursuit of the way is the history of the constant struggle between faith and doubt. As our true and sincere pursuit of the way the history of the Pure Land is not only a matter of the perpetuation of the faith; it is where faith and doubt are locked in perpetual combat that the holy working of the magnificence of the Pure Land undergoes infinite unfolding. This configuration is what lies at the heart of Shinran's perception of Buddhist history; that is, it was this configuration that Shinran perceived as operative in Buddhist history, hence it was on this basis that he established the teaching revealing this truth known as the Jōdo Shinshū. This, in any case, is what my thoughts lead me to assert.

As I was saying, Shinran surveyed the two thousand years of Buddhist history that preceded him. For us it is now closer to two thousand five hundred years, close to three thousand. What, then, is the core of the Buddha-*mārga* undercurrent to this span of Buddhist history?

According to modern Buddhist studies as it has come down to us in the past sixty or so years since the Meiji era (1868–1911), there was, first, the pure form of the basic Buddhist teachings propagated by the founder Śākyamuni. After his passing, the Theravāda Buddhist disciples he left behind compiled the Buddhist Tripiṭaka, the so-called three baskets, which spawned numerous schools of thought, giving rise to a narrow form of Buddhism focused on individual salvation and a subjective understanding of the teachings. To offset the excesses of this trend, a kind of revivalist, return-to-Śākyamuni movement occurred, known as Mahāyāna Buddhism. This movement initially had its inception in the desire of seekers for the world-saviour future Buddha, Maitreya, to appear in this world; next to come into vogue was the belief in attaining birth in the eastern Pure Land of Akṣobhya Tathāgata; and finally there arose the belief in the western Pure Land of Utmost Bliss of Amida Buddha. And here it is thought that the impetus behind the Mahāyāna Buddhist movement, having run itself out, had reached completion. Now all of this sounds very *plausible*, and though to call it plausible may seem so rude as to be insulting, my making silly emotional shows of my foolish self is how I respond whenever I have no way of confirming the truth of such matters as these, plausible though they may be. This plausible explanation of matters, set forth with an air of certainty even, as if all the facts were all but certain, has come to be acknowledged as conventional. I do not intend to take that explanation apart piece by piece. Instead, let us proceed first by regarding that explanation as one version of Buddhist history. But, by creating a Buddhist history along such a point-to-point itinerary, Buddhism becomes the object of a historical materialistic view of history.

Let us say it is acceptable to speak of a historical-materialistic concept of Buddhist history. While that would doubtless be *one* version of Buddhist history, would not such a historical-materialistic version of Buddhist history be limited to being only that and nothing more? Indeed, can a historical materialism that refutes the spirit of the Buddha-*mārga* be the situation we truly desire? If a person like myself, a man of little learning and less merit, were completely misguided in setting forth this line of argument, he would end up the laughing stock of the community and the statements above would stop there. But, as I see it, the greater part of Buddhist research as presently pursued tends to subscribe to the line of reasoning I describe above. Thus, as a result, Buddhism as a consistent body of truth is, as it were, nowhere to be found. If Buddhism is pursued on the basis of historical materialism that has no underlying spirit of the Buddhist *mārga* to unify it, soon the only thing left will be a banal Buddhist history of academic stamp. To be certain, this example of Buddhist history is also a variety of Buddhist historical concept, I will grant you that. However, a Buddhist history that takes as its basis a religion-denying materialism is a historical materialistic concept of Buddhism that aims to explain the extinction of Buddhism. While admitting it is a variety of Buddhist historical concept, I would think we must define it more precisely as applicable only when elucidating Buddhism as a past phenomenon. Beyond this I have no further claims to make. Indeed, the precise standpoint that we take is important, and should we at first, unwittingly, take the standpoint of historical materialism, it should be sufficient merely to have this pointed out to us, in order to remedy the situation. In the past it may well have been there was only one [standard] version of Buddhist history, but with the gradual sophistication in historical research, assumed or unconscious elements have been brought to light. Although I have no idea what novel concept of Buddhist history has now come into vogue, from what I gather from the lively discussions among the newer students to Buddhism, there is a fresh, new concept of historical materialism in the making. If this is true, I believe it a welcome sign.

With regard to Shinran's concept of Buddhist history, the majority of people would not be opposed to such a concept of Buddhist history. Those people could be counted as being on our side.... Generally speaking, though, people these days imagine that the Truth Buddhism teaches did not exist prior to Śākyamuni, that Śākyamuni was the one who suddenly discovered that Truth, and that Śākyamuni is fundamentally the patriarchal founder of Buddhism. These points are of course irrefutable, and I have no differences with them. Śākyamuni is the patriarchal founder of Buddhism. The Buddhist teachings in this sense could with little difference be called Śākyamuni's teachings. And so when the Buddhist teachings are mentioned, they are understood to mean the teachings explained by the Buddha, that is the teachings comprising the statements made by the Buddha. Thus, as the realization of [the enlightenment of] the Buddha, the Buddhist teachings are the teachings through which the Buddha explains what that realm [of enlightenment] is like. And so the Buddhist teachings are generally thought to be the Dharma as the recorded testimony of the Buddha or as the recorded statements of the Buddha. However, the Buddhist teachings according to Shinran are not merely the teachings explained by the Buddha or the teachings the Buddha realized. Shinran's Buddhist teaching is the teaching that one directly becomes a Buddha oneself; it is the teaching of the nature of the Buddha. It is the teaching of how the Buddha, while truly living in accordance with the Buddha-mārga as such, at the same time [discloses the path for] the ordinary unawakened being[7] to live in accordance with the Buddha-mārga as such. What the Buddha bestowed upon us through his realization of enlightenment as a true Buddha was the revelation of the causal path by which all humankind could equally attain Buddhahood. The method of research applied by the Buddhist scholars of today regards Buddhism so called as the teachings explained by the Buddha, and so scholars are only interested in determining whether it is what the Buddha taught or not. Although their chosen problematic of determining what is and what is not the Buddha's teaching is a highly important one, an even more important issue is that the Buddhist teaching so called is the teaching of how to become a Buddha, the teaching that explains the nature of the Buddha. Ultimately, the Buddhist teaching according to Shinran is the teaching of one's realization of one's own Buddhahood, the teaching of one's own explanation [of the nature of the Buddha]. Otherwise expressed, it is the teaching of the Buddha actively being realized and actively explaining [that experience]. It is important to clarify where one stands in terms of this active–passive distinction.[8] However, recent Buddhist scholarship has stripped away this aspect of how to become a

---

7. The ordinary unawakened being refers to "sentient beings," who form the target of the Buddha's awakening activity. Soga here expresses the Mahāyāna Buddhist principle that the true Buddha is one who not only attains the goal of awakening for himself but also demonstrates the path of awakening for all living beings; unless that contingency is met, true awakening is not achieved.
8. The active–passive (nōsho 能所) distinction is one found, among other places, in Shin theological discussions. It generally can be understood as the actor (nō) and the ground acted upon (sho), or as the acting subject (nō) and the object acted upon (sho). Soga introduces it here to distinguish different kinds of relationships that exist in the study of religion, where the active form of the Buddhist teachings would be Shinran who "lives" Buddhism, while the passive form might be identified with the empirical approach of Buddhist scholars who talk "about" Buddhism.

Buddha, of explaining the nature of the Buddha, and seeks to determine only what the Buddha taught, and so working on the hypothesis of approaching Buddhism through what the Buddha taught, it has limited itself to what it assumes is the path shown by these statements of the Buddha's realization. Or let me put it this way. There are those of us whose research deals with the problem of determining solely what the Buddha taught. Since we may be said to engage in such research out of the belief that, were we to put into practice what the Buddha teaches, we too, like the Buddha, would surely become Buddhas, there is no necessity for us to voice our thoughts on these matters, and we might even be reprimanded were we to attempt to do so. To be reprimanded for my views is, for me, a matter of course and does not disconcert me in the least. Though not disconcerting, I must admit I am surprised to find people today who, though they acknowledge the problem, still persist in their outmoded way of thinking.... Setting as their sole criterion whether it was the Buddha who said it or not, they ignore the matter of whether they will become Buddhas or not by putting that teaching into practice. Thus, I feel it necessary to ask ourselves whither such Buddhist research is headed. Aged as I am, there may be those who do not want to listen to the advice offered by the elderly, but I truly feel the present situation to be regretful. There are many who say that Buddhism today is undergoing a revival, that this is a golden age for Buddhist research, but these people are like the empty barrel that rattles the most. Once a barrel has been emptied of all its wine, the drunken revellers pound the barrel, dance, sing and make merry. But, while it may only be natural that they should beat the barrel and sing in their drunken dance once all the wine has been drunk, I suspect that there are those who, even without the influence of drink, would still go about performing their silly song and dance. This is the kind of doubt I have about such people...

Returning to our topic, Buddhism is the path by which one becomes a Buddha. When Śākyamuni became a Buddha, he contemplated within himself[9] the way he became a Buddha, and clarified that path by which all living beings could equally become Buddhas. On the basis of having realized enlightenment for himself, whilst actively realizing enlightenment, actively explaining his realization he strove to bestow on us the truth that ordinary unawakened beings could also become Buddhas. In explaining how to become a Buddha, though, he did not merely give people superficial advice as to how to do it, but putting himself in the place of one pressing forward along the path he

---

9. The phrase "contemplated within himself" (admittedly somewhat redundant) is intended to render the term "*naikan*" 内観, lit. "introspection," a key word in the Kiyozawa lineage of Shin thought to which Soga belongs. It was used by Kiyozawa Manshi (1863–1903), a religious philosopher of the Meiji period, who emphasized spiritualism, in contrast to the materialism of his day. Soga's early essays exploring Shin spirituality can be said to reflect the influence of Kiyozawa.

extolled how to become a Buddha, clarifying the true way of practice leading to Buddhahood; this total phenomenon is Buddhism. To speak of a Buddhism that truly and sincerely has bearing on our lives, there must be an undercurrent of the unfolding of the Buddha-*mārga*.

As regards Buddhism, in its large literary corpus a few of the works are thought to be Śākyamuni's exhortations. There are those who become attached to the single criterion that they are the teachings of Śākyamuni, but this is merely materialism, the materialistic foraging in history for suitable documents. The Buddhist canon, in that it is comprised of documents written on paper, is of material form, and as a material thing is no different from this cup on the table. The materialist examines the Buddhist canon seeking to determine when this material document came into existence. While the fact the documents are material is not mistaken, the teaching-of-the-Dharma appears on the basis of the material, through the material, by transcending the material, by preceding the material, for here we find the spirit in concrete form. What that form is, is not the problem, but when researchers merely analyse the document as a thing, we must ask what kind of philosophy such thinking engenders. Applying a concept-driven system to analyse a document, they ask when this canon appeared and proceed to do research. When they pursue research in this vein they arrive at foregone conclusions. The only problem here is the questionable methodology they apply.

Generally, man's philosophical systems go from simple to complex. Applying the so-called theory of evolution, the founder Śākyamuni should have gone no further than teaching a simple and vivid path of praxis contemplated within oneself. Śākyamuni was a person of a profound philosophical bent of mind, who lived a rather humble life style. He had about him an aura of energy and profundity that was difficult to describe in words, but to what one can attribute the source rippling with such energy and profundity I have no idea. At any rate, whenever he explained matters, what he said was so extremely persuasive that anyone who heard it found it reasonable, the path he described being extremely lucid and simple. What he explained was not the so-called theoretical or mystical path, but a moral and practical path that anyone could proceed upon with assurance. As the religion gradually became increasingly philosophical and mystical, this gave rise to what is known as Mahāyāna Buddhism. This I relate as my own thoughts on the subject.

Conceived in this way, though, there is absolutely no allowance for a notion such as ordinary unawakened beings becoming Buddhas. Those who follow that line of thinking would feel that this offers conclusive proof that the problem of becoming a Buddha was absent from the beginning. With this fundamental problem missing from the outset, their approach has as much life to it as stale beer, for it paves the way for treating the documents empirically as so much material. To treat what is material as material would seem entirely proper, but while that may be so, they make no effort to determine the nature of that so-called material by contemplating within themselves its contents; to them it is just so much empirical material and nothing more.

Applying this kind of superficial, abstract, generalized treatment, they know nothing of the material either inwardly or concretely. There is a way of looking at things by categorizing them. Since, as far as the method goes, it is no different from the method applied in the natural sciences, this would mean looking at the Buddhist canon in the same way that natural science looks at the material world. If we scientifically analyse the water in this cup, we end up with hydrogen and oxygen molecules, which are completely different from the original water; the original water is completely gone. When we think of how the Buddhist canon is being treated, we soon recognize that Buddhist research as it is presently being pursued is unmistakably burdened with the same method of research. But, when things turn out this way, I think it does not take much thought to realize what kind of results to expect.

The Buddha-*mārga* sought by our Shinran, that is the heritage of our spiritual ancestors, the so-called two thousand five hundred to three thousand years of Buddhist history, is not like that. The Buddha-*mārga* is what each of us, as the ordinary unawakened being lost in delusion, must seek over and over again, until finally, we realize the attainment of the long-sought goal as a history-changing event in our lives.[10] Our spiritual ancestors, their minds at one [with the Buddha],[11] sought for that path, trod it with unwavering concentration, to create the history of the Buddha-*mārga* as a place of practice. Never once did our spiritual ancestors ever conceive of the history of the Buddha-*mārga* as some sort of evolutionary development starting from fundamental Buddhism and going to Theravāda/Hīnayāna Buddhism and then to Mahāyāna Buddhism and Ekayāna Buddhism, or from *jiriki* Buddhism to *tariki* Buddhism. As far as our true and sincere involvement in the Buddha-*mārga* is concerned, the evolutionary view is a denial of the history of Buddhism. The true and sincere unfolding of Buddhist history is properly the historical process making Buddhas out of ordinary unawakened beings, that is the historical process of bringing the Buddha-*mārga* to fulfilment. Out of a desire "to devote himself to the holy cause of Buddhism and to increase the spiritual welfare of all beings"[12] is history thus made over a period of three thousand

---

10. "A history-changing event in our lives" renders Soga's term *rekishiteki jishō* 歴史的事証 "the realization of a historic event."
11. Ed. The translation has been slightly adjusted here.
12. From the opening passage of "The Life of Shinran Shōnin" (*Godenshō*, 1295), which describes Shinran, aged nine, deciding to abandon the secular world for monastic life on Mount Hiei. For the translation used here, see "The Life of Shinran Shōnin", in D.T. Suzuki (ed.), *Collected Writings on Shin Buddhism*, trans. D.T. Suzuki and Sasaki Gesshō (Kyōto: Shinshū Ōtaniha, 1973 [1911]).

years by the countless buddhas and bodhisattvas beginning with Śākyamuni who have trodden this path. I am sure my statement is not mistaken.

And so, when the modern Buddhist scholar asserts that Mahāyāna Buddhism was produced out of the theorization and mystification of Theravāda/Hīnayāna Buddhism, this deprives the religion of the kind of factual, real-life aspiration [whereby a person devotes himself totally to the resolution of the religious question]. If we were to think of a simple argument to refute my claim, it would not be impossible for us to conjure up some argument that would do so. But, when we imagine the consequences of such a schema, there is no argument that we can make that would justify interrupting the three thousand years of Buddhist history. From the beginning, where there was a Buddhist congregation, there was Buddhist history so called. Where there is no Buddhism, is not Buddhist history, as it were, simply a dream, a subjective notion? Of what possible significance would it be to create a history of Buddhism stripped of the fact of Buddhist experience? Truly, it is when Buddhism as the object of our investigation is made vivid by the experiences of one's very ancestors that the methodology of what we call Buddhist history is established. In other words, what we call Buddhism and what we call Buddhist history, which are respectively the object and the methodology, are one. This being the case, caught in the flow of time while transcending time, we refer to the former as Buddhist history while we call the latter Buddhism. These two are none other than the same phenomenon seen from two different perspectives.

To clarify what I mean by Buddhism, as an easy-to-understand example of what I mean, I have on numerous occasions introduced the problem of *nipponseishin* ("the Japanese spirit"), once known as *yamatodamashii*, which is a slogan we hear chanted incessantly these days.[13] But where exactly do we locate this Nippon-seishin? As a country Japan is said to have come into existence with the reign of Emperor Jinmu (660–585 BCE); that is, the history of Japan is said to begin with the ascension of Emperor Jinmu. But the real Japan does not begin with Emperor Jinmu. Although there is little so-called historical information on the period preceding Emperor Jinmu, prior to this founding of the nation by Emperor Jinmu the origins of Japan go deep back into the past. And it goes without saying that those inexhaustible sources even today gush forth uninterrupted.[14] It is here, in this unique historical fact truly and sincerely presenting itself, that the Spirit of Japan (*Nippon seishin*) is to be found. Now, to clarify the significance of the Spirit of Japan, one must go back before Emperor Jinmu as recorded in the legendary account of the

---

13. Around the time Soga wrote these words (1935), the notion of *Nippon seishin* 日本精神 was the centrepiece of the militarist and right-wing ideology.
14. The imagery of the inexhaustible wellspring gushing forth is a recurrent one in Soga's writings and draws its inspiration from the Earth-sprung Bodhisattva of the *Lotus Sūtra*.

Kojiki, for this is where you find the wellsprings of the Spirit of Japan. As to the chronology given in the *Kojiki*, whether one looks at its temporal or spatial aspects, it should strike one as a dubious account in that all the emperors reigned for such long periods of time and all ruled over such wide domains. It is like hearing a fantastic story. It may be fantastic, but we must verify the account, view it with reasonable doubt, in order to arrive at the hard facts. For I will not allow even a drop of doubt to be mixed in when it comes to historical fact...

Once again turning our attention to the problem of Buddhism and Buddhist history, it has long been thought and said that Buddhism begins with Śākyamuni, but in my view the position accorded Śākyamuni would be exactly like the one accorded Emperor Jinmu. Generally speaking, there is no call for anyone to make radical statements such as this one, but if you give any thought to the matter I think you will arrive at a similar conclusion.

If we wish to truly understand Buddhism, we must look at the situation prior to Śākyamuni's arrival on the scene. For Śākyamuni to truly assume the role of the Buddha, Śākyamuni cannot merely be Śākyamuni the man, and yet as Śākyamuni the man he truly assumes the role of the Buddha Śākyamuni. Prior to Śākyamuni, there must have been countless living souls who assumed the role of Buddhas and were worshiped and revered as such, but what proof is there of this? Here we come upon an issue of central importance.

While the *Jātaka* stories of the previous lives of Śākyamuni abound in Mahāyāna Buddhism, they are also found in the Theravāda canon in considerable number. But are these to be considered merely simple tales as might be told to children? What significance do these stories hold? It might be well, I feel, to let our thoughts dwell on this matter at length. In the *Avataṃsaka Sūtra* legend of Sudhana, relating the process of his spiritual search, at each place he visits he encounters many spiritual teachers – what can we surmise from this? In the revelation of the Original Gate in the *Lotus Sūtra*, there are the Earth-sprung bodhisattvas; the great Earth splits open and out of it springs a stream of bodhisattvas infinite in number – what significance does this hold? Letting them engage our thoughts, what do these stories tell us? In the *Larger Sūtra of Infinite Life*, there is the account of Amitābha Tathāgata who, though enjoying the stage of the highest fruit of awakening, takes the name of Dharmākara Bodhisattva to abide in the stage of causation [where he must work out his salvation] – what does this story tell us? Is there not in the offing an especially important problem that we should take time to ponder? Buddhism starts from Śākyamuni, the history of Buddhism starts from Śākyamuni – it is correct to say that Buddhist history so called begins with Śākyamuni. However, the wellsprings of this Buddhism go back to even before the beginning of Buddhist history. Ever distant the source, ever extending its flow, might well describe this case. Only when our thoughts become one with the flow can we understand for the first time how distant is the source.

As to the *Jātaka* tales of Śākyamuni's previous lives in Mahāyāna Buddhism, such legends are found in the *Prajñāpāramitā* and *Avataṃsaka Sūtra*s, but were all these legends composed after the Buddha's demise, as commonly accepted? Could it be that that such a vast collection of stories was produced in just a few hundred years after the Buddha's death? Or were those stories actually the traditions handed down for several tens of thousands of years before the Buddha? This is a matter we should deeply ponder. While it goes without saying that such pursuits apply to those who seek truly and sincerely to pursue the Buddha-*mārga*, even for those who only casually wish to study Buddhist history as an academic study or who are doing empirical (materialistic) or intellectual research, I think we can say there is some value for them to let their thoughts dwell on these matters. Even were they to view them materialistically, I think they would agree they are materials of extremely high value. The vast, boundless world of the *Avataṃsaka samādhi* has come down to us in the form of the *Avataṃsaka Sūtra*, and I think it an extremely valid research topic to determine how many years after the Buddha's death the *Avataṃsaka Sūtra* literature was compiled, and I would also approve of studies to determine the dates of the *Larger Sūtra of Infinite Life*, and I have no doubt in my mind that what Buddhist scholars are saying today is true. I know we have no right to stick our noses into their business. Ours, though, is not a problem of form, but a problem of content. To ignore the content while arguing about the form – that is like a caterpillar going round and round the rim of a potted plant; it goes around in circles, like the circle of transmigration, until, its life force spent, it dies, having accomplished nothing. This, at least, is what I think.

(Translated by Wayne S. Yokoyama)

Part II
Thinking about Zen Buddhism in the 1960s

6

Zen: Its Meaning for Modern Civilization

Hisamatsu Shin'ichi

1. ZEN AND THE BUDDHIST *SŪTRAS*

As to the question, "What is Zen?," if one is to be brief, it may perhaps suffice to utter just one word or, indeed, to utter no word at all. If, however, one is to elaborate, it may be said that no amount of elaboration can ever prove to be exhaustive. The intention here, however, is to be as simple and as plain as possible.

In the common view, Zen is a school of Buddhism which was founded by Bodhidharma in the sixth century in China. Speaking from the side of Zen, however, Zen is not one particular school within Buddhism; it is, rather, the root-source of Buddhism. There is a good reason for this.

Each of the various schools of Buddhism has a basic expression to characterize its fundamental teaching. Zen's basic expression, dating from the early period of Zen's introduction into China and attributed to Bodhidharma, is

Not relying on words or letters,
An independent Self-transmitting apart from any teaching;
Directly pointing to man's Mind,
Awakening his (Original-) Nature, thereby actualizing his Buddhahood.[1]

---

1. Ed. This famous statement may be found in various, sometimes more succinct versions. Suzuki Daisetsu once translated the lines as
    A special transmission outside the scriptures;
    No dependence on words and letters;
    Direct pointing to the soul of man;
    Seeing into one's nature and the attainment of Buddhahood.
   ("Zen Buddhism as Purifyer and Liberator of Life," *The Eastern Buddhist* 1.1 [May 1921], 20).

This expression attempted at once to do several things: to criticize and to break through radically the kind of Buddhism prevalent in China at the time of the rise of Zen; to express verbally the true nature of Buddhism; to return to the true source of Buddhism and to produce anew, therefrom, a genuine Buddhist creation.

This mode of creative criticism raised by Zen Buddhism fifteen centuries ago may provide a suggestive precedent not only for present-day Buddhism but also for present-day religion in general; for it is an authentic and appropriate way to revive and make fully alive again religions which have succumbed to formalization and conventionalization.

As regards the first part of Zen's basic expression, "Not relying on words," this is not to be taken simply literally. "Not relying on words" does not mean the complete negation (as ordinarily understood) of words. Rather, it is to be taken to mean "prior to words" in the sense of not depending on words, not being bound or caught by words. It must be explained that as here used the term "words" refers to the Buddhist *sūtras*, which are all expressed in words. Ordinarily, the Buddhist *sūtras* are treated as records of the oral expositions of Śākyamuni and are considered to be the source of and the authority for Buddhism. Today, however, modern research into the historical actualities of the compilation of the scriptures has made clear that what is spoken of as the *sūtras* are not all the direct discourses of Śākyamuni, but also include *sūtras* which were composed many centuries after Śākyamuni. Until this realization, however, the *sūtras* were generally regarded by Buddhists as the ultimate foundation and authority of Buddhism. When each of the various schools of Buddhism was about to be founded, the founder always sought in the *sūtras* the final authority for the truth to be embodied in the new Buddhist form. In the traditional Buddhist view, the final norm of truth was contained in the *sūtras*; that which had no basis in the *sūtras* could not be called truth.

Accordingly, each Buddhist school has its own particular *sūtra* (or *sūtras*) as the ultimate authorization of its teaching. For example, the Avataṃsaka School has for its authoritative scripture the *Avataṃsaka Sūtra*;[2] the Tiāntái (J. Tendai) and the Nichiren Schools, the *Saddharmapuṇḍarīka Sūtra*;[3] and the Pure Land School the "three Pure Land *Sūtras*." To prove that they are Buddhist and that their teaching is true, the various schools have recourse to their authoritative scriptures. In this regard, the same is true of Christianity. For Christianity, the Bible is the exact counterpart of the Buddhist *sūtras*; it constitutes for Christianity the final criterion of truth and is itself absolute truth. Zen, however, has no such authoritative *sūtra* upon which it is based.

---

2. I.e. the *Kegongyō* 華厳経.
3. I.e. the *Hokekyō* 法華経.

This does not mean that it arbitrarily ignores the *sūtras*, but rather that it dares to be independent of the *sūtras*. Zen severely condemns that Buddhist *sūtra*-dogmatism or *sūtra*-magic which makes the *sūtras* the final norm of truth. Zen rather casts off such dogmatism and magic and seeks to return to the source of the *sūtras* – that is to that which is "prior to" the *sūtras*. In this, Bodhidharma's response of "No-Merit!"[4] was a great criticism of the Buddhism of his time; indeed, it was revolutionary. When I say here "prior to" the *sūtras*, this "prior to" is liable to be taken temporally or historically. But, of course, I do not mean historically "prior to." I mean, rather, the source which is "prior to" the *sūtra* expressions. In Zen, this source is expressed by the term "Mind," which is, however, radically different from what we today commonly call mind. It is, for Zen, this "Mind" which is the root-source of the *sūtras*, and, thus "prior to" the *sūtras*. It is this Mind, the "Mind" as the source of the scriptures, which is meant in the previously mentioned, "Directly pointing to man's Mind, Awakening his (Original-) Nature and thereby actualizing his Buddhahood." By the word Nature in "Awakening his (Original-) Nature" is meant man's original nature, that is his true way of being. This is generally called, in Buddhism, Buddha-Nature or Mind-Nature. In Zen, however, it is called Self-Nature or "one's Original-Face," expressions which are far more intimate to us humans. Self-Nature is our own original human nature, which original nature is no other than "man's Mind." For Zen, it is precisely this original nature of man which is the Buddha-Nature; it is precisely "man's Mind" which is the "Buddha-Mind." Apart from this "Mind of man," there is nothing which is truly to be called "Buddha." Again, Buddha is not to be sought outside of this "Mind."

Consequently, "Awakening his (Original-) Nature" means, finally, that we human beings "see" that original nature of man himself. This does not mean "objectively" to see, to contemplate, to cognize, nor, of course, to believe in the nature of some Buddha which is wholly other to man. That is though we say "to see one's original nature," this does not mean to see with the eyes. Nor does it mean to contemplate, as in the case of "contemplating the dharma." As Dàzhū[5] (a Chinese Zen master of the ninth century) said, "the Awakening or Seeing is itself the (Original-) Nature." This "seeing" is man's awakening to his own original nature. In Zen, apart from the one who has awakened to his original nature, there is no Buddha to be called Buddha. It is the awakening of man's original nature which is the actualization or attainment of Buddhahood; hence, "Awakening his Original-Nature, thereby actualizing his Buddhahood." As is well known, the term "Buddha" means, in Sanskrit, "the Awakened-One." This "Awakening" means, again, man's awakening to

---

4. See further below.
5. Dàzhū 大珠 (+831). Japanese: Daiju.

his own original nature, that is to his Buddha-Nature. Śākyamuni is called "Buddha" only because of his awakening to this original nature.

Returning to the matter of the Buddhist *sūtras*, there are written within those *sūtras* many things which are no longer acceptable today, however much one may try to make them acceptable by forced interpretations. Especially today when the influence of Western religion, philosophy and science has entered into Buddhist countries, if one is taken up with the words of the *sūtras*, then one is caught and bound by words expounded in the past; this, then, becomes an obstacle to an understanding of the original meaning and, consequently, it becomes impossible to give that original meaning a new and free contemporary expression. Rather than rely on what has been expressed in the past, that is rather than rely on the *sūtras*, it is far better to enter directly into the source "prior to" what is expressed, that is into what is "before" the *sūtras*. Then, equipped with the living "eye with which to read the *sūtras*," one can interpret them freely and, according to the particular situation or occasion, give a new and truly spontaneous expression of their "source." So it is said, in Kumārajīva's translation of the *Mahāprajñāpāramitā Sūtra*, "To use words to expound the dharma which is without words."

Zen, thus, does not rely on the *sūtras* but rather makes its main concern the direct entering into the Mind which is "prior to" the *sūtras*. To repeat, Zen does not stand on any authoritative *sūtras*. This, after all, is what is meant by the phrase "apart from the teaching" in the expression, "An independent Self-transmitting apart from any teaching." This phrase, "apart from the teaching," stands in contrast to "standing within the teaching." "Teaching" here means, again, that teaching which has been established with the written *sūtras* as its basis. In contrast to that Buddhism which relies on the *sūtras* and is therefore said to "stand within the teaching," Zen, not relying on the *sūtras* but entering directly into the Mind which is the source of *sūtras*, is said to be "apart from or outside the teaching." "Apart from or outside the teaching" thus does not mean apart from or outside Buddhism; rather, it means the inner source of that which is "within the teaching." In other words, considered from the side of the *sūtra*-expressions, Zen is "apart from" or "outside"; considered from the source of what is expressed in the *sūtras*, Zen is rather even more "inner" than what is ordinarily called "within or inside the teaching." Thus, in contrast to that which is ordinarily considered to be "within the teaching," that which is within this ordinary "within" therefore becomes "apart from or outside the teaching." If we think in terms of base or foundation, it may therefore be said that Zen's base or foundation is that root-source which is even more "inner" than the *sūtras*.

2. THE ZEN UNDERSTANDING OF BUDDHA

In fact, however, Zen does not only not rely on the *sūtras*; it does not rely on anything. In an expression of Línjì, a famous Chinese Zen master of the ninth century,[6] Zen is "Self-sustaining Independence." This derives from the basic nature of "Mind" itself. If there were "that which relies" and "that which is relied upon," or, again, if it were just a matter of not relying on the *sūtras*, then it would not be ultimately not relying on anything. In Zen, however, the true authority is that Self which is itself the authority and does not rely on anything. Zen's authority consists in the non-duality of "that which relies" and "that which is relied upon." True authority is where there is no distinction between that which relies and that which is relied upon. Accordingly, since there is no distinction between that which relies and that which is relied upon, there is, in fact, no relying. Thus, true-relying is "not-relying." It is as Huángbò[7] has said, "During the twelve divisions of the day, not relying on anything."

In this respect, Zen greatly differs from Christianity and even from the Shin or Jōdo Shin school of Buddhism. Christianity and the Shin school are religions which rely absolutely either on God or on Amida Buddha. In these religions, that which relies is always that which relies, and that which is relied upon is always that which is relied upon. Their duality is never removed. It is for this reason that Christianity is called a religion of absolute dependence and the Shin school a religion of the absolute "other power." Consequently, the understanding of man in these religions is that of a being absolutely dependent upon and supported by God (in Christianity) or Amida (in the Shin school). This is not the Zen view of man which Línjì has described to be "Self-sustaining and Independent." Línjì has further characterized such a man as the "Independent Man of *bodhi*" and also as the "True-man." He has, moreover, asserted that other than such a man there is no Buddha to be properly so called. And in a very severe statement he has declared,

> Encountering a Buddha, killing the Buddha; encountering a Patriarch, killing the Patriarch; encountering an Arhat, killing the Arhat; encountering mother or father, killing mother or father; encountering a relative, killing the relative: only thus does one attain liberation and disentanglement from all things, thereby becoming completely unfettered and free.

---

6. Línjì 臨濟 (+867). Japanese: Rinzai (臨済).
7. Huángbò 黄檗 (+850). Japanese: Ōbaku.

In a later period, Wúmén[8] similarly pronounced, at the beginning of his "Gateless Gate",[9]

> Encountering a Buddha, killing the Buddha; encountering a Patriarch, killing the Patriarch: therein does one attain the Great-Freedom at the brink of life-and-death and actualize the *samādhi* of sportive-play in the midst of the four modes of birth in the six realms of existence.

These expressions emphasize that the Zen true-man is emancipated even from Buddhas and Patriarchs; he is a man of absolute non-dependence – of absolute independence, beyond the Buddhas and the Patriarchs.

In the *Discourse on the Direct-Lineage of the Dharma*[10] attributed to Bodhidharma, we read,

> Topsy-turvy beings do not know that the Self-Buddha is the True-Buddha. They spend the whole day in running to and fro, searching outwardly, contemplating Buddhas, honouring Patriarchs, and looking for the Buddha somewhere outside of themselves. They are misdirected. Just know the Self-Mind! Outside of this Mind there is no other Buddha.

The Sixth Patriarch of Zen, Huìnéng[11] also says, in his *Dharma-Treasure-Platform Sūtra*,[12] "The Self-Buddha is the True-Buddha. Your Self-Mind is the Buddha."

Mǎzǔ[13] likewise declares, "Outside of the Mind, no other Buddha; Outside of the Buddha, no other Mind." Huángbò, in his *The Pivotal Point of Mind-to-Mind Transmission*,[14] asserts, "Your Mind is the Buddha; the Buddha is this Mind. Mind and Buddha are not separate or different." Yǒngjiā,[15] in his *Song of Actualizing Bodhi*,[16] says, "In clearly seeing, there is not one single thing; / There is neither man nor Buddha."

To talk in this way may appear at first glance to be negating Buddha and to be extremely anti-religious. From the standpoint of Zen, however, the self which is still dependent on Buddha or dharma is not the truly emancipated, free, self-supporting, independent Self.

---

8. Wúmén 無門 (1185–1260). Japanese: Mumon.
9. *Wúménguān* 無門關. Japanese: *Mumonkan* (無門関).
10. Xuèmàimòlúnlùn 血脈論. Japanese: Kechimyakuron.
11. Huìnéng 慧能 (638–713). Japanese: Enō.
12. Fǎbǎotánjīng 法寶壇經. Japanese: Hōbōdankyō. Ed. Often referred to as *The Platform Sūtra*.
13. Mǎzǔ 馬 (707–786). Japanese: Baso.
14. Huánzhuànxīnfǎyào 傳心法要. Japanese: Denshinhōyō.
15. Yǒngjiā 永嘉 (665–713). Japanese: Yōka.
16. Xīnfǎyào 證道歌. Japanese: Shōdōka 証道歌.

The fundamental aim of Buddhism is to attain freedom from every bondage arising from the dualities of life and death, right and wrong, good and evil, and so forth. This is the meaning of ultimate emancipation as understood in Buddhism. Thoroughgoing emancipation is thus not being bound by anything, not depending on anything, not "having" anything – that is being in unhindered freedom from everything. The expression in the *Prajñāpāramitāhṛdaya Sūtra*,[17] "The Mind has no obstruction," has no other meaning than this.

Zen emphasizes, further, that this ultimate emancipation is not to be sought only as a future ideal which can not be actualized in the present. On the contrary, Zen insists upon its actualization in the present. The self which is dependent on Buddha is not yet the true Buddhist-Self, that is, is not yet the Mind spoken of in Zen. The Mind spoken of in Zen is not dependent on any Buddha or dharma outside of itself; rather, this Mind is the Buddha Itself which is the root-source of all.

In Buddhism, Buddha is considered the most honourable. But even that which is most honourable, if it is outside of us, would bind and obstruct us. When we are bound by something which is insignificant, we easily become aware of it. When we are bound by something very important and honourable, however, we tend to be blinded by it and fail to notice our bondage.

In Buddhism, however, the ultimate is for us to awaken the Self which, not being bound by anything – not even by its "not being bound" – works freely. Indeed, it will be even more correct to say that just because it is not bound by – or to – anything it can work freely.

Ordinarily, the above-quoted Zen phrase, "Killing the Buddha, killing the Patriarch," would be an expression of the most extreme anti-religiousness. To draw even one drop of blood from the body of a Buddha is considered by Buddhists to be one of the five deadly sins. Thus, to kill a Buddha or a Patriarch is, from the viewpoint of Buddhist faith, absolutely inadmissible. From the standpoint of Zen, however, this utterance most thoroughly expresses Zen's being "out-side the teaching," which means being free even from Buddha-bondage or dharma-bondage. Indeed, this phrase is rather to be regarded as expressing the ultimate position of true faith. The third Zen Patriarch, Sēngcàn,[18] meant this when he said, in his *Xìnxīnmíng* (*Verses on the Faith-Mind*),[19] that "Faith and Mind are not two; / Not two are Faith and Mind."

In Buddhism there are, ordinarily, innumerable forms of Buddha. In Zen, however, the true Buddha, as stated above, is the Mind which is emancipated from every kind of bondage and is completely free of all forms. Zen denies not only that Buddha figures depicted on paper, in earthenware, in wood, or in metal are the true Buddha, but even those most sublime Buddhas possessing

---

17. *Hannyashingyō* 般若心経.
18. Sēngcàn 僧璨 (+606). Japanese: Sōsan.
19. Xìnxīnmíng 信心銘. Japanese: *Shinshinmei*.

the so-called 32 major and 80 minor marks of excellence. For Zen indeed such Buddhas as the Buddhas of the recompense body, the response body, or the transformation body are not to be called the true Buddha.[20]

In the Shin School which has as its central religious concern the Buddha-with-form called Amida Buddha, it is likewise recognized that the source of Amida is the *dharmakāya*, which is without form. Shinran (1173–1262), the founder of the Shin School, writes in his *Yuishinshōmon'i*, "The *dharmakāya* is without shape, without form, and, accordingly, beyond the reach of the mind, beyond description in words. That which takes form and comes forth from this Formless-Suchness is called the *upāya-dharmakāya*."[21] Again, in his *Jinenhōnishō*, which he wrote at the age of 86, Shinran says,

> The Supreme Buddha is without form. Because it is without form, it is called Self-effected. When we represent it with form, it can not then be spoken of as the Supreme Nirvana. It is to make known this Ultimate Formlessness that we speak of Amida-Buddha.

Here it is made clear that the *upāya-dharmakāya* expressed in form, that is Amida-Buddha, is not the Supreme Buddha or Supreme Nirvana. Again, in the fifth book, "The True Buddha and His World," of his main work, *Kyōgyōshinshō*, Shinran, quoting from the *Larger Sūtra of Eternal Life*, says that attaining rebirth in the Pure Land is "enjoying the Self-effected, Unlimited Dharma Body of Emptiness." This is quite reasonable if, in the Shin School, rebirth is considered, as it should be, equivalent to attaining Nirvana. They call the attainment of Nirvana the "going aspect." Since, however, Nirvana is the Self-Nature, the Original Way of life of all beings, the attainment of Nirvana is also spoken of by Shinran (in his *Yuishinshōmon'i*) as "the returning to the capital of Dharma-Nature."

From this we can see clearly that a Buddha which has form is not the ultimate or true Buddha, that the true Buddha is without form. It is in this sense that for Zen the Buddha without form is the true Buddha; and it is just the true Buddha which is the true Self, the true Man. Therefore, Zen has nothing to do with idols – and this in a most thoroughgoing fashion. Accordingly, Zen Buddhism does not worship, pray to or believe in any Buddha with an objective form, whether material or ideational. Rather, for Zen, Buddhism is awakening to the True, Formless Mind; that is awakening to the True-Buddha. It is this awakening to the True-Buddha that Zen calls Seeing One's Nature or awakening to One's Original Face. According to Zen, it is precisely the Original Face of man – of any one of us human beings – which is the True-

---

20. Ed. The preceding two sentences have been edited for the sake of greater transparency.
21. Ed. I.e. the *hōben-hosshin* 方便法身. Shinran did not use the Sanskrit term which is presumably a retrospective construct here.

Buddha. The True-Buddha is no other than the Original Way of human life, or, in other words, the True-Self. Awakening to one's Original Face is "Seeing man's Nature and becoming Buddha." By the Seeing of one's Nature we do not mean any objective contemplation, objective awareness, or objective cognition of Self-Nature or Buddha-Nature; we mean the awakening of the Self-Nature itself. Since there is no Buddha apart from this awakening, to "become Buddha" means to come to the true Self-Awakening. Thus it is that the term "Buddha" literally means "the Awakened one." Since, for Zen, there is no true Buddha outside of the man who is awakened to his True Self, Línjì calls this awakened one the "True Man." All Buddha-forms, like the so-called recompense body, response body, or transformation body, are but different modes of expression of this "True Man" and have meaning only as such.

It is in this sense that we can say that Zen is neither a theism which sets up a transcendent god, nor a humanism centred on man in the ordinary sense, but that it is rather "True-Man-ism," centred around the True Man awakened to his Original True Self.

3. THE METHOD OF ZEN

As has already been made clear, Zen does not rely on any authority. If we are to speak of any authority in Zen, its basic authority is the True Self, that is the True Man. This authority, however, is to be called the authority of no-authority. Accordingly, the method of Zen is to get oneself – and to get others – to awaken to the True Self, which all men are in their primal nature. This is what is meant by "Directly pointing to man's Mind." Zen takes its occasions or opportunities to come to this awakening not simply from within the teaching but freely and directly from life itself in its every aspect and action, such as walking, abiding, sitting, lying, hearing, seeing, raising the eye-brows or blinking the eyes. If one looks into the Zen occasions and Zen opportunities which appear according to the different places and different times in Zen history, this becomes clear at a glance. Such occasions and opportunities are simply too numerous to be counted. A few well-known examples are Nánquán's "Killing the cat"; Zhàozhōu's "Have a cup of tea" and his "Cypress tree in the garden"; Lóngtán's "Blowing out of the lantern"; Yúnmén's "What is the meaning of wearing a clerical gown at the bell-signal?" and his "Dried dung stick"; and Shǒushān's "Bamboo spatula." Thus, according to the time and place, Zen makes use of any of the innumerable phenomena of life as the occasion to awaken oneself or to awaken others to man's true Self-Nature.

To seek for the Buddha externally is wrong in its very direction. Nánquán, in his Zen teaching-expression, "The ordinary mind is the Tao-awakened," goes so far as to say to Zhàozhōu, "Even to set upon the quest for awakening is to go contrariwise." Línjì, often using the example of Yajñadatta (who once went about searching for his face), also admonishes that in searching externally for the Buddha one only goes further and further away from him. The *Discourse on the Direct Lineage of the Dharma* cited above states that so long as one searches externally, not knowing that the Self-Mind is the Buddha, even if one is busy the whole day contemplating the Buddha and making obeisance to the Patriarchs, one misses the True-Buddha.

For Zen, that Śākyamuni is a Buddha is only because he is awakened to his True Self-Nature. And not only Śākyamuni, but anyone without exception who is awakened to his true Self-Nature is, for Zen, a Buddha. Here lies the sameness quality of being a Buddha. In the Buddha-Nature every man is completely equal. The Buddha who is the mode of being only of some particular person or who is transcendent does not represent the true mode of being of the True Buddha. Conversely, the man who is not a Buddha does not represent the true mode of being of a True Man. Thus it is even said that man as he truly is is Buddha, and that not being a Buddha is to be in *māyā* or "illusion." The same is meant by the Sixth Patriarch when he says in his well-known verse, "Originally not-a-single-thing, / Where can dust collect?" (*Platform Sūtra*).

When historians say that Śākyamuni lived in India 2500 years ago, they are referring to the Śākyamuni with form. Śākyamuni as Buddha is not the Śākyamuni who existed temporally and spatially 2500 years ago in India, but is the Formless True Man who is not delimited by time or space. In this sense Śākyamuni is the eternal "right-now," the infinite "right-here." Śākyamuni as Buddha cannot be understood by those historians who would negate the Self-Buddha through their use of the categories of time and space. Śākyamuni as Buddha can be known never as an object but only as Self-Awakened Existence, as the Awakening awakened to Itself.

This means that wherever and whenever any man is awakened to his True Self-Nature, the Buddha is there and then, Śākyamuni as Buddha is there and then. This "there and then" is the root-origin of Buddhism which is "prior to the *sūtras*." From this root-origin there can be created newly and freely, appropriate to the time and place, dharma-expressions which are not bound to the already established dharma-expressions of the past, such as the Buddhist *sūtras* and Buddha-images. Zen's "not relying on words" means freedom not only from the already established forms but, indeed, from every form; further, it means that while continually creating forms in Self-expression, one is not captured by those forms or by their creation. It is just in this meaning that the *Vimalakīrti-nirdeśa* speaks of "Giving rise to every dharma from the root of the non-abiding," and that the Sixth Patriarch says, "Just with 'no dharma to be attained' to give rise to all dharmas."

Zen thus may be said to have two aspects: one is the aspect of the true emptiness of the True-Self which, unbound by any form, is completely free from all forms; the other is the aspect of the wondrous working of the Self which, unbound by any form, actualizes all forms. These two aspects constitute the "substance" and "function" of the True Self. True emptiness is the "abstraction" of all forms; the wondrous working is the free formation of every form. This is the Self-expression of the absolutely Formless Self. It is here that we have the ground for the non-dualistic oneness of thoroughgoing abstraction and thoroughgoing expression. Ordinary abstraction is not completely free from form, since it is still only a stage in the process going toward the liberation from all forms. Ordinary expression is not yet a free expression which is not bound by anything, since it is still an expression deriving from some kind of form. Herein lies the Zen basis for a thoroughgoing abstract art and a thoroughgoing expressionism.

When Zen arose in the sixth century, much had been going on in Chinese Buddhism in the way of translations into Chinese of the *sūtras*, the construction of Buddha images, of the building of monasteries, and the giving of offerings to the monks. Emperor Wǔ of the Liáng dynasty had achieved so much in the line of these Buddhist works that he was called the Buddhist-minded Son-of-Heaven. It was just during this Emperor Wǔ's reign that Bodhidharma came to China from India. Bodhidharma was asked by the Emperor what kind of merit he could expect from the innumerable good works which he had sponsored since his enthronement, such as the construction of monasteries, the copying of *sūtras*, and the ordination of monks. Bodhidharma replied that all these accomplishments were of "No-Merit." This single phrase of "No-Merit!" may be said to be a basic and thoroughgoing criticism of the mode of Buddhism of those days. For Bodhidharma, these works were trivial fruits attained within the birth-and-death-bound cycle of *saṃsāra*, and were still causes producing defilement. They were not to be regarded as ultimate realities. Upon being asked further by Emperor Wǔ what, then, was the true merit, Bodhidharma answered, "The Wisdom of Purity being perfect in its functioning, the Functioning Self is empty and calm." What this means is that this Empty-Calm-ness is the root of all merits, the merit at the heart of all merits; that if this is neglected, however devotedly one undertakes the construction of monasteries, the reproduction of *sūtras* and the ordination of monks, these achievements must be said to lack the essential point. The Empty-Calm-ness of the Functioning Self, spoken of by Bodhidharma, is nothing but the Original Face of the truly Empty Self mentioned previously. Awakening to this Self is, for Bodhidharma, the highest merit, the essential meaning of Buddhism. This radical criticism by Bodhidharma together with the later spread of Zen brought about a great change in Chinese Buddhism, redirecting it from its diversion toward accidentals back to its basic source.

This direction toward the root-source, however, does not mean the *process* of going toward the root-source, but rather means, as is expressed in the Zen phrase "Directly pointing to man's Mind," directly *entering into* the root-source, that is directly awakening to the Original Face of the Self. That is why direct and straightforward ways to open up this awakening came to be so greatly emphasized. The innumerable occasions of *satori*, that is of Seeing one's True Nature, which appear in the history of Zen are so many instances both of this unique method and of its actual fruition in Self-Awakening.

The examples of the so-called *kosoku* (ancient case)-*kōan* which are recorded in and make up many of the Zen texts such as the *Bìyán lù* ("Blue-Cliff-Records"), the *Wúménguān* ("Gateless Gate") and so forth, constitute no more than a very small portion of these Zen occasions. These occasions, it is to be emphasized, all involve the concrete things of the ordinary world of man, including such extremely common things of the natural world as the sky, the earth, mountains and rivers, various trees such as the bamboo, the peach, the pine, the cypress, various animals such as the dog, the cat, the wild duck, the ox and the tiger, or the daily activities of the monks – travelling about to different monasteries, begging alms, drinking tea, taking meals, taking a bath, talking, keeping silent, raising the hands or stretching out the legs. This concreteness of the occasions, however, is no mere concreteness.[22] As the *sūtra*-expression "Concrete matter is itself empty" indicates, it is only the occasion according to the time and place for the direct entering into True-Emptiness; that is this concreteness is no more than the moment for the direct awakening to the true Emptiness-Formlessness, which is the "abstraction" which emancipates concreteness. This abstractness, in turn, as indicated by another *sūtra*-expression "Emptiness is itself concrete matter," is not simply the negation of concreteness. It is, rather, the very basis of the turning away from the concreteness which is to be negated (i.e. the false being) to the concreteness which is to be affirmed (i.e. the true being).

We have said that natural things and human affairs serve as the occasions and the opportunities for Zen. There are, however, not a few instances in which phrases from the various Buddhist scriptures, such as the *Vimalakīrti-nirdeśa*, the *Vajracchedikā Sūtra*, the *Avataṃsaka Sūtra* and the *Saddharmapuṇḍarīka Sūtra*, also serve. For example, Zen makes use of the following *Sūtra* sayings:

> The Original Being is consummate and fulfilled in Itself;
>   why the going astray and being unawakened? (*Vimalakīrti-nirdeśa*)
>   To enter the Dharma-gate of Non-Duality (*Vimalakīrti-nirdeśa*)
>   The fourfold Dharma-World is originally all pure. Why come there to be mountains, rivers, and the great earth? (*Avataṃsaka Sūtra*)
>   Not to abide anywhere and yet to activate that Mind (*Vajracchedikā Sūtra*)

---

22. Ed. With the word "concreteness," the writer refers invigoratingly to what is more conventionally translated as "form," as in the expression "form itself is emptiness" in the *Heart Sūtra*. See the next sentence.

> If one sees Me with form or seeks Me identifying Me with sound or voice, that one practises the wrong way and can never see the Tathāgata.
> (*Vajracchedikā Sūtra*)
> No eyes, no ears, no nose, no tongue, no body, no consciousness.
> (*Prajñāpāramitāhṛdaya Sūtra*)

These phrases, which are so-called "*kōan* from inside-the-teaching," are not quoted, however, out of respect for what is written in the *sūtras* or for the purpose of indulging in verbal comments or textual exposition. Zen rather takes over these phrases and makes them its own, using them as its own occasions and opportunities according to the requirements of the time and place. In this usage, these scriptural phrases are given a treatment completely different from the close, logical reasoning they receive in Indian Buddhism and the textual exegesis and commentaries they receive in Chinese Buddhism. The Indian and Chinese treatments are "inside-the-teaching"; the Zen treatment is a living usage "outside-the-teaching." That is, in Zen even the scriptural phrases are used as Zen's own unique and direct moments to bring about the Seeing of one's Nature and the attainment of Buddhahood through the direct pointing to man's Mind, which is at once separate from and the source of all the *sūtra*-expressions.

Often, the occasions for the functioning of Zen take the form of *mondō* question-and-answer exchanges. A *mondō* question-and-answer exchange is not a dialectical or theoretical dialogue or discussion; nor is it of the question-and-answer mode of daily conversation. It is a kind of question-and-answer exchange wholly unique to Zen, developed for the purpose of bringing about Self-Awakening in the unawakened or, when used by the already awakened, for the purpose of taking the measure of each other's awakening. This kind of question-and-answer exchange is the total Self-hurling, so to speak, of true Emptiness-at-Work. It is the free play of Zen functioning, which takes everything and anything for its occasion depending on the time and place. It includes all the functions of man and is not, as is generally the case with ordinary questions and answers, based merely upon words. For example, there are many instances in which the *mondō*-exchange involves the blinking of the eyes, the raising of the eyebrows, the cupping of the ears, the raising of a fist, a blow with a stick, the shouting of a *katsu*, eating a meal, drinking tea, bowing in homage, lifting up a mosquito-driver and the like. What must be emphasized is that in this kind of *mondō* question-and-answer there is the vivid, dynamic Self-presentation of true Emptiness-at-Work. In short, what is being unfolded in the *mondō*-exchange is the direct, vigorous Zen action of "directly pointing to man's Mind, and seeing into his Nature," thereby to attain oneself and to have others attain Buddhahood. The uniqueness and marvelousness of the Zen *mondō* lies in its never being mere talk or silence, sitting or lying, drinking tea or taking a meal, using a stick or shouting; it is always the Wondrous-Working of True-Emptiness. If it were not for this – and if this is not understood – the Zen *mondō* would be nothing but a falsehood, a boast, a madness or, at best, a kind of wit or riddle.

4. THE ZEN UNDERSTANDING OF MAN

It is a characteristic of man that the more he becomes involved in complexity, the more he longs for simplicity; the simpler his life becomes, the more he longs for complexity; the busier he becomes, the stronger is his desire for leisure; the more leisure he has, the more boredom he feels; the more his concerns, the more he feels the allure of unconcern; the more his unconcern, the more he suffers from vacuousness; the more tumultuous his life, the more he seeks quietude; the more placid his life, the lonelier he becomes and the more he quests for liveliness.

It is a characteristic feature of modern civilization that everything is becoming more and more complicated, that the degree of busyness increases day by day, and that the mind becomes too overburdened with concerns. Consequently, there is an increasingly strong desire on the part of people to seek simplicity, leisure, freedom from concern and quietude in order to offset the common trend of modern life.

Recently, in the United States, which has assumed the lead in modern civilization, not only ordinary buildings but even churches have changed their architectural style from a heavy, complex and intricate style to a straight-lined, simple, smart, modern style. That this tendency toward modernization in architecture is sweeping over not only America but also the older cities of Western Europe and, indeed, even Japan, is not simply because of practical utility, but also undoubtedly because it responds to a natural desire of modern man, who finds himself further and further enmeshed in the extreme complexities of modern life. More specifically, the fact that houses in America are gradually becoming one-storied, simple, and clean-cut, influenced by Japanese architecture, is probably because of the desire to escape complexity and to find serenity. Further, that intricate and involved painting and sculpture have given way to forms which are unconventionally informal, de-formed or abstract may also be considered to signify a liberation from troublesome complexity, elaborateness and formality. So, too, the change from overly heavy colours to monotone colours in the manner of monochrome *sumie* paintings, thus making for a beauty of simplicity, one of the special characteristics of modern art, may also be considered another aspect of this same liberation.

In the same vein, it is inevitable that modern man, thrown more and more into a whirl of pressing concerns, should seek and in fact greedily demand leisure time, a phenomenon which has found its expression in the current term, "leisure-boom." Indeed, all of the following recent phenomena – the deep interest in the extremely primitive art of uncivilized people, the popularity of folk songs and of children's songs, the appeal generated by the rustic colloquialisms of the local dialects in contradistinction to the standard language of the cities, the attraction of the free and open world of nature (the mountains, the fields, the oceans) as opposed to the uncomfortably close and crowded urban centres, the marked tendency in recent art toward naïve artlessness, simplicity and rustic beauty – can probably be similarly attributed to a longing for artlessness by modern men, who are suffering from the excessive contrivances and artificiality of modern civilization.

Oneness and many-ness – or, unity and diversity – are mutually indispensable moments within the basic structure of man. They must necessarily be one with each other and not two. Oneness without many-ness is mere vacuity without content; many-ness without oneness is mere segmentation without unity. Here lies the great blind spot in the mode of modern civilization. The so-called diseases of civilization – uprootedness, confusion, frustration,[23] instability, bewilderment, scepticism, neurosis, weariness of life and so forth – are largely due to this blind spot. The greater the multiplicity, the stronger in direct proportion must be the oneness or unity. When, on the contrary, the actual situation is a relation of an inverse proportion, then man has no other alternative than to seek to escape into a oneness or simplicity alienated from many-ness, whether by turning to the primitive or by simply negatively withdrawing from many-ness. This, however, is no more than a superficial solution to the problem of segmented dissociation. Herein may also be found one reason that today, although anachronistic to our time, premodern, non-civilized cults and superstitions still command a following, a drowning man will grasp even at a straw, although objectively considered it is clearly untrustworthy. The attempts by contemporary man to escape from civilization or to return to the primitive, to the non-civilized, and the non-modern, may be viewed as natural but superficial countermeasures to try to compensate for the lack of unity in modern civilization. To turn from such superficial countermeasures to a genuine solution, there is no other way than by establishing within the multiplicity that oneness or unity which is appropriate to the multiplicity.

If the direction of the development of civilization is toward more and more multiplicity, more and more specialization, then no fixed, static oneness or unity will ever do. The oneness or unity must be sufficiently alive and flexible to respond freely and appropriately to the growing multiplicity. It is not enough that the oneness, while not being alienated from multiplicity,

---

23. Ed. The original has "prostration," but this was presumably a printer's error based on the similarity to "frustration" in Japanese phonetics.

merely serve as the static basis within multiplicity. It must be a dynamic and creative oneness or unity which, as the root-origin of multiplicity, produces multiplicity from itself without limit; a oneness that can eternally produce multiplicity out of itself freely and yet remain unbound by what is produced; a unity which while producing multiplicity yet remains within multiplicity and can accord with that multiplicity appropriate to the particular time and place. Only then can the multiplicity, while unlimitedly taking its rise from such a oneness, never lose that oneness, and only then does the oneness, while producing the multiplicity, ever remain within and unalienated from the multiplicity which it produces.

Multiplicity, in such a case, continuing to contain within itself, even as multiplicity, a oneness or unity, will thus not become disjointedly fragmented. Accordingly, there will be no need to escape from multiplicity to a hollow unity which is alienated from multiplicity. On the other hand, since the oneness even as oneness is the inexhaustible source of, and is never separated from, multiplicity, there will be no need, because of any feeling of ennui or because of having fallen into a mood of emptiness or loneliness, to seek for a liveliness within a many-ness alienated from oneness. The true oneness is a oneness in many-ness; the true many-ness is a many-ness in oneness. There is a Zen expression: "Within Nothingness (there is contained) an inexhaustible storehouse." Only when such a relation obtains between oneness and many-ness, the two elements of the basic structure of man, will man, however much he may diversify toward multiplicity, be free from disjointed fragmentation and, at the same time, in his oneness never suffer from emptiness or loneliness. Then can he be at once a unity and a multiplicity without hindrance, free from all pressure and self-contented, the true Subject eternally giving rise to civilization. Man as such a Subject is Man in his True mode of being. Precisely this Man is the human image which is the inner demand, whether or not he is conscious of it, of modern man, standing as he does right in the midst of a civilization which continues to diversify more and more as it develops. Such a human image is the Original-Subject which, even as it freely and unlimitedly creates civilization and is ever present appropriate to the time and place within the civilization which has been created, is always completely emancipated and never bound by the civilization.

This Original-Subject, which must awaken to itself and form itself right in the midst of modern civilization, is no other than the Zen image of man. It is this Man that the author in his previous writings has called "Oriental Nothingness," "Active Nothingness," and "Formless-Self." It is the Man which Huìnéng, the Sixth Patriarch, already very early in the history of Chinese Zen, spoke of as "The Self-Nature which, unmoved in its base, is able to produce all things," and, again, as, "Not a single thing to be obtained and, precisely thereby, able to give rise to all things." It is the same image of Man which is referred to when Yŏngjiā, a contemporary of Huìnéng, says that "Walking is also Zen, sitting is also Zen. Whether talking or silent, whether in motion or rest, the Subject is composed." The same Man is meant by Huángbò when, in his *The Pivotal Point of Mind-to-Mind Transmission*, he declared, "Just the one who the whole day, though not apart from things, does not suffer from the world of things, is called the Free Man." In that it infinitely creates civilization and forms history, this human image may be said to be humanistic. In that – even while it is immanent in, and the root-origin of, what is created or formed – it is not attached to or bound by, but is always free from, the created, it may be said to have the religiousness of Línjì's "Self-awakened and Self-sustaining (Man)," that is the religiousness of being the truly Emancipated-Subject. Only when they come to be this Emancipated-Subject can the subjects spoken of in the Avataṃsaka teaching as the subject which "returns to and takes rise from Itself," and in the Pure Land teaching as the subject which in its "going aspect" actualizes Nirvana and in its "returning aspect" "plays freely amid the thick woods of what formerly constituted self-agonizing illusions," lend themselves to a modern application. Of course, by modern here I do not mean anything temporal, that is [being] of any particular generation or period of history. Rather, I mean a modern Self-formation-actualization of the Eternal-Subject which is the root-origin of, and beyond all, historical periods. In the *Vimalakīrtinirdeśa*, this is expressed as "taking form in response to the thing confronted." Here there can be established a newer and higher humanistic religion which, on the one hand, does not degenerate into the modern type of anthropocentric, autonomous humanism which has forgotten self-criticism and, on the other, does not retrogress back toward a premodern, theocentric theonomy completely unawakened to human autonomy.

The realization of such a new, yet basic and ultimate, human image will enable us to do two things. First, it will enable us to turn away from the superficial attempt to cure the disease of modern civilization through an anachronistic, simple-minded, world-renouncing mode of escape to a naïve, premodern oneness which is in estrangement from civilization. Second, it will enable us to make a more proper attempt at a radical cure of the modern predicament through the Self-awakening of that oneness which, contrary to being in estrangement from civilization, accords with, and is the source and base of, civilization. Such an image of man entertained by Zen will also sweep away every internal and external criticism or misunderstanding of Buddhism which takes it to be world-weary, world-renouncing and removed from reality, longing for some ideal world in a sphere other than the historical world of time and space. It will, at the same time, be worthy of being presented to the Occident as a new Oriental prescription for the disease of modern civilization. For the recent surging of Zen interest in the West in such areas as psychology, the arts, the handicrafts, invention, philosophy, religion and so forth is not accidental but derives from an inner necessity of modern civilization.

5. FORMLESS BEAUTY

Zen is, thus, the awakening to the above-described human image which is beyond time and space, but which works freely and without hindrance according to each particular time and place. For Zen, therefore, this awakening-working is the ultimate active truth, active good and active beauty, which transcends all limitation; it is the root-origin of every particular – and therefore limited – instance of truth, good and beauty. Although we shall confine our remarks here to beauty, what is said in this regard applies as well to truth and goodness.

Supreme or ultimate beauty is not a particular beauty belonging to the realm of art in the narrow sense, but is, rather, the beauty of the awakened, working human Self. It is a formless beauty which never becomes an "object" – either of vision, of any of the other senses, or indeed of any mode of consciousness. It is Active-Subject-Beauty, that is the beauty which is the free functioning itself of that which is emancipated from all forms; it is neither merely the concept of beauty nor the idea of beauty. That is, it is the beauty of our being the human Self which is actually awakened and is at work; it is not any objective beauty which arises from seeing or otherwise sensing that Self as an object. It is the beauty which becomes aware of itself only when it becomes the awakened Self itself. In other words, it is the beauty of the Formless Self.

In Buddhism, the so-called 32 major and 80 minor physical marks of the Buddha are ordinarily regarded as the perfect features of Buddha. But perfect as the features may be, any Buddha with form is not the true Buddha. As Línjì has said, the true Buddha is formless; being without form is the true form. Formlessness is the genuine mark of the true Buddha, and is true beauty. The Buddha beauty which is sought in objects of perception by the eye, ear, nose, tongue, body or consciousness, that is through shape, voice, smell, taste, touch or idea, is not the true Buddha beauty. In the *Vajracchedikā Sūtra* it is written, as already noted, that "If one sees Me with form or seeks Me identifying Me with sound or voice, that one practises the wrong way and can never see the *tathāgata*." The true beauty of *tathāgata* cannot be sought for through the above-mentioned sixfold mode of sense perception (or consciousness) or their objective referents.

It must never be forgotten that in Buddhism there is an ultimate beauty of formlessness which goes beyond the beauty of form to be found in such things as Buddha images, Buddhist music, incense-burning, ceremonial meals, worshipping, verses, the various *mudrā* expressions of the fingers and so forth. It is precisely this beauty of formlessness which is the beauty truly unique to Buddhism, the beauty of the true human Self. Buddhist aesthetics or the true beauty of form in Buddhism must be a formless beauty expressing itself in form, which is then known through the six modes of sense-perception or consciousness – that is it must be the Self-expression of formless beauty which freely takes on form in any of the objective realms of sense-perception or consciousness. Formless beauty, because it is formless, not only is not conditioned by any already established form but is never conditioned by any form whatsoever. Therefore, it can freely take on any form in Self-actualization. True Buddhist aesthetics is to be found in this beauty of formlessness which freely actualizes itself within form while never being bound by any form.

Accordingly, true Buddhist aesthetics, from the side of the active creation, is formless beauty expressing itself in form; from the side of appreciation, it is the apprehension within form of the formlessness which transcends form – that is the apprehension of the form as the expression of formlessness. In short, true Buddhist beauty is none other than the beauty of the human Self awake and at work. Awakened formless beauty, through its working, expresses itself in, so to speak, "a subtle form-beauty," the beauty of mere form returning, thereby, to the beauty of formlessness. True Buddhist art is the beauty not of mere form but of "subtle form." It is this latter beauty alone which enables Buddhist art to be directly connected with the true human Self and to have a necessary intrinsic relation with the awakening of this Self; it is this beauty alone which can enable Buddhism to become the backbone for a healthy development of contemporary civilization and to become the eternal source for the creation of future civilization.

(Translated by Richard DeMartino and Gishin Tokiwa)

7

The Awakening of Self in Buddhism

Nishitani Keiji

I

At present Japanese Buddhism is exerting little influence upon people's lives. This fact is claimed as proof of the decline of Buddhism. The impact of Buddhism upon society has become feeble because it has penetrated too pervasively into our daily life; it has changed into a sort of social custom and has fallen into a state of stagnation. The major reason for this perhaps may be traced back to the religious policy of the Tokugawa Shogunate.[1] Some people say that the cause of the decline of Buddhist influence lies in its negative doctrine of resignation. But upon looking back on its past history, we find that Buddhism has been a great force for moving society, as have been Christianity and Mohammedanism. Of course, by "moving society" it is not meant that Buddhism has a social theory of its own or that it attempts a social revolution. Buddhism is not a so-called "social movement"; it rather transforms man's inner mind radically, and develops man's most basic being into a flowering that it has never reached before. In short, it has become a moving force in society by opening up a way to transform man himself. It might be said that, so far as its religious function is concerned, Buddhism has exerted a really deep and most lasting influence upon society although, in appearance, it may seem to be an indirect and devious influence.

---

1. Ed. 1600–1867. The point is that while the main Buddhist denominations which had come into existence by then were privileged through the system of household registration at Buddhist temples, this in turn led to a certain ossification. At the same time Confucianist and Neo-Confucianist studies were encouraged, while from the eighteenth century onwards there were major stirrings of Shintō revivalism.

At present, most people think that to transform society is one thing and to transform man is another, and that the former should be achieved before the latter. But in reality, these two aspects cannot be separated from each other so easily.

To take an example, many "progressive" men in our country say that the present-day crisis concerning atomic warfare results from modern capitalism which obstructs the inevitable direction of history, or especially, from international capitalism which has become monopolized in the stage of its development as "imperialism." Those who think thus believe that the only way to overcome the crisis lies in a social revolution. But is this really so? Is it not rather that the crisis does not result exclusively from the capitalistic society alone but arises also from the very thought of those who think that the crisis derives exclusively from capitalistic society? The viewpoint which regards the conflict of social ideologies as ultimate and social revolution as necessarily prior to anything else constitutes one of the major factors in the very crisis that it is attempting to overcome. The very thought that social revolution should take precedence over man's inner transformation is not an insignificant part of the crisis itself. We recall, for example, that Malenkov, as premier of the USSR, once declared that the use of the latest weapons might result in the destruction of both the Soviet Union and its enemies, and even of civilization as a whole. The following year, when he resigned the premiership, he was severely criticized in *Pravda*. What he had declared before, the Communist press said, was ideologically untenable: only the West would be destroyed while the Soviets would survive.[2]

Behind such an incident, we can perceive a way of thinking which might be called a sort of "pseudo-messianism" (Berdyaev)[3] in which the communization of the world is regarded as the inevitable direction of history, the realization of which would ensure the solution of all the problems of mankind. Such a fanatical attitude is closely bound to a black and white way of thinking in which social revolution and the transformation of man are naïvely regarded as two distinct problems while, in truth, the one presupposes the other. If such an over-simplified separation were not made, the conflict of ideologies could not be regarded as ultimate, and there would be opened up a way of mutual understanding between the "two worlds."

Therefore, matters concerning man's inner life are not so detached and remote as they appear to be at first sight.

---

2. Ed. Parts of this paragraph have been grammatically modified for the sake of transparency. Malenkov (1901–88) held the post of premier of the ministerial council of the USSR between 1953 and 1955.
3. Ed. Nikolai Berdyaev (1874–1948).

II

Since Buddhism opened up an entirely revolutionary view of the essential nature of man, it is not surprising that it should offer a more basic and permanent principle of social transformation than could ever be offered by a mere ideology. From its very beginning, Buddhism was a religion that indicated the path to transcend the "world." According to Buddhism, the only thing necessary is emancipation from the innumerable bondages which come forth spontaneously from within ourselves and tie us to things of this world, that is to say, nirvana, the extinguishment of the fire. This Buddhistic way of transcending the "world" as well as the "self"-in-the-world, in spite of its so-called "other-worldliness," means an awakening in which we become aware of our original and authentic nature (our dharma-nature) and live in conformity to it. The possibility of attaining this enlightenment depends entirely upon ourselves; the ability to attain it lies buried deep in the dharma nature of each of us. The only thing required for us is to cut down the threads of attachment and to become "homeless" in the world. It was thus natural that the community of Buddhists, the samgha, was from its start based on the absolute negation of all sorts of "worldly" differentiations, social as well as psychological, such as the rich and the poor, the learned and the unlearned and so forth, and especially the distinction of the castes, "the primal distinction that Brahmanism presumed to have originated in the mystical depths."[4]

As is well known, the first disciples who gathered around the Buddha came from various castes. They must have been fully conscious of the fact that their own establishment of "brotherhood" was a historical event of revolutionary character and that it was made possible only by a wholly new basis of human relationship being opened up beyond the rigid Brahmanical framework of castes – a basis wherein man is free from all bondage, ultimately independent and truly equal as man to man.

> As the great streams, O disciples, however many they be, the Gaṅgā, Yamunā, Aciravatā, Sarabhū, Mahī, when they reach the great ocean, lose their old name and their old descent, and bear only one name, "the great ocean," so also, my disciples, these four castes, Brahmans, Nobles, Vaiśya and Śūdra, when they, in accordance with the law and doctrine which the Perfect One has preached, forsake their home and go into homelessness, lose their old name and old paternity, and bear only the one designation, "Ascetics who follow the son of the Śākya house."[5]

---

4. H. Oldenberg, *Buddha*, trans. W. Hoey (1881). Ed. Here 7th printing, 172 n.
5. Oldenberg, *Buddha*, 152.

This way of awakening to one's self on a plane beyond the world, and the same absolute denunciation of the caste distinction, have been maintained throughout the development of Buddhism. To quote an example: there is within the *Tripiṭaka* a short tract entitled *Kongōshinron* (*Diamond Needle Tract*), supposedly written by Aśvaghoṣa, who flourished as a thinker and poet from the first to the second century CE. In this tract, he disapproved, from the Buddhist standpoint, of the class distinction of the four castes in India. He rebuffed one by one the mythico-religious or socio-conventional assertions that defended the authenticity of class distinction, and set up an entirely new universal and religious standard of the nobility of man's basic character based upon morality. We find herein a revolution in man's viewpoint from the external to the internal. We can also see an example of the religious reformation that has transformed the concept of man as a social being.

Needless to say, the establishment of the caste system in India is due to the historical circumstances in which the aboriginal Dravidian race was conquered and enslaved by the invading Aryan race. The enslaved aborigines were then called Śūdras, upon which the other three castes (Brahmans, Kṣatriyas and Vaiśyas) were superimposed according to the differences of their professions. As is well known, this caste system was so strict as to prevent anyone born in one caste from ascending to a superior one, and also from marrying anyone of another caste. Moreover, this fixed idea of a caste system seems to have been given various kinds of justification by the Brahmins.

As to the grounds for their justification, seven items – life, blood, body, knowledge, custom, practice and Veda – are mentioned in the *Diamond Needle Tract*. Since it is not necessary here to dwell upon each one of these, we shall only refer to the first one, that is "life."

For example, an argument advocated by the Brahmins runs as follows. Those who die in the Heavenly Realm are reborn in the Heavenly Realm; those who die in the Human Realm are reborn in the Human Realm. So is it with the beasts. According to their life philosophy, heavenly beings, humans and animals are reborn in the same realm as before. The argument seems to mean that they are predestined to be reborn in the same realm eternally.

It seems that such a philosophy was expounded on the basis of the Brahmanical canons, thereby establishing the priority of class distinction. Aśvaghoṣa, however, repudiates such a philosophy by quoting from the same canons in which it is stated that Indra himself was originally a kind of creature, and he retorts by asking what is meant by "life" at all. In some cases he argues by producing counter-evidence. For instance, he says that in spite of the Brahmins' insistence that their superiority is maintained by "blood," there are, among Brahmin families, not a few whose ancestors are identified with some mythological figures other than Brahman; or, again, that in spite of the Brahmins' insistence upon their superiority by "knowledge," there are, among the Śūdras, some people who are possessed of all the knowledge to be learnt by the Brahmins, and so forth. He observes that after all, all of their grounds for arguments are "not in accordance with the right Reason." More important is what he maintains positively.

According to Aśvaghoṣa, what determines man's position is "virtue." Nothing but "virtue" is the standard for classifying man essentially as man per se. A man's nobility is determined only by whether or not he is possessed of virtue. He says, "Therefore, it is to be known that one is called a Brahmin, not according to his lineage, conduct, practice, blood, but according to his virtue." "Virtue," as he called it, is that which can be developed in the Buddhistic life. He declares,

> Those who have mastered their senses and extinguished their defilements, who are detached from the differentiation of "self" and "others," and are altogether free from craving, anger, and ignorance, *they* are worthy of the name of Brahmins in the true sense of the word.

He also asserts elsewhere that those who are endowed with the five characteristics of perseverance, endeavour, contemplation (*dhyāna*), wisdom (*prajñā*) and compassion are Brahmins; others who, being devoid of these five characteristics, are attached to the differentiation of "self" and "others," are all Śūdras. Thus he declares conclusively that on these grounds a Brahmin can be called a Śūdra, and a Śūdra can be called a true Brahmin.

III

The revolutionary change expressed in this tract by Aśvaghoṣa is that human existence emerged from behind the fortified caste system which it had inherited throughout a long period of history and which it had regarded as fixed, as if belonging *a priori* to man himself. By this change, the realization of man as "man" emerged for the first time. Especially to be noted here is the fact that the realization of man was brought about on the basis of none other than the Buddhist standpoint of non-ego. The event is fundamentally different from its Western counterpart which occurred at the dawn of the modern era and in which man's realization of himself took place in the form of the realization of ego.

In the case of the West, the realization of "man" came into existence mainly through the process of the so-called "secularization" of culture, and through man's separation from the religious outlook toward himself. The result was that man, rather than a God-centred being subservient to the Will of God, came to be regarded as an independent, self-centred being who has his motivation within himself. This "self" came to its own consciousness as an autonomous being whose independent existence is sustained only in relation to itself, not as a "created" being whose existence is founded upon its relationship to God. Such are the implications of my above-mentioned statement that the self-realization of man took place in the form of the realization of "ego."

The opinion often advanced by historians might well be justified that such a realization of man, despite its far-reaching discord with Christianity, has, after all, originated in the Christian view of man. This Christian view includes man's *personal* relationship with God, the essential equality between man and man in the presence of God, man's freedom attained in the faith of being a son of God and so forth. But it must also be noted that man's autonomous existence could be brought about only through the process of social and cultural "secularization," detaching itself from its religious background. This circumstance shows that the aforesaid "self-realization" comprised a great question-mark from the very beginning of its effectuation. It means that as man came to realize himself as autonomous "man," he left out the most essential moment of his being. This is the moment of "love," which is united as one with freedom and equality in the existence of religious man. Or, at least, love ceased to be an essential moment of that self-realization. This was, indeed, unavoidable. Because whereas freedom and equality can maintain their identity (although in the rather paltry guise of "liberty" and "equal right") in spite of the transition from the religious to the irreligious and secular way of living, this can not be the case with love.

Through that transition, love undergoes a qualitative change. In Christian terms *agapē* changes itself into *eros*. Religious love (*agapē*) is so particular to religion that as man's realization of himself occurred apart from the religious background, this realization necessarily had its motive apart from love. Thus, liberty and equality without the moment of love came to be claimed as man's "right," inherent a priori in his being a man. Liberty and equality have been established in the form of the insistence upon "human right." Man's grasp of himself has been brought about as the realization of his "self" as *ego*. In the meantime, love has manifested itself as the *fraternité* of the French Revolution, as the "love of humanity" expounded philosophically by Feuerbach, as the so-called spirit of "service" of modern Americans, and in many other forms of disguise. But this love never succeeded in assuming such an essential significance as to break through the boundaries of the enclosure of ego; nor did it succeed in becoming a driving force in the formation of societies and individuals, as did the assertion of liberty and equality. In view of such circumstances, it can be said that beneath the various critical problems faced by modern peoples, there lies the fact that the realization of man by the West in modern times was effected by such a realization of ego as has been stated above.

The reason why the realization of "man" in the modern West was only brought about in that particular fashion is that the religious (Christian, in this case) outlook of man prior to this event was dogmatically God-centred, and that it contained in itself something that made it impossible for man's autonomy to function fully. Because of this deep-seated discrepancy, it was inevitable that the realization of "man" should finally become detached from the religious background. In this respect, it comes to assume a great significance for contemporary man that the realization of man, as discussed in the above-mentioned *Diamond Needle Tract*, was made possible by the evolution of the religious standpoint of the "non-differentiation of self and others," as expounded in Buddhism.

IV

If one phase of the vital revolution appearing in the above-mentioned tract lies in the fact that the realization of "man" manifested itself in overcoming the caste system previously regarded as almost predestined, another phase lies in the fact that a new standard for deciding man's essential value came to be discovered within that same realization. As Aśvaghoṣa says, "on account of that reason" (i. e. on account of the presence or the absence of the Buddhist virtues), "a Brahmin can be called a Śūdra, and a Śūdra can be called a true Brahmin." This is a complete revolution in the estimation of value according to an entirely new standard. Śūdras, who have been regarded as the lowest in the rank of man, are now true Brahmins if only they possess the Buddhist virtue; and Brahmins, regarded as the highest of men, are in truth Śūdras if they are lacking in it. Here we see a discovery of a new sense and a new reason in regard to the "truth" of man. The claim that the Brahmins are the standard for the value of man undergoes a radical revolution by this discovery. The idea of the true Brahmin or the "man" par excellence is established by thoroughly overturning the conventional outlook of caste distinction. It is even stated, "If those Caṇḍālas were equipped with the characteristics of a king, they can be called true Brahmins." Caṇḍālas are especially lowly men among the Śūdras. By kingly characteristics may be meant the above-mentioned Buddhistic virtues. Anyone who is equipped with those virtues is said to be king-like in his essential being as a man. What it means to be a "true" Brahmin is clear. It means that, as regards the truly essential in man, even the lowly can possess kingly characteristics. Herein is revealed the cause of Buddhism as a religion.

It must further be remembered that Buddhist monks voluntarily took to the mendicant way of life. They possessed no private property at all, except an alms-bowl and a robe that consisted of rags. They imitated therein their Master who was thought to have rejected the throne of Cakravarti-rāja, the world ruler, and to have chosen a life of begging.[6] And "the begging-bowl was

---

6. Ed. The meaning of *cakravarti* is "wheel turner," and a person with the karmic prerequisites for becoming a Buddha is considered to have the option of becoming either a mon-

the Buddha's badge of sovereignty.... He obtained it as the reward of rejecting the position of world ruler. Teachers often gave their begging-bowl to their successor as a sign of the transmission of authority."[7] It is also asserted in the same tract that there is no essential distinction among human beings belonging to any of the four castes, just like four children born of the same parents. The author of the tract repeatedly admonishes, saying, "Having been born of the same one father, why the conceited attachment to the difference of the four castes?" The statement that even the lowly, in their essential being as man, can be equipped with a king's characteristics should especially be noted.

The "lowly" in the modern West are the modern "proletariat" who are said to have become estranged from humanity in the capitalistic society. In order to recover their lost humanity, modern revolutionary ideology preaches the way in which the proletariat, who have been exploited so thoroughly that nothing more remains to be lost, should in turn exploit their exploiters. It is a recovery of human rights and at the same time an actualization of the movement of man's realization carried out in the form of the realization of "ego" brought into the material phase of economics. In this case also, the "humanity" whose recovery is being sought is humanity of "ego"; it is not the realization of "man" as "non-ego" referred to in the passage on the possession of kingly characteristics in terms of the Buddhistic virtues.

However materially enriched and culturally elevated the recovered humanity might be, as long as it is restricted to the realization of "ego," there remains, if that statement is viewed from the standpoint of the realization of man in "non-ego," room for the statement, "those Brahmins can also be called Śūdras." Even when the proletariat have reached the highest possible standard of living and have ceased to be the proletariat, seen from the more essential viewpoint, they still remain proletarian. Needless to say, the aristocracy and the bourgeois, from this viewpoint, are equally proletarian. While, on the contrary, even the lowly are capable of being possessed of kingly characteristics as a true man.

It is not only Marxism but all other modern social ideologies as well which have failed to recognize the possibility of such a paradox. They may have reached to the concept of "Nothing" in a material sense, as implied, for example, in the idea of "Proletariat," but they are unable to know anything of the Nothingness as the religious Self-realization of "Human-Being"-ness. It is not in their knowledge that even the lowly who have nothing materially can be possessed of kingly characteristics in the "Nothing" of the religious sense. Hence their interpretation of religion as an opiate. Such an interpretation can only be derived from the various ideologies, in whose perspective

---

arch (*rāja*) who rolls out the wheel of empire or an enlightened person who sets in motion the wheel of Dharma.

7. E. Conze, *Buddhism: Its Essence and Development* (New York: Harper, 1959), 55.

man appears only as an "ego." They only know the realization of man on the level of "ego," not on the level of "non-ego." The way of thinking referred to at the beginning of this thesis, in which social revolution is considered apart from the transformation of man, derives also from this blind spot.

In the contemporary West, the conflict between the theocentric standpoint of Christianity and the man-centred realization of "ego" of the various sorts of atheism, seems to be the most basic problem. Would not the Buddhistic realization of "man" involve something that can contribute to the solution of this difficult problem?

(Translated by Bandō Shōjun)

8

Introducing Martin Heidegger

Nishitani Keiji

Note from the Editors of *The Eastern Buddhist* (1966)

The Eastern Buddhist is honoured to have the privilege of presenting these texts of two speeches by Dr Martin Heidegger.[1] The first, "Ansprache zum Heimatabend," is an address given 22 July 1961 at Messkirch, Germany, the small town near the Bodensee where he was born. The occasion was the 700th anniversary of the town's founding. The second, entitled "Über Abraham a Santa Clara," was delivered to an alumni meeting at Messkirch on 2 May 1964. Both were published as pamphlets by the town of Messkirch, however their distribution was, for the most part, limited to those present at the speeches. We are therefore very grateful to Professor Heidegger and to Mr Siegfried Schühle, the mayor of Messkirch, for their kind permission to reprint these valuable addresses, little known even in Germany. While there is no doubt that the presentation of two speeches by one of the most eminent thinkers of the present age is significant enough in itself, still the reason for their appearance in a Buddhist magazine may require some explanation. Although Professor Heidegger makes no reference whatsoever to Buddhist thought and although his original motivation surely was not connected with Buddhism, we nevertheless feel that the thoughts expressed in these speeches contain various points of contact with Buddhistic thought and thus they should be capable of contributing to the mutual understanding of East and West.

---

1. Ed. In the original edition of *The Eastern Buddhist* both texts were published in German, but in this volume only the first is given, and in English translation. This is partly for reasons of length, but also because (a) such biographical details about Abraham a Santa Clara which are necessary for Nishitani's argument were explained by him as required, and (b) some of the other parts, fascinating in themselves, involve many plays on words which interested Heidegger himself but could only be reproduced with substantial annotations not relevant to this book. Abraham a Santa Clara is the monastic name of a German monk, originally Ulrich Megerle (1644–1709), who grew up in the same small town of Messkirch and later lived in Vienna, where he wrote robust sermons in an inventive style. Nishitani picks out the parts of Heidegger's address which are of immediate interest for a comparison with Zen Buddhism. Readers interested in German thought will find the seriously playful use of words a fascinating clue to the understanding of Heidegger's own thought.

Nishitani Keiji's introduction:

I

With the encounter of East and West proceeding in all fields of human activities at a surprisingly rapid tempo, mutual understanding is, needless to say, one of the most important tasks facing mankind today. Among the many difficulties lying hidden along the way of this task, the greatest appears when, trying to penetrate in some degree the inner thought, feelings and purposes of our co-partners, we find words and concepts, the inevitable vehicles of this communication, rising up time and again to bar the way. In that region near the innermost core of the mind, in the region of things spiritual, the above-mentioned difficulty becomes almost insurmountable. It is especially so in the case of encounter between world religions, such as Buddhism and Christianity, where the differences between the religious faiths, residing in the innermost mental core of both sides, are concerned. In each of them, their own faith or insight has long been formulated into creed and authoritatively laid down as dogma predominating over all that men think, feel or will, so that people become firmly convinced of their own opinions and come to have great confidence in themselves. Often their conviction and self-confidence are armoured by sharp analysis and subtle dialectics which are developed in dogmatics. In short, the religious faith or insight is translated into words and concepts and these give birth to dogma and dogmatics, which, in turn, serve to confirm that faith or insight. Here is a process in which faith is brought closer and closer to itself, thereby becoming more firm and more self-confirmed, and thus more enclosed within itself. Such is the process that occurs in most cases within the innermost mind in religious thinking, and therein arises the extreme difficulty of mutual understanding between minds of different religious faiths. Of course, dogmatics has not always been narrowly enclosed by dogma. By the very causes that make the establishment of dogmatics necessary (the need, for instance, of defending the dogma against criticism from without), religion is compelled to accept from philosophy as many concepts and theories as are useful to its purposes. Dogmatics comes in this way to contain elements which make a dialogue with "outsiders" possible; it becomes in this way more or less open-minded and is enabled to exist as an open system. But however open-minded it may become, even when its system is made as open as possible, so long as it remains dogmatic, that is so long as it stands on an exclusively closed basis of faith and dogma, it can never avert the above-mentioned procedure: it must produce, in all its own efforts to become "open," a means to confirm itself alone. And thus, as it becomes more "open," it must become all the more firmly closed. It is compelled to return to its original enclosure, making futile all its "openness." It thus betrays itself, and allows mutual understanding to remain despairingly difficult. But however hard it may be, in order to pave the way to mutual understanding, we must descend to the region of faith and dogma, where the aforementioned extreme difficulty appears; because that region is, after all, the deepest plane mankind has yet attained in his long history. The encounter of East and West cannot be ultimate as long as it does not plumb that region where resides the marrow of the mind of men. But, as we have seen, this region is at the same time the very place where the most troublesome aporia arises to thwart mutual understanding. The encounter cannot truly take place there, for on that plane (of faith and dogma) even a world religion, however open it may be within its own confines, still remains closed against any other world religion. And between two closed systems there can be only collision, not an encounter in any true sense. We should, therefore, after once arriving at the plane of faith and dogma, break through it and search beyond it on some deeper plane for the possibility of encounter and mutual understanding in a true sense; an entirely new plane, where perhaps the innermost core of man's mind, as we usually understand it, should also be broken through. We are standing today before a trenchant requirement; to transcend our innermost spiritual forms and norms, the rigid framework of dogma and dogmatics. This requirement is a trenchant one, because it calls upon us to return to our basic "self" beyond all dogma, to strip ourselves once and for all of those fixed forms and norms enclosing our thoughts, feelings and volitions within ready-made and seemingly eternal frames. It calls upon us to return to the most basic plane where man is solely man or is merely a son of man, no more, no less, where he is thoroughly bare, bare-headed, bare-backed, bare-handed and bare-footed, but where he can bare his innermost heart as well. It is as if we were demanded to walk bare-footed the city of "the variegated cow" as Nietzsche called it – a world multi-coloured with miscellaneous forms. However hard it may be, to descend in ourselves to such a basic plane seems necessary in order to prepare the open place for the true encounter in question. But granted that such a procedure is today necessary, can we find in the actual world any clue at all for making the realization of that procedure possible? If so, what is it and where can we find it? Now, that possibility seems to be comprised in no other than the basic historical circumstance, which at present is necessitating an encounter of Buddhism and Christianity. I mean by this the situation in which now the whole world is rapidly becoming One world. Today, in almost all fields of human life, in industrial, economic and political activities, and in the arts, morality and philosophy, the One world is more and more emerging as the stage of their plays. There is no need to speak in this regard of science and technology. Their new inventions are making communication easier and speedier between distant parts of the globe. They are bringing at the same time, by their essential character of "objectivity," the minds of all peoples on to a common plane of thought and intention. They are the main actors in the drama of the emergence of the One world, necessitating the encounter of various cultures and religions. This general current has been able to arise only through the process of "secularization," the process in which various sorts of man's activities have become emancipated one by one from the ban of religious dogma and dogmatics that have long commanded them. Today religion, with its dogma and dogmatics, stands aloof in the world, encased in itself, the sole exception to the world's general trend. In such a situation, the only possible way of a true encounter and mutual understanding of East and West in the most basic locus of human existence – in the innermost kernel of man's mind, heretofore shackled by dogma and dogmatics – seems to be discovered solely through candid self-exposure to the deep complexities of the actual world and by grasping therein some new point of departure. That would mean, in truth, to delve into the basis of existence itself through and through until we reach the hidden source; the source, in which originates the present emergence of the One world with its thorough and universal secularization of human life, and from which are arising now all sorts of social "progress" through the rapid development of science and technology, as well as the devastation of traditional culture progressing side by side with the "pro-gress" of modern civilization. To expose oneself candidly to this situation of the actual world would then signify that we, every one of us, become in the most simple and radical sense a "son of man" who has nowhere to lay his head. The word "simple" here means being a "son of man" stripped of all his traditional forms and norms, or, as expressed above, a "bare" man; the word "radical" means to be a "son of man" to whom all religious dogma and dogmatics would be the holes of foxes or nests of birds which he has not. Today no real encounter with Jesus seems to become possible without a descent to the deepest plane of our existence, on which every one of us has nowhere to lay his head and is "homeless." Today "man should," as Bonhoeffer has said, "live in the presence of God, as if there were no God." On that plane alone can we become qualified for the commencement of the quest for the way to exist truly in the emerging One world and thus notified to search for a way of true encounter between East and West.

II

In the former of the above-mentioned speeches at his native place Heidegger begins with the problem of the *Heimat* ("home" in the sense of native place). In our age of modern technology, we are, he thinks, essentially reduced to the state of homelessness. By television and radio, for instance, we are continually transported abroad, although we think ourselves always to be at home. We live in truth amidst *das Unheimische* (the undomestic, un-"home"-like).

Heidegger speaks then of *das Unheimliche* (the uncanny) that reigns in the sphere of *das Unheimische*, haunts man wandering there, and draws him into the state of homelessness (*Heimatlosigkeit*). What then will man be like in the future? Heidegger says, "Perhaps man is settling into homelessness. Perhaps the connection with the *Heimat* is vanishing from the existence of modern man." But he then continues, "Perhaps, however, in the midst also of the pressing *Unheimische* a new relation to the *Heimische* is being prepared." What does he indicate by that? Within our constant escape into something new, newer and newest, there lurks a deep boredom (*Langeweile*) in which Time hangs heavy upon us; this boredom floats within the abysses of existence like a fog driven to and fro. In this boredom is concealed a home-sickness. Boredom is the veil of the home-sickness, which is a longing to the Home, a drive towards the Home. In the midst of the homelessness, there occurs a drive towards the Home. The fact that man is perpetually on the way of escape into the *Unheimische* indicates the presence of an impelling drive to the *Heimat*, which is none other than Home-sickness. Perhaps deep boredom is the hidden, unconfessed drive to the *Heimat*, the drive which we thrust away and yet are unable to evade. In the depression of the hidden Home-sickness, the Home presents itself with more pressure upon us than anywhere else. Therefore, Heidegger says further, "Thus in all un-home-like things the Home we seek, although veiled, yet comes to us." Because it comes to touch us in such a form again and again, we should go out to meet it. But how? In such a way that we are willing to preserve That, whence we have come. Right in the midst of that homelessness which, lurking in the future, comes to haunt us at present, we can find a way to the place of our origination. That place, the Home, is no other than that which "sustains us in the core of our existence (*was uns trägt im Kern unseres Daseins*)." Stepping forward into the future to meet it, we tread backward towards it. Thus alone we can preserve our Home in the midst of our homelessness.

    Buddhism also knew, from its beginning, this homelessness. Moreover, the Buddha and his disciples chose voluntarily the life of the homeless. In order to emancipate themselves thoroughly from this world with its suffering, from the transitoriness of all things and the birth and death of their own being, they made up their minds to sever all threads of attachment. This was a turnabout similar to that stated above: the turnabout consisting of the return to the "son of man" in the simple and radical meaning. The Buddha said, "Hear ye who have ears; give up thine own faith (*saddhā*)." While the teachers of the *Upaniṣads* gathered around them only limited groups of men who accepted some definite faith, the Buddha broke that limit, established a universal standpoint and preached to all kinds of men. He went down to the basis of human existence prior to any sorts of "Home." There, he then transcended all attachments, became completed and was emancipated into the great Repose called Nirvana. He became the Awakened One; he became "the knower of all," "the conqueror of all," and "the one who knows himself." This awakening, this attainment of Repose in the midst of Transitoriness, can mean a way of discovering the Home in the immediate midst of homelessness, as is also pointed out by Heidegger. Of course, this does not signify an escape from this world to some other world. The transcendence of this world was compared, to be sure, to an escape from a burning house,[2] but the true meaning of it lies in becoming truly awakened, in becoming the awakened one, or in awakening to the true Self. Nirvana signifies living as an awakened one (as the Awakened One) in this world, that is to say, to "live" in the true sense. Apart from this "life," the "other world" could be only a world of fancy conceived by a man remaining attached to this world; it cannot be our "Home." Needless to say, the above-stated way of awakening in the Buddha was afterwards inherited and developed in Mahāyāna Buddhism. It would here suffice to be reminded of the famous phrase in the sayings of Rinzai, "not to leave one's house, while being on the way" and "not to be on the way, while leaving one's house." In Pure Land Buddhism, the Pure Land used to be called "the Home." In this case also, the concept of the "Home" is essentially connected with the Awakening of the Amida Buddha, although it has assumed the character of the other world in the devout aspirations of the converts. The vocation of Buddhists today is two-sided. On the one side, a Buddhist must seek, amidst the uncanny homelessness of the present technological age, amidst the widespread situation of man's estrangement from himself, the way back to his *Heimat* or, as Heidegger has put it, to that which sustains man in the core of his existence. On the other side, he must essay to recover, in and through the same situation of estrangement, his own authentic way of Awakening and to revive Buddhism for the present age. This effort is at the same time an effort to shed all ready-made dogmas and dogmatics, because the above-said situation of estrangement acts as a cathartic fire for Buddhism as well as for other religions. As the Buddhistic way of Awakening itself signifies the return to and repose in the *Heimat*, it is clear that these two sides are united in one and the same task. Christianity also is certainly burdened today with the same task of indicating the way home to a wandering mankind. Man, in becoming a wanderer, can be said essentially to have become self-indebted, and his deliverance from that debt is now the common task of all potent religions. This task is the debt with which religions today are saddled for the sake of mankind. Thus far, we have tried to take up, in regard to Heidegger's first address, the most fundamental point that seems to be in contact with Buddhism, which may help somewhat the mutual understanding of East and West.

---

2. Ed. E.g. in the allegory of the burning house in *The Lotus Sūtra*.

III

In his second address, "Über Abraham a Santa Clara," instead of expressing his own thought, Heidegger speaks of a seventeenth-century preacher who had also been a pupil of the school of Messkirch. The drastic speeches here quoted of this vigorous Catholic preacher contain words which might deeply impress Buddhists. For instance, he speaks of the mass deaths of the plague in Vienna:

> I have seen that Death is a mower, who cuts down with his scythe not only the low clover but also the high-growing grass. I have seen that Death is a gardener, who breaks to pieces not only the violet clinging to earth but also the high-ascending larkspurs.... I have seen that Death is a thunderbolt, that hits not only the transparent straw-huts but also the most translucent houses of monarchs.

What he continues to say is especially interesting:

> I have seen *Leiber* (bodies of living beings), not *Leiber*; I will say *Körper* (bodies material), not *Körper*; I will say bones, not bones; I will say dust, not dust; I will say the Nothingness (*das Nichts*) of the crowned kaisers and monarchs.

But the most interesting is the phrase which is quoted next: "man – this five-foot-long Nothingness."

Heidegger comments on this passage, a passage poignant and humorous at the same time: "The very contradiction between the Nothingness and the length of five feet tells the truth, that earthly magnitude and the emptiness of its meaning belong together."

To men of Zen, however, this phrase may sound almost like Zen. But Zen would then contrive further to turn the interpretation advocated by most Christians, including, perhaps, Abraham a Santa Clara himself. This turnabout would be made possible by breaking through the Nothingness here mentioned and by opening beyond it a still deeper dimension of the Nothingness, namely that of Buddhistic *śūnyatā*, as it is curtly stated in the basic Mahāyāna thesis, "Form is no other than Emptiness; Emptiness is no other than Form." (We may also say "things" instead of "Form."[3]) Here, a turnabout must necessarily occur. Standing on this new dimension, Zen approaches the same phrase, "man – this five-foot-long Nothing-ness," from the opposite direction, so that it is now taken up in a wholly new light, the accent being put

---

3. Ed. This is drawn from *The Heart Sūtra*.

on the "five-foot-long" instead of the "No-thingness." It would then further become possible to come back from the length of five feet to dust, not dust; I will say bones, not bones; I will say corpses, not corpses; I will say living bodies with flesh and blood. The "five-foot-long Nothingness" is, as such, a five-foot-long living body. Jōshū, the Chinese Zen master of the ninth century, when asked, "Is there the Buddha-nature in a dog?," answered, "None (Nothingness)." This is a well-known *kōan*. The Nothingness in this answer does not mean, of course, that which is conceived of merely as something opposite to Being. It lies beyond the alternative of "to be" and "not to be." Therefore Jōshū could on another occasion answer, "here is (Being)," to the same question. Whether in the case of "None" or in that of "Being," we must not remain on the dimension of the alternative, where both termini are taken up merely as words or concepts and drawn into logical or semantic interpretations. When the words "Being" or "Nothingness" are presented from the dimension beyond the Duality to us, by some one, say Jōshū, who stands existentially on that dimension, then we ought at the same time to fix our eyes on the one who is there speaking. We must pay attention to the whole of the actual occasion, or, rather, to the togetherness in the whole: to that whole consisting of the chance theme, "a dog" for example, the words spoken, ourselves who just are listening, and especially the speaker himself. Jōshū, the speaker on that occasion, standing beyond all alternatives, embodies absolute freedom and can give to the dog or rob him of his essential "Being" (namely the Buddha-nature inherent to it) as he likes. This Jōshū, embodying absolute freedom, exists in his five-foot-long body side by side with all other bodies and sits near the questioning monk and, also perhaps, near the dog in question. He looks at them, hears the question and speaks the words of answer, He is there, and where he is, there is also the place whence his words come, with which he bestows or takes back "Being" freely; the place whence the Being of a dog originates, and its two-foot-long Nothingness; the place, whence the Buddha-nature in all living beings comes forth and whence even all Buddhas originate – the above-mentioned *Heimat*. The same one, Jōshū, whose body is sitting there on a chair, is at the same time nowhere; he is the very "Nowhere," *śūnyatā* (Nothingness) making the place of his Being, whence come also his words of answer. In this Nowhere he is absolutely free. And in this absolute freedom he is everywhere. He is, on the occasion mentioned above, there, where the dog is. He is wholly together "with" it, even while sitting next to it. All of this together expresses the state of *satori*. We have above quoted Heidegger's comment on the phrase, "man – this five-foot Nothingness." He asserts that in the very togetherness of the contradictory factors, the Nothingness and the five-foot length, the truth becomes manifest: the truth of the togetherness of earthly magnitude and the emptiness of its meaning. We can not see clearly, at least from this address alone, the thorough implication he gave here to the words "truth" and "together."

He, too, may have interpreted the phrase along the line of usual interpretation; namely to the effect of the meaninglessness of earthly things, of *vanitas vanitatum*. Heidegger says, however, in another place of this address, "There awoke in the second half of the seventeenth century a new spirit of creative affirmation and formation of the world (*schöpferische Weltbejahung und Weltgestaltung*) – the spirit of the Baroque." It may be then not altogether impossible to sense this new spirit behind the above-mentioned phrase. We may be able to attribute some positive meaning to the gathering of those contradictory factors. Heidegger's saying about the "truth" of their togetherness may be interpreted as hinting not only at a negative truth but rather more at a positive one. Howsoever it may be, Zen at any rate can take the phrase as expressing a positive truth about man's essential mode of being. The spirit of world-affirmation, man's positive attitude to the world, seems to be found in its full manifestation in another word quoted of Abraham a Santa Clara: "A man who dies before he dies, does not die when he dies." Heidegger comments on this sentence that it brings forward a decisive thought. This sentence would not sound strange if it had come from the mouth of a man of Zen. In fact, the same thought, in literally the same mode of expression, has been pronounced, we suppose, by a great number of Zen teachers. There is, for instance, a well-known Japanese *waka* of Shidō Bunan, a Zen master of the seventeenth century: "Become a dead man, remaining alive; become thoroughly dead; then do what you like, according to your own mind; all your works then are good." The first part of the poem, "To become a dead man, remaining alive," is an exhortation toward the Great Death as is so called in Zen. The latter part indicates the mode of man's being in *satori*, a life of work, absolutely free. The poem expresses that the way to *satori* is through the Great Death. In the above-mentioned saying of the Christian preacher the spirit of creative world-affirmation through Death is breathing, it seems to me, as lively as in the poem of the Zen teacher. It might be in this sense that Heidegger found in this saying a decisive thought. That was certainly the reason that we have dared in our interpretation to attribute a positive meaning to the phrase, "man – this five-foot Nothingness."

IV

Finally, Heidegger remarks on the following profoundly poetic saying of the preacher, "Come here, you silver-white swans, who are rowing about on the water with your wings, in defiance of snow." He [Heidegger] says,

> Everyone knows that snow melts in the water and disappears. Swans, on the contrary, preserve a "pure" whiteness with their very feathers. They thus carry the snow on, so to speak, over the waters. Swimming,

they prevent the snow from sinking into the waters. The movement of the white swans on the waters is an image of the Permanence in the most transitory things (*das Unvergängliche im Vergänglichsten*).

This reminds us of some similar poetical metaphors that are familiar in Zen, such as "A white horse enters the flowering reeds" or "The thousand mountains covered with snow, why is a solitary peak not white?" We can at first sight hardly discriminate a white horse, trotting through the broad shallows covered with white reed-flowers; there being only One colour. It is difficult to search for it, But after a time, as our eyes get accustomed to the scene, the figure of the horse gradually becomes discernible and stands out conspicuously in the One colour; like that "silver-whiteness" of the swans who defy the snow and its whiteness. From the ground of One colour emerges something which is equally coloured, yet distinguishable from all other things; something solely different in the midst of the Indifference of All. The above-mentioned metaphor of "a solitary peak" remaining unwhitened amidst the snow-covered thousand mountains is, therefore, an indication of the mode of being as in the metaphor of the white horse, seen there only from the opposite side. Both sides – the One white colour, on the one hand, and the silver-white-ness of the swan or the figure of the white horse, standing out in prominence within the reed-flowers, on the other hand – or, in terms of philosophical categories, the side of Oneness and the side of Otherness, and likewise the side of Indifference, Identity, Universality and that of Difference, Distinctiveness, Singularity, are equally essential. Although the latter side "defies" the former and stands in contradiction against it, the Otherness being the negation of the Oneness, the Difference the negation of the Indifference, it must have in the former the ground that sustains it; it can only subsist, as a relief, by standing out in prominence within its own ground. The latter must, at the same time, "preserve" (*bewahren*) the former, elevating it to a higher plane, as swans preserve with their snow-covered wings "a pure whiteness." The whiteness of the snow appears on the swan's wings as shining silver-whiteness. The whiteness of the snow appears here in a truer degree of itself than is found in itself. It appears in its own ultimate reality, that is as a "pure" whiteness. This silver-whiteness belongs, however, not only to the snow, as its heightened true colour; it is also the colour of the swans and also belongs to them. It is they that preserve, through their very swimming, the snow and prevent it from disappearing in the waters. "The movement of the white swans on the waters is an image of the Permanence in the most transitory things." Isn't it also an expression of the spirit of the world-affirmation? Isn't it permissible to view this movement of the white swans as an image of a man who "dies before he dies and does not die when he dies"? If so, we could see here also an attitude deeply similar to that of Zen. But, although it is too hasty to say here "yes," the words of Abraham a Santa Clara and Heidegger's commentary on them are certainly moving, without their knowing of it, in the neighbourhood of Zen and contain various points of contact with it. The second speech can serve especially to the true contact between Christianity and Zen Buddhism, while the first implies a valuable suggestion as to the basic plane on which the encounter of Eastern and Western thought in general ought to occur. Of course, it is absurd to think that the possibility of contact is to be found in one particular thinker only. Anyone somewhat versed in Mahāyāna Buddhism and in its religio-philosophic thought developed in the various speculative as well as devotional schools must certainly find in almost all great Western thinkers, as well as religious teachers, so many points of contact as to surpass expectation; so much so that it would be rather misleading to mention here any name whatever. But nevertheless, in regard to the imminent problem of the encounter of East and West, we think that Heidegger's thought is doubtlessly one of those which can most help this encounter. Even the two short speeches here presented will suffice, we believe, to convince us of this fact.

9

Home: The Seven-Hundredth Anniversary of the Town of Messkirch

Martin Heidegger

The evening, whether of a day or a lifetime, is the time and hour for meditation.[1] To meditate means: to gather oneself into reflection. Here and now we have only a moment for that. But it is enough even if it is quickly covered over by everything the week of festivities has to offer. Perhaps for some of us the moment of meditation will come back again later, at a different time and place.

But what can we meditate on at this time, specifically so that this moment of reflection might, in its own way, fit in with this evening celebration of home?[2] The most obvious suggestion is that we meditate on home. But generally speaking, all too much has been said and written about that. The theme of "home" has meanwhile become boring, not just incidentally but for deep-seated reasons. It might be worthwhile for us to reflect on this fact.

For the seventh-centennial jubilee of the town a book about our home has appeared. It tells the story of "Messkirch yesterday" and brings news about "Messkirch today." So it would seem that everything has already been said about our home. Everything? Messkirch yesterday and today – that's all to the good. But Messkirch tomorrow? If we pursue this question, we might come up with a small appendix to the book about our home.

---

1. Ed. An address given on 22 July 1961 on the occasion of the seven-hundredth anniversary of the city of Messkirch: "Ansprache zum Heimatabend, am 22, 7, 1961, anläßlich des 700-jährigen Jubiläums der Stadt Meßkirch." English translation © Thomas Sheehan. An earlier version of this English translation was first published as "Messkirch's Seventh Centennial," in *Listening* 8.1–3 (1973), 40–57.
2. Ed. On the term "home" (*Heimat*) and related vocabulary see the Translator's Note (Thomas Sheehan) at the end of the article.

But right away everyone will ask a question in return: How can we know anything about tomorrow? Can anything be determined about the future? Not even the wisest person on earth can predict the future. Even those among us who are more skilled in reflective thought know no more about the future than the rest of us. At best he or she is clearer on the fact that and the reason why we can know nothing about it. That notwithstanding, we dare to stick with the question: Messkirch tomorrow? In the future?

Whether and to what extent we are in a position to give a reliable answer to this question about home depends on how we understand the meaning of the word "future."

If by "future" we mean the span of the coming years and decades that follow upon today, then we will never be able to indicate how this time will be filled out, not even (and emphatically so) when we try to calculate how the town's economic situation will look in the coming years, or how agriculture and the farming class will change, or which paths the schools and education will take, or what position and efficacy the Christian faith and the churches will have in the future. When we try to reason out tomorrow in this fashion, we take the future merely as the extension of the present, one in which everything remains uncertain.

But what if we understand the future as that which is approaching us today? In that case the future is not just something that follows today but rather is what projects into today. In that case, today is not a segment of time standing on its own, self-contained on all sides. Today has its origin in what has been and still is, and at the same time is opened out onto what is approaching it.

What approaches us concerns and determines us continually without our properly paying attention to it and without our being able to say unequivocally what this approaching might be. Nonetheless there are multiple signs of it everywhere. One of them is, for example, the TV and radio antennae that we can see almost lined up in rows on the housetops in the towns and villages. What do these signs point to? They indicate that people are no longer at home precisely in those places where, from the outside, they seem to "dwell." Instead, by the day and the hour people are being pulled away into strange realms – enticing, exciting, at times also entertaining and educational. But these realms offer no lasting, reliable abode; they change ceaselessly from the new to the ever more new. Captivated and absorbed by all this, one "moves out," as it were, from one's home and moves into the alien. The danger looms that what we once called home is dissolving and decaying. The power of the alien seems to so overpower us that we can no longer hold out against it. How can we protect ourselves against the onrush of the alien? Only by ceaselessly awakening the bestowing, healing, conserving powers of home; only by tapping the powerful springs of home over and over again and securing the correct course for their flow and influence.

Such a task is most readily possible and most enduringly effective where the powers of encompassing nature and the echo of historical tradition live side by side and where the origin and the customs fostered from ancient times determine human existence. Today only the rural areas and the small country towns are up to this decisive task – provided they recognize ever anew their extraordinary calling, provided they know how to draw the line against life in the big cities and the gigantic areas of modern industrial complexes, and provided they do not take these as their guiding model but instead hold firm to what is their own and conserve home. For that, two things are necessary.

First, we must recognize the alien as what it is, that is in what produces and determines it. Second, we must prevent the powers of home, which of their essence are unpretentious, from lying fallow and perishing.

This centennial festival could be a good occasion, that is the proper celebration, for meeting both demands.

First of all it is a matter of seeing the alien with utter clarity, seeing the impelling threat it brings and the power at work in it.

There exists the possibility, which is corroborated more each day, that soon enough there will be a state of affairs in which we no longer recognize what home means, that we no longer need it because we no longer miss it. What then, when home inevitably withers away? There would not be nothing more that is alien. There would be only the frantic change from the newest to the newest of all, which one would chase after with his ever self-surpassing machinations. If we are ready to save and foster home, we certainly may not shut our eyes to this possibility.

All around us we constantly see in its varied forms what is determining the actuality of today's world. It is modern technology, now already uniformly dominating the whole earth and even regions of the universe beyond the earth. If today the much-discussed underdeveloped peoples are to be endowed with the achievements, outcomes and useful features of modern technology, we have to ask whether what is their own-most and their heritage is not thereby taken from them and destroyed and whether they are not in this way being dislodged from their home and banished into the alien. Perhaps "aid for developing countries" is basically nothing else but the race run by the seemingly highly developed peoples and nations with the sole aspiration of getting into the world-market as quickly and decisively as possible, thereby gaining a means of power in the struggle of the great powers for the domination of the earth. The form of such domination will be shaped by the absolute technological state.

It is no accident that we speak of the technological age. This age itself is subject in its history to the puzzling frenzy that constantly propels all modern technology out beyond itself. Only a short while ago the modern age was still called the "atomic age." The name is already out of date, replaced by the "space age." Overnight another name will surface.

Everyone is familiar with the phenomena of technological production. We look at them with astonishment. And yet no one knows what in truth this thing is by which man today is being provoked in increasing degree to such boundless activity. What so overpowers man cannot itself be a mere human product. For that reason it remains puzzling and uncanny. Yet it is precisely this "uncanny" that dominates in the alien and that, through the alien, comes towards us, determining our future. Tomorrow is not only the tomorrow that follows immediately upon today; rather it already dominates within the affairs of today.

Messkirch tomorrow? It will be entangled in the network of the technological era. The question will arise – not only for this town, or for our country, or for Europe, but for all peoples of this earth – as to whether, under the domination of modern technology and amidst the world-transformation it brings about, there can still be home in any sense at all. Perhaps we are settling into homelessness. Perhaps the relation to home, the pull of home, is vanishing out of the existence of modern man. But it may also be the case that, amidst the pressing force of the alien, a new relation to home is being prepared. Perhaps just such a festival as ours could cooperate in this preparation and thereby gain its meaning for tomorrow. Many may doubt this precisely because the supreme power of the alien and the uncanny seems to neutralize anything like the pull of home. But the truth of the matter is quite different.

Our language has a name for the pull of home: we call it homesickness. In homesickness home is more forcefully present at home than anywhere else. Yet it seems that for people today home has died out, since they are at home everywhere and nowhere. In many ways that seems to be the case; however, we should guard against the claim that modern man and woman no longer knows about home and homesickness. The pull of the homeland is still alive, in fact most alive where we least suspect it – alive, yes, but in a peculiar way that we scarcely notice.

Let us give it long and deep thought: homesickness is alive where people are constantly in flight into the alien that is supposed to entertain and bewitch them, fill up their time and wile it away for him. Of and by themselves they can do nothing more with their free time, since time is continually becoming too long for them. What does that mean? It says something very striking. People today do not have time for anything more, and yet when they have free time, it right away becomes too long. They must kill long periods of time by wiling them away through pastimes. Whatever passes the time is supposed to get rid of the boredom, or at least cover it over and let it be forgotten. What kind of boredom? Not the kind that comes up now and then, and quickly passes away, when we are bored (i.e. left unoccupied and unnecessarily delayed) by some specific thing: a book, a film, a lecture.

We easily get over such boring things and their boredom. But it is quite different with that kind of boredom we have in mind when we speak of ennui.

There we find nothing specific that bores us, not this or that thing or person or event. Rather, in this ennui nothing appeals to us anymore, everything has as much or as little value as everything else, because there a deep boredom penetrates our existence to the core.

Is this possibly our final condition, that a deep boredom, like an insidious fog, creeps to and fro in the bottomless depths of our existence?

We ask this question, but why precisely now during this evening celebration of our home? Because for a moment we are reflecting on whether and how there still is home amidst the alienation of the modern technological world. Yes, there still is home, and it affects us, but *as that for which we are searching*. The hardly noticed but fundamental mood of deep boredom is probably what drives us into all the time-killing which the strange, the exciting and the bewitching offer us daily in our alienation. Moreover, this deep boredom – in the form of the passion for killing time – is probably the hidden, unavowed pull of home, shunted aside but still inescapable: our hidden homesickness. Our language speaks more knowingly than we suppose. When a person is homesick, our language says, "Time weighs long and heavy on him." The long time that weighs on us is none other than the long while in which nothing any longer appeals to us, yet in which at the same time we seek for what addresses itself to us in a way that claims us so totally that time never lies empty and there is no need to kill time.

The phrase "in a little while" means "in a short time." A long time means boredom. Probably the following two belong together: the alienation of the technological world and the deep boredom that is the hidden pull of a sought-for home. For no technological equipment and none of its achievements or aids, neither the powers of invention pushed to their limits nor endless activity, have the power to give us our home in the sense of what sustains us, determines us and lets us grow in the core of our existence.

Deep boredom, the long time and homesickness: these attest ceaselessly and quietly to the pull of the homeland, our indestructible belonging to it.

Thus in all the forms of the alien there still comes towards us the home that we seek, although disguised. How? By being ready and disposed to guard that from which we *originate*. There are also signs of this origin.

When we old and older citizens of Messkirch want to find again our friends, loved ones or acquaintances, we now have to search for many of them in the cemetery, the *Friedhof* or "garden of peace." This word speaks to us; but even more expressive is the name that is slowly fading out of use, "God's acre" [*Gottesacker*]. This word can be interpreted in various ways. For example: In this acre there is sown ever anew the remembrance of what has been and still is. So there grows in this acre recollection of all the forces and powers that bestow the healing, the fruitful and the abiding, at times also the meaningful. From out of this origin we must go forth and confront the alien that approaches us. Against the noisy and frantic we bring to bear the quiet and restrained. For this reason the exhibition of the works of the Master of Messkirch forms the focal point of our town celebration. The exhibition is a real "occasion," that is the festival in the authentic sense. For these works are an occasion for us not only to rejoice in the beauty of the pictures and to wonder at the artistic accomplishment of the Master. The exhibition is the occasion for us to find our way back, in the presence of these works, into rest and ingathering, that is into home. Therefore it is to the high credit of the Bürgermeister of our town that he not only came up with the idea of this exhibition but also has brought it to fruition. Likewise the performance of the recently discovered orchestral Mass of Conradin Kreutzer is an event that calls us back to the powers of home that quietly hold sway. Finally, if I may be allowed a personal note: Archbishop Gröber, when he was the town curate in Constance, gave me as a 17-year-old high school student, a philosophy book that was to be decisive for my whole path of thinking. Thus one thing intertwines with another if only we carefully attend to and foster that which works in silence.

In the midst of the alien we are taking a turn back into home. If we abide carefully and without haste on its way, such a return home has the power to outstrip again and again everything that sweeps us up into the alien.

Through meditation on tomorrow we awaken the healing power of yesterday correctly understood and genuinely appropriated. By such paths we first reach into the today that we must live out between the future and the origin. Such a living out helps us to become committed to that which remains firm against all change.

This evening – a time of meditation, a moment for reflection. Thinking is indeed a serious matter, but at the same time a festive one. For in thinking, the insight into that-which-is is freed up, that is given a free day for celebration. Meditation is not melancholy but a gladsomeness in which everything is gladdened, everything becomes clear and transparent.

And so may what I have just said be nothing else but a small light kindled this evening in the midst of our hometown, whose inhabitants have bedecked their houses so richly and carefully with flowers, a further sign that they are disposed to cherish the meaning of dwelling aright.

How long the small light kindled here will shine, how soon it will be extinguished, this is up to each one of us whom this evening celebration of home has brought together for joyful play and friendly conversation.

(Translated by Thomas Sheehan)

Translator's Note: I translate *Heimat* as "home," *Zug zur Heimat* as "the pull of home" and *Heimkehr* as "return home." Three key terms in this address are *das Heimische, das Unheimische* and das *Umheimliche*:

1. *Das Heimische*: The adjective *heimisch* means literally "home-bred, domestic, homelike, native" and so forth. I always translate it as "home." It functions primarily as a philosophical *terminus technicus* – not primarily as a geographical or even as an emotional category but as what the early Heidegger called an "existential" of the relation of man and being. Its meaning emerges in the text, specifically in terms of *Herkunft/Herkommen* – the ontological origin that comes towards us as *Zukunft* or future – and *das Gewesene*, another ontological term, which refers to what is "always already" the case with the man–being relation. I translate it as "what has been and still is," with the unspoken supplement "what has always-already been prior and ever will be such."
2. *Das Unheimische*: (As an adjective *unheimisch* is rare in German, the more common form being *unheimlich*; see below.) I translate this as "the alien," occasionally but reluctantly as "alienation," although not in the Hegelian or Marxist sense but rather as the opposite of "home."
3. *Das Unheimliche*: I translate this as "the uncanny." It refers to being (*das Sein*) as the overpowering that still approaches us in the *Unheimisches* of the technological epoch.

10

Zen and Compassion

Abe Masao

I

An English translation of the *Línjì lù*[1] was a long-cherished project which Dr D.T. Suzuki had so wished to complete during his lifetime. Unfortunately, however, he passed away before his wish could be realized.[2] The *Línjì lù*, as Dr Suzuki says, is "regarded by many as the strongest Zen treatise we have."[3] And traditionally it has been called the "King of Zen Sayings." Yet, the collection of Zen Sayings which Dr Suzuki prized most was the *Zhàozhōu lù*.[4] To Dr Suzuki the *Zhàozhōu lù*, while sharing the same vital Zen-Realization with the *Línjì lù*, expressed so well the compassionate side of Zen.

As for the *Línjì lù*, Dr Suzuki published a book in Japanese, *Rinzai no Kihon Shisō*[5] ("The Fundamental Thought of *Línjì*"), the subtitle of which is *Rinzairoku ni okeru "nin" shisō no kenkyū* ("A Study of the Idea of 'Man' in the *Línjì lù*"). This is one of the most important of all of Dr Suzuki's extensive writings in Japanese or English. In this book he presents an original and penetrating view

---

1. *Línjì lù*: 臨済録. J. *Rinzairoku*, or "Sayings of *Línjì*"; i.e. Línjì Yìxuán 臨済義玄, J. Rinzai Gigen (-867). Ed. The original abbreviations have been left in the footnotes to this essay: J. for Japanese and C. for Chinese. However, Chinese pronunciations have been given in *pīnyīn*, as usual, and other slight alterations are made to increase comprehension.
2. We can, however, see his English translations of some important passages of the *Línjì lù* in his *Essays* I (New York, 1948), 332-3; *Essays* II (London, 1933), 33-5; *Essays* III (London, 1934), 30-33; *Zen Buddhism and Psychoanalysis* (New York, 1950), 33-43 (hereafter *ZBP*).
3. *Essays* III, 30.
4. *Zhàozhōu lù*: 趙州録. J. *Jōshūroku*, or "Sayings of *Zhàozhōu*"; i.e. 趙州眞際. C. Zhàozhōu Zhēnjì, J. Jōshū Shinsai (778-897).
5. *Rinzai no Kihon Shisō*: 臨済の基本思想 (Tokyo: Chūōkōronsha, 1949); hereafter *RKS*.

of the *Línjì lù*, an approach which elucidates "Man" as being the crucial point of this work and the nucleus of genuine Zen spirit.

Dr Suzuki did not publish a separate volume of interpretation on the *Zhàozhōu lù*, although he quoted it as often as the *Línjì lù* in his writings. However, the last critically edited text with Japanese translation which Dr Suzuki published was the *Zhàozhōu lù*.[6]

In memory of Dr Suzuki, I would like here to consider his appreciation and interpretation of the *Zhàozhōu lù* on the basis of what Dr Suzuki called the idea of "Man" (*nin* 人 *rén*), which he found to be common both in the *Línjì lù* and the *Zhàozhōu lù*.[7]

Before going on, however, it would be well to note that Dr Suzuki was more concerned with Línjì and Zhàozhōu as Zen personalities than he was with the *Línjì lù* and the *Zhàozhōu lù* as collections of Zen sayings. More than that, what concerned him was the genuine and vivid "Zen" which manifests itself in Zen texts or in and through Zen Masters, which can and should manifest itself in any one, present or future, East or West. But even more than that it is, after all, in terms of the true way of human existence that Dr Suzuki was concerned with "Zen."

Throughout his extensive writings Dr Suzuki used Zen texts only to show what genuine and vital Zen is. It was simply because he believed genuine Zen was well expressed in them that he appreciated the *Línjì lù* and especially the *Zhàozhōu lù*.

II

One day Rinzai (Línjì) gave his sermon, "There is the true man of no rank in the mass of naked flesh, who goes in and out from your facial gates [i.e. sense organs]. Those who have not yet testified [to the fact], look, look!"

A monk came forward and asked, "Who is this true man of no rank?" Rinzai came down from his chair and, taking hold of the monk by the throat, said, "Speak, speak!"

The monk hesitated.

Rinzai let go his hold and said, "What a worthless dirt-stick this [true man of no rank] is!"[8]

---

6. *Jōshūzenjigoroku* 趙州禅師録. C. *Zhàozhōu chánshī yǔlù*. Edited in collaboration with Ryūmin Akizuki (Kamakura: The Matsugaoka Bunko, 1962). Republished by Shunjūsha (Tokyo, 1963).
7. *RKS*, 137, 195–7.
8. *ZBP*, 32.

This is one of the famous sermons from the *Línjì lù* to which Dr Suzuki attached great importance. The subject matter of this sermon is "the true man of no rank."[9] It is here that Dr Suzuki found the pivotal point of the *Línjì lù* and the culmination of Zen thought. He says, "The true man of no rank" is Rinzai's term for the Self. His teaching is almost exclusively around this Man (*nin* 人 *rén*) or Person, who is sometimes called "the Way-man" (*dōnin* 道人 *dàorén*).[10] He can be said to be the first Zen master in the history of Zen thought in China who emphatically asserts the presence of this Man in every phase of our human life-activity. He is never tired of having his followers come to the realization of the Man or the real Self.[11]

Dr Suzuki's idea, that *Línjì*'s "Man" is the culmination of Zen thought in China, may be clarified by summarizing his discussions in the *Rinzai no Kihon Shisō* as follows.

While "Mind" (*shin* 心 *xīn*) was transmitted as being the core of Zen by Bodhidharma, "Seeing into one's Self-nature" (*kenshō* 見性 *jiànxīng*) was emphasized by the Sixth Patriarch, Huìnéng. This is probably because "Mind" was and is apt to be understood as static when grasped only in terms of *dhyāna* (meditation). It may not be wrong to say that Huìnéng emphasized the oneness of *dhyāna* and *prajñā* (Wisdom) in "Seeing into one's Self-nature" as the nucleus of Zen to avoid the static implication in the term "Mind."[12] Huìnéng's "Seeing," because of its emphasis on *prajñā*, was on the one hand replaced with "Knowing" (*chi* 知 *zhī*) by Shénhuì.[13] "Knowing," however, has a tendency to become conceptual and abstract, and this is incompatible with the nature of Zen.[14] And so Huìnéng's "Seeing" was developed on the other hand by Mǎzǔ[15] into "Activity" (*yū* 用 *yòng*). While the school of Shénhuì which emphasized "Knowing" declined, that of Mǎzǔ developed vigorously because "Activity" is nothing but Zen itself.[16]

"Activity" alone, however, is not entirely satisfactory. There must be something living behind "Activity." "Activity" is to be "Man." In Mǎzǔ's Zen, "Man," although working behind "Activity," was not clearly realized as "Man." It is Línjì who vividly took "Man" out as "Man." See Him where Línjì, grabbing the monk, says, "Speak! Speak!" in reply to the question, "Who is the true man of no rank?" Thus Dr Suzuki says, "In this 'Man,' 'Seeing,' 'Knowing'

---

9. J. *ichimui no shinnin* 一無位真人.
10. Ed. The author showed this and other such terms below in the sequence Japanese/the characters/Chinese. This has been followed but for Chinese the modern transcription (*pīnyīn*) has been used, replacing the Wade-Giles of the original.
11. *ZBP*, 32.
12. *RKS*, 27.
13. Shénhuì: i.e. Hézé Shénhuì 荷沢神会 (668–760); J. Kataku Jinne.
14. *RKS*, 112.
15. Mǎzǔ: i.e. Mǎzǔ Dàoyī 馬祖道一 (707–786); J. Baso Dōitsu.
16. *RKS*, 112.

and 'Activity' are integrated in a concrete way. In this respect Línjì may be said to be a great thinker."[17]

According to Dr Suzuki, the *Línjì lù* is a record of the sermons and activities of this "Man," and Línjì established his religion upon the one notion of "Man." The destiny of Línjì's school may be said to depend exclusively upon "Man."[18] Now, what really is "Man"?

III

Let us return to *Línjì*'s sermon as quoted above: "There is the true man of no rank in the mass of naked flesh, who goes in and out from your facial gates [i. e. sense organs]. Those who have not yet testified [to the fact], look, look!" This is Línjì's declaration of "Man" as the most concrete and living Self. He also calls Him "the One who is, at this moment, right in front of us, solitarily, illuminatingly, in full awareness, listening to this talk on the Dharma."[19] If one, however, takes the concreteness of this "Man" in terms of sensation as differentiated from intellectualism, he is entirely off the mark. Again one is wide off the mark if he understands "the true man of no rank who goes in and out from your facial gates" as a psychological self.[20] Interpreting Línjì's "Man" as the real Self, Dr Suzuki says,

> The real Self is a kind of metaphysical self in opposition to the psychological or ethical self which belong in a finite world of relativity. Rinzai's Man is defined as "of no rank" or "independent of (*mue* 無依 *wúyī*)," or "with no clothes on," all of which makes us think of the "metaphysical" Self.[21]

If one, however, taking up the term "metaphysical Self," assumes "Man" to be consciousness in general or an abstract humanity, one's view is "dead wrong."[22] Neither consciousness in general nor an abstract humanity is a

---

17. *RKS*, 113. By way of introduction, Dr Suzuki writes, "With all his rejection of letters and words, Línjì himself, having delivered sermons using thousands of words, must be said to have had some thoughts. One may say that the shout (*katsu*) and the stick (*bō*) rush out from beyond thought. With this alone, however, the problem of the human being is not settled. It is because there was the thought to be transcended that one could transcend even the thought. If there is nothing from the beginning, there can be no problem of transcending. So thought must become an issue" (4).
18. *RKS*, 17.
19. *ZBP*, 13, 33.
20. *RKS*, 221.
21. *ZBP*, 32.
22. *RKS*, 236.

living "man," a concrete existence. Being intellectualizations they are abstractions, devoid of vital activity. On the contrary, Línjì's "Man" is "The One who is, at this moment, right in front of us, listening to this talk on the Dharma." He is neither a philosophical assumption nor a logical postulate, but one who is working, fully alive, here (right in front of us) and now (at this moment). This is why Línjì says, "Look, look!" and "Speak, speak!" In order to realize Línjì's "Man," therefore, one must transcend the discriminative consciousness. Human consciousness is always imprisoned in objectivity and relativity. Zen urges us to "advance further from the top of a hundred-foot pole";[23] it urges human consciousness or human intellect at the far edge of its own field to leap and thereby effect a "turning-over," called *parāvṛtti*[24] in Buddhist terminology.

This turning-over as a leap from the very field of consciousness is nothing but the realization of "absolute subjectivity" which itself cannot be objectified – it being the root-source of one's objectification in terms of the consciousness or intellect. In other words, the realization of "absolute subjectivity" takes place at the moment one realizes that the intellect's endless proceeding is nothing but its complete turning back. Línjì's "true man of no rank" is no more than this absolute subjectivity. Since "Man" in Línjì's sense is the very root and source of one's objectification, he himself has no root and yet is most active and creative as the source of one's objectification.

Thus Línjì says of "Man,"

> He is the most dynamic one except that he has no roots, no stems whatever. You may try to catch him, but he refuses to be gathered up; you may try to brush him away, but he will not be dispersed. The harder you strive after him the further he is away from you. When you no more strive after him, lo, he is right in front of you. His super-sensuous voice fills your ear.[25]

Dr Suzuki characterizes this "Man" as absolute subjectivity; "*reiseiteki jikaku*,"[26] "the Cosmic Unconsciousness"[27] or "*prajñā*-intuition."[28]

Línjì's "Man" is not a man who stands over and against nature, God or another man, but is rather one's absolute subjectivity, as *prajñā*-intuition,

---

23. *Wúménguān:* 無門関; J. *Mumonkan*, Case 46.
24. *RKS*, 239, 252.
25. *ZBP*, 41.
26. *Reiseiteki jikaku:* 霊性的自覚. This term, though it may be translated as "Spirituality," has no appropriate English equivalent. The literal translation of it is "spiritual Self-realization."
27. *ZBP*, 16–17, 19, 51. *Zen and Japanese Culture* (New York: Pantheon, 1959), 165 n., 192–3, 199, 226, 242–3, 250.
28. *ZBP*, 57–8. *Studies in Zen* (New York: Delta, 1955), 80ff., 147, 159–60.

which goes beyond the dualism of all forms of subject and object, self and the world, being and non-being. "If the Greeks," says Dr Suzuki,

> taught us how to reason and Christianity what to believe, it is Zen that teaches us to go beyond logic and not to tarry even when we come up against "the things which are not seen." For the Zen point of view is to find an absolute point where no dualism in whatever form resides. Logic starts from the division of subject and object, and belief distinguishes between what is seen and what is not seen. The Western mode of thinking can never do away with this eternal dilemma, this or that, reason or faith, man and God, and so forth. With Zen all these are swept aside as something veiling our insight into the nature of life and reality. Zen leads us into a realm of Emptiness or Void where no conceptualism prevails.[29]

By saying this, Dr Suzuki does not mean that Christianity, for instance, is dualistic in the ordinary sense. He says this by way of comparison with Zen's "Emptiness" or "Void," the realization of which is called *satori*, "Seeing into one's self-nature" (Huìnéng) or "Man" (Línjì).

This can be seen when one takes seriously the following question raised by Dr Suzuki: who was it that heard God speak and then wrote down, "God said, 'Let there be light' and there was light"?[30] There must be a witness to God's creation hidden in the biblical account. The Christian idea of God is certainly beyond the duality of subject and object, transcendence and immanence, being and non-being. There is, however, a hidden duality between God, who is creating the universe, and a veiled seer of His Creation. Even when God before creation is talked about, who is it who talks about "God before creation"? This hidden and final dualism is a great and serious problem which Zen believes must be thoroughly overcome for man to attain a complete liberation. Zen is properly concerned with the very origin before duality takes place. Since the hidden duality is the final one which is concerned with God Himself, the veiled "seer" of God's creation can be neither God nor man as a creation. This seer is, in Línjì's terms, "the true man of no rank," whereas other terms such as "Emptiness," "Void," "Mind," "Seeing," "Activity," "Knowing," have been traditionally used in Zen.

The veiled seer is called "Emptiness" or "Void" because, being the ultimate seer, it cannot be objectified. It is called "Mind," "Seeing," "Knowing," "Activity" and so on because, although it cannot be objectified it is not sheer

---

29. *Zen and Japanese Culture*, 360–61.
30. *Shinrankyōgaku*, No. 6 (Kyōto: Bun'eidō, 1965), 105. The same kind of question is found in Dr Suzuki's review of Father H. Dumoulin's book *A History of Zen Buddhism* (*The Eastern Buddhist* New Series 1 [September 1965], 125).

emptiness but the absolute subjectivity as the root-source of human objectification. Línjì calls the ultimate seer "Man" or "The true man of no rank" to express its living concreteness.

In his Song of Enlightenment,[31] Yǒngjiā dàshī[32] describes the inner light[33] as follows: "You cannot take hold of it, nor can you get rid of it; while you can do neither, it goes on its own way."[34] This "it" is precisely the ultimate seer, or "Man" in Línjì's sense. The ultimate seer or "Man" can neither be taken hold of nor forsaken. Yet, right in these impossibilities "it" or "He" already *is*. So Línjì's "true Man of no rank" as the ultimate seer stands neither before God's creation nor after God's creation. He is standing and working right here and now "prior to" *any* form of duality such as before and after, time and eternity, God and man, seer and the seen. The ultimate seer is nothing but "Seeing" itself. "Seeing" is the absolute Activity prior to both personification and deification. "Seeing" in this sense, however, is not something whatsoever but "No-thingness" or "Void." For this very reason "Seeing" is really the absolute activity which can never be objectified. Being the absolute activity "Seeing" does not see itself, just as an eye does not see itself. "Seeing" is *non-seeing* in regard to itself. It is because of non-seeing in regard of itself that "Seeing" is "Seeing which is absolutely active."

From this "Seeing" as the absolute Activity spring God's words "Let there be light" – that is God Himself and His creation. In the "Seeing," God sees the light and the light sees God; God sees God and the light sees the light. Since "Seeing" is always working regardless of *before* and *after* and thereby is working right *here* and *now*, Línjì, taking it in the most existential way, calls it "Man." Hence he addresses "The One who is, at this moment, right in front of us, listening to this talk on the Dharma" and shouts "Look, look!" and "Speak, speak!" seizing the monk by the throat.

Accordingly, Dr Suzuki emphasizes that Línjì's "Man" is supra-individual[35] as well as individual.[36] "Man" is supra-individual because Línjì's "Man" is identical with "Emptiness," "Seeing," or to use Dr Suzuki's terminology, "Cosmic Unconsciousness." At the same time, "Man" is an individual, a concrete living existence such as Línjì, Déshān, you or I.

"Man" has two aspects – he exists as a finite individual, and at the same time he is a "bottomless abyss." It is not possible to take hold of "Man"

---

31. *Zhèngdaò ge:* 證道歌; J. *Shōdōka* (証道歌).
32. Yǒngjiā dàshī 永嘉大師 (665–713); J. Yōka Taishi.
33. Inner light: *língjué* 靈覺; J. *reikaku*.
34. D.T. Suzuki, *Manual of Zen Buddhism* (London: Rider, 1956), 98.
35. "Supra-individual" indicates being free from all limitations including form and colour, time and space, "I" and "you," one and many, and so on while "individual" is limited by these conditions.
36. *RKS*, 13, 30.

on the plane of the individual alone. For the [finite] individual inevitably goes hand in hand with the "bottomless abyss," and we must go through this "abyss" [aspect of him] if we are to be individuals in the true sense.[37] The bottomless abyss is, needless to say, "Emptiness," "Void" or "Cosmic Unconsciousness" which is supra-individual. One often takes Emptiness, Void or Cosmic Un-consciousness as something separated from an individual existence. Línjì, however, says that it "goes in and out from your facial gates. Those who have not yet testified to the fact, look, look!" The supra-individual Emptiness or Cosmic Unconsciousness cannot manifest itself directly unless it materializes in an individual existence. On the other hand, an individual existence is really individual only in so far as the supra-individual Emptiness or Cosmic Unconsciousness manifests itself in and through it. Línjì's "Man" is nothing but a living individual who is always (therefore, right here and right now) Emptiness, Cosmic Unconsciousness or Seeing. In other words, the living oneness of the individual and the supra-individual is "Man." Hence Línjì's saying,

> O Followers of the Way, the One who, at this moment, right in front of us, brightly, in solitude, and in full awareness is listening [to the talk on the Dharma] – this Man tarries nowhere wherever he may be, he passes through the ten quarters, he is master of himself in the triple world. Entering into all situations, discriminating everything, he is not to be turned away [from what he is].[38]

Here is the liberated and creative activity of "Man." Acting through the five senses, "Man" goes beyond them without being trapped in them. Acting in accord with consciousness, "Man" transcends consciousness without being confined by it.

> When conditions arise let them be illuminated. You just believe in the One who is acting at this very moment. He is not employing himself in any particularly specified fashion. As soon as one thought is born in your mind, the triple world rises with all its conditions which are classifiable under the six sense-fields. As you go on acting as you do in response to the conditions, what is wanting in you?[39]

---

37. *RKS*, 117.
38. *ZBP*, 33–4.
39. *ZBP*, 38–9.

Thus Línjì says, "He is master of himself wherever he goes. As he stands all is right with him."[40]

The above is an outline of Línjì's "Man" insight which Dr Suzuki elucidates as the core of the *Línjì lù* and as the most concrete basis of Zen. Here we can see what Dr Suzuki thinks to be the true way of human existence.

IV

As I said earlier in this paper, Dr Suzuki believes that Zhàozhōu shares the "Man" idea with Línjì, although the former does not use the term "Man" so explicitly as does the latter. Dr Suzuki illustrates this by the following *mondō* (question and answer) from the *Zhàozhōu Lù*:

Zhàozhōu was once asked by a monk, "What is my self?"
Zhàozhōu said, "Have you finished the morning gruel?" "Yes, I have finished," answered the monk.
Zhàozhōu then told him "If so, wash your bowl."[41]

Zhàozhōu's instruction here is not simply to wash a bowl after a meal, but to awaken to the "Self" in eating and washing. Commenting on the *mondō* Dr Suzuki says,

The eating is an act, the washing is an act, but what is wanted in Zen is the actor himself; the eater and the washer that does the acts of eating and washing; and unless this person is existentially or experientially taken hold of, one cannot speak of the acting. Who is the one who is conscious of acting, and who is the one who communicates this fact of consciousness to you, and who are you who tells all this not only to yourself but to all others? "I," "you," "she," or "it" – all this is a pronoun standing for a somewhat behind it. Who is this somewhat?[42]

We may also see from the following *mondō* that Zhàozhōu clearly grasped the same core of Zen as Línjì:

Zhàozhōu once asked a new monk, "Have you ever been here before?"
The monk answered, "Yes, sir, I have." Thereupon the master said,

---

40. *Rinzairoku* (Tokyo: Iwanami Bunko, 1966), 52.
41. ZBP, 29.
42. ZBP, 29.

"Have a cup of tea." Later on another monk came and he asked him the same question, "Have you ever been here?"

This time the answer was quite opposite. "I have never been here, sir." The old master, however, answered just as before, "Have a cup of tea." Afterwards the Inju (the managing monk of the monastery) asked the master, "How is it that you make the same offering of a cup of tea no matter what monk's reply is?"

The old master called out, "O Inju!" who at once replied, "Yes, master." Whereupon Zhàozhōu said, "Have a cup of tea."[43]

I think I am right in saying that Zhàozhōu's "Have a cup of tea" is the same as Línjì's "Look, look!" or "Speak, speak!" in that both are trying to help another to awaken to his true "Self" – that is to "Man."

Of Zhàozhōu it was said, "His Zen shines upon his lips," because the utterances he made were like jewels that sparkled brightly. This characteristic of Zhàozhōu is often contrasted with the somewhat militant attitude of Línjì and Déshān as seen in their use of the shout (*katsu*) and stick (*bō*). Dr Suzuki's appreciation of Zhàozhōu's Zen may be said to depend partly on his personal affinity for Zhàozhōu's above-mentioned characteristic. But the more important and more essential reason for his appreciation of Zhàozhōu's Zen is of course beyond such a personal matter. It can be found in the following words of Dr Suzuki:

> It ought to be said that the most distinguished character of Zhàozhōu's Zen lies in his teaching on "suffering from passion for the salvation of all living beings." Other Zen men, of course, say the same thing, because those who do not declare this can not be Zen men. In Zhàozhōu's Zen, however, the emphasis is striking.[44]

In this connection Dr Suzuki quotes the following *mondō* involving Zhàozhōu:

> Jōshū (Zhàozhōu) was approached by an old lady who said, "Women are considered to be heavily laden with the five obstructions. How can I be freed from them?"

---

43. *An Introduction to Zen Buddhism* (London: Rider & Co., 1948), 81.
44. *Jōshū-Zen no Ichitokusei* ("A Characteristic of Zhàozhōu's Zen"). *Gendai bukkyō kōza* (Series on Modern Buddhism; Tokyo: Kadokawa shoten, 1955), I, 308.

The master said, "Let all the other people be born in Heaven, but may I, this old woman, be forever drowned[45] in the ocean of suffering."[46]

Someone asked, "You are such a saintly personality. Where would you find yourself after your death?"

Jōshū the Zen master replied, "I go to hell ahead of you all!"

The questioner was thunderstruck and said, "How could that be?"

The master did not hesitate, "Without my first going to hell, who would be waiting there to save people like you?"[47]

Referring to the first *mondō*, Dr Suzuki says, "This expresses the *praṇidhāna* (Original Vow) of vicarious suffering."[48] As for the second *mondō* he makes the comment,

> This is, indeed, a strong statement, but from Jōshū's Zen point of view he was fully justified. He has no selfish motive here. His whole existence is devoted to doing good for others. If not for this, he could not make such a straightforward statement with no equivocation whatever. Christ declares, "I am the Way." He calls others to be saved through him. Jōshū's spirit is also Christ's. There is no arrogant self-centred spirit in either of them. They simply, innocently, wholeheartedly express the same spirit of love.[49]

In the view of Dr Suzuki, the Zen man is apt to seem to make too much of *prajñā*, the Great Wisdom, rather neglecting *karuṇā*, the Great Compassion. However, Dr Suzuki emphasizes that "What makes Zen as such is that various *upāya* (good devices for salvation) naturally come out of the Great Compassion with the quickness of the echo following a sound."[50] In Zen, properly speaking, *prajñā* and *karuṇā* are not two but one. Says Dr Suzuki, "Vimalakīrti's words 'I

---

45. A literal translation of this portion is, "may the old woman be forever drowned in the ocean of suffering" referring to the other party of the *mondō*. In so saying Zhàozhōu, though apparently pitiless, is trying to save the old woman by cutting off her attachment to her own liberation from the "five obstructions." Zhàozhōu's seemingly harsh reply springs from Great Compassion in which distinction between Zhàozhōu and the old woman does not exist and in which Zhàozhōu himself is willing to suffer much more than or in place of anyone else. I understand it was to emphasize this point that Dr Suzuki translated this portion as "may I, this old woman, be forever drowned in the ocean of suffering." Ed. Commas have been inserted before and after "this old woman" to eliminate purely grammatical incomprehensibility.
46. *The Essence of Buddhism* (Kyōto: Hōzōkan, 1948), 91.
47. ZBP, 69.
48. *Jōshū Zen no Ichitokusei*, 308.
49. ZBP, 69.
50. *Jōshū Zen no Ichitokusei*, 308.

am sick because my fellow-beings are sick' expresses the essence of religious experience. Without this there is no religion, no Buddhism, and accordingly no Zen. It must be said that Jōshū's Zen well realizes this insight."[51] One can be rightly called "The true Man of no rank" when in him the Great Wisdom is backed up by the Great Compassion and the Great Compassion is backed up by the Great Wisdom. As proof of the clear realization of this idea in Zhàozhōu (Jōshū), Dr Suzuki quotes another *mondō*:

> Somebody asked Jōshū, "Buddha is the enlightened one and teacher of us all. He is naturally entirely free of all the passions (*kleśa*), is he not?"
> Jōshū said, "No, he is the one who cherishes the greatest of all the passions."
> "How is that possible?"
> "His greatest passion is to save all beings!" Jōshū answered.[52]

From this point of view Dr Suzuki, especially in his later years, stressed affinity between Shin Buddhism (Pure Land True Buddhism)[53] and Zen Buddhism. Indeed he emphasized the basic oneness of the very root of Amida's *praṇidhāna* (Original Vow) and Zen's Realization of the true "Man."

With heartfelt sympathy, Dr Suzuki often quoted in his writings and lectures Zhàozhōu's story of a stone bridge.

> One day a monk visited Jōshū and said, "O Master, your stone bridge is noted all over the empire but, as I see it, it is nothing but a rickety log bridge." Jōshū retorted, "You see your rickety one and fail to see the real stone bridge." The monk asked, "What is the stone bridge?" Jōshū, "Horses pass over it; donkeys pass over it."[54]

The following comment by Dr Suzuki on this story well expresses his view of Zen and man's way of life. Jōshū's bridge resembles the sands of the Ganges, which are trampled by all kinds of animals and incredibly soiled by them, and yet the sands make no complaint whatever. All the foot prints left by creatures of every description are effaced in no time, and as to their filths, they are all effectively absorbed, leaving the sands as clean as ever. So with Jōshū's stone bridge: not only horses and donkeys but nowadays all kinds of conveyances, including heavy trucks and trains, pass over it and it is ever willing to accommodate them. Even when they abuse it, its complacency is

---

51. *Jōshū Zen no Ichitokusei*, 309.
52. ZBP, 69.
53. Ed. i.e. Jōdo Shinshū.
54. ZBP, 68.

not at all disturbed. The Zen-man of the "fourth step"⁵⁵ is like the bridge. He may not turn the right cheek to be struck when the left one is already hurt, but he works silently for the welfare of his fellow beings.⁵⁶

Dr Suzuki, in my view, not only appreciated Zhàozhōu's story of a stone bridge; he himself was the stone bridge over which men and women, scholars and laymen, artists and psychoanalysts, Easterners and Westerners all passed for the extraordinary length of his life of 95 years. In any case, he, or "the true Man of no rank" realized in him, will serve timelessly as a stone bridge, spanning especially East and West, for all his fellow beings.

---

55. The "fourth step" is *kenchūshi* 兼中至, the fourth of the "five steps," known as *goi* 五位 in Zen training. *Kenchūshi* is the step in which the Zen man, completely going beyond the noetic understanding of Zen truth, "strives to realize his insight to the utmost of his abilities" (ZBP, 60) by stepping into the actual world of duality. For a discussion of the "five steps" see ZBP, 59–76.
56. ZBP, 68.

Part III

Responses to Suzuki Daisetsu

11

The Stone Bridge of Jōshū

Kondō Akihisa

In the *Hekiganshū*, one of the most important writings of Zen literature, there is a passage as follows:

A monk asked Jōshū, "The stone bridge of Jōshū is famous. But what I see is just a log bridge. Why?" Jōshū answered, "You see only the log bridge, but cannot see the stone bridge." The monk asked, "What is then the stone bridge?" Jōshū answered, "That which lets the asses and horses pass."

The stone bridge of Jōshū represents the ever-functioning dynamic spirit of Zen – Zen in action – which has been transmitted, from mind to mind, from generation to generation, in the history of Zen.[1]

Throughout his long life of 95 years, Dr. Daisetz Teitarō Suzuki[2] lived a life of the stone bridge in the exact sense Jōshū meant.

It is a well-known fact that he exerted his effort in expounding the meaning of the enlightenment experience, *satori*, and the importance of *prajñā* (Wisdom) in Zen. *Satori*, in other words, means awakening to *prajñā*.

Thanks to his effort no one doubts today the importance of the enlightenment experience in Zen. Therefore, it is quite understandable that, given this importance, the attainment of enlightenment is apt to be taken as the ultimate goal of Zen practice.

---

1. Ed. Jōshū is the Japanese pronunciation for Zhàozhōu 趙州.
2. Ed. The standard spelling of Suzuki's Buddhist name is Daisetsu; the alternative spelling "Daisetz" is sometimes used as an aid to correct pronunciation, and is left at various places according to the preference of the authors.

However, if one simply aims at the attainment of enlightenment and is gratified with it, he does not really understand the full purport of the meaning of *satori* experience.

As Dr. Suzuki so correctly pointed out, enlightenment is important, but its importance lies in the fact that it is not merely the moment of fulfilment of one's long-cherished aspiration but it is the moment of his rebirth, the beginning of his spiritual life as a new being, to live not for himself but with other sentient and insentient beings, to share their sufferings and sorrows with them, and to help them become enlightened so that they too can liberate themselves from the bondage of troubles and pains, their anxieties and their feeling of meaninglessness. In other words, with his awakening to *prajñā*, his new life with and for the people begins in direct response to the irresistible urge of *karuṇā* (Compassion), the immediate self-expression of *prajñā*. This kind of life is called the life of the Bodhisattva, which Jōshū, in his plain but graphically concrete Zen term, calls his "stone bridge."

In this sense, after his enlightenment experience, Dr. Suzuki walked the way of the Bodhisattva throughout his life with his undaunted, tireless spirit. By virtue of his version of Jōshū's stone bridge, not only asses and horses but people in the West as well as in the East, irrespective of the difference of nationality, colour, race, class, culture, language, intelligence, age, sex, profession, richness and other worldly values, were able to deliver themselves from the shore of ignorance to the other shore of truth.

In the East, around the time he began to write about Zen, it was a fact that Zen was just for practising. Any intellectual elucidation or noetic approach was considered somewhat blasphemous or at least useless and obstructive. Of course, so far as Zen experience is concerned, as long as it is something to be experienced, practice is important. But if no noetic elucidation is allowed, there is a danger, in Zen practice, of falling into a kind of seemingly mystical state of self-complacency, a Zen sickness, which is a far more harmful obstacle to real *prajñā* awakening.

Since even intellection – *vijñāna* in Buddhistic terms – is one of the functions of *prajñā*, it ceases to be a hindrance, if it does not assert its conceited claim for supremacy and is operated in its legitimate function by a person who has achieved its mastery by awakening to *prajñā*. On the contrary, intellection will serve as one of the most efficient tools to discern the nature of enlightenment experience and promote the correct understanding of Zen practice.

It is true that you cannot make a horse drink water, but you can at least lead him to the water. Any effort, therefore, to contrive means and ways – *upāya* – to take him to the water is meaningful because it will give him a chance to drink when he wants it. In this sense Dr. Suzuki's elucidation of Zen through his voluminous writings was illuminating and helpful for those who were in need of guidance and instruction. His style of writing in Japanese was extremely plain, clear and readable. Without using difficult Buddhistic terms unnecessarily, his works were permeated with profound wisdom. He wrote with a touch of warmth, which was a reflection of his personality, so that people could feel themselves closer and more intimate with the spirit of Zen which had been existing intrinsically in their veins but which they had erroneously taken as something mysterious and incomprehensible that belonged entirely to the possession of a selected few.

His noetic approach was more appealing and instructive to the younger Japanese who, being brought up in the rationalistic Western way of education, did not feel so syntonic with the traditional authoritative atmosphere of Zen, even though they respected its value.

Generally speaking, his books not only stimulated those in the temple, but also helped common people appreciate Zen as a traditional asset benefiting their own lives. His contribution in this regard is quite significant in view of the present state of Japanese culture which is being "modernized" under the strong influence of the West, because any change could not be successfully accomplished in any country not attuned to its basic cultural assets embedded in the hearts of its people.

To the West, where analytical, intellectual ways of thinking had traditionally prevailed, his analytical way of elucidation was not nearly as strange as it was to the East. However, the subject he introduced to the West was not something with which Western minds were familiar. Therefore, it was quite understandable that people in the West at first took what he talked about as just another esoteric product of the mysterious East.

It seems a strange but interesting coincidence that in the year of 1900, when he published in the United States his first book in English about Zen, Aśvaghoṣa's *Discourse on the Awakening of Faith in the Mahāyāna*,[3] Freud published his first book on psychoanalysis, *The Interpretation of Dreams*.

But perhaps this is not so strange or accidental. Because, though they did not know each other at all and were not aware what they had in common, they had started on the same mission, the criticism of the pathology of modern Western culture, especially of the supremacy of reason, to which both offered remedies in their own way. Freud stressed the meaning of the unconscious, the forces of emotion, as opposed to the conscious, the power of reason, and their conflict as the source of neurosis. Suzuki specifically clarified the dichotomous and discriminating nature of reason at the source of human suffering.

---

3. Ed. In fact this work is now widely presumed to have been composed in China (in Chinese) and was only piously ascribed to Aśvaghoṣa. Moreover, while popular in East Asia, it is not really about Zen. It is more of a compendium of major strands in Mahāyāna Buddhist thought up to the time of its composition, but relevant here is a distinct emphasis on the role of consciousness.

Because of Freud's audacious and ruthless exposure of the problem, Western minds began to open their eyes to the alienation of man from his wholeness as a human being as revealed in the form of numerous cases of psychic disturbances. The forerunners of Freud, Nietzsche, Marx and Kierkegaard, had foreseen the phenomenon even though it had been well covered by the glory of the materialistic achievements called progress.

Freud's approach to the solution of the problem was by means of psychoanalysis. It was guided by the principle of bringing the unconscious into consciousness, the unreasonable into the realm of reason, that is according to his phrasing, "Where there was *id* – there shall be *ego*."

In that sense he was still in the traditional rationalistic cultural pattern of the West. With all his colossal laborious works in psychoanalysis, however, he came to a pessimistic conclusion about the future of human civilization because he found by his critical observation the existence of the self-destructive tendency which he believed intrinsic in human nature. He concluded also, by his rationalistic thinking, that religion is an illusion and a sort of infantilism.

Suzuki's contribution in this regard was, of course, the way of Zen. He stressed the importance of awakening, and he used the word "conscious" as Freud used it. However, in his case, what he means by conscious is different from Freud's notion of bringing the libidinal unconscious into consciousness. Suzuki's term means to become conscious of "the Cosmic Unconsciousness," which is achieved by awakening to *prajñā*.

As Buddhism essentially originated from the realistic observation and understanding of the state of mankind as suffering, it can agree with Freud in the respect that man's state of existence is pessimistic at present as well as in the future so long as man is driven by his self-destructive tendency which is ultimately rooted in his ignorance.

According to Buddhistic understanding, man's existential state of suffering comes out of two kinds of ignorance, both of which are inseparably related. One is the ignorance of the fact that he is alienated from the Buddha-Nature, and the other is the ignorance of the truth of the existence of the Buddha-Nature in every human being. In short, man is ignorant of his ignorance of the Buddha-Nature with which he is bestowed. And just because of this ignorance, he surrenders himself blindly to the instinctual impulses which are governed by the principles, in Freud's terms, of pleasure and death. The more he is driven by these impulses and pursues their fulfilment, even with the resistance of reason by way of repression, the more he is alienated from his real self. The way by which man can liberate himself from his self-alienation, according to Zen Buddhism, is not by repression or sublimation through reason, but by breaking through his ignorance and realizing the Buddha Nature through his experience of awakening to *prajñā*. In this sense, even though Zen, as a school of Buddhism, shares the same view of the existential state of mankind with Freud, it begins to develop its own doctrine of liberation from the very point where Freud ended with pessimism. It helps man to see his original face, according to its expression, to have a rebirth as a whole human being and to enable him to attain a new spiritual life beyond the death and pleasure principles, transcending the dichotomy of reason at the same time. To experience this and live in it, helping others to get enlightened, is the religious life of Zen. For Suzuki, the religion he believed in and practised is not an illusion or infantilism. Religion is for him the way of maturity and realism in the sense that one can live his life fully with it as a new whole being helping his fellow men to restore their wholeness.

At that time when the West was beginning to be coloured by the rosy notion of progress based on the belief in the supremacy of reason, it was most opportune that a message was conveyed from the East. Zen stated that by becoming aware of his state of self-estrangement resulting from the supremacy of reason, man is able to free himself from his ignorance so that he can realize his Buddha-Nature. In that sense it is nothing to be afraid of to be exposed to the emptiness and meaninglessness of his existential state, for it is to be taken as the turning point that opens the way for his ultimate awakening to *prajñā* as prepared in Zen. This was the message conveyed by Suzuki in person to the world – a message for the resurrection of man himself.

Perhaps more than any other group, those engaged in the treatment of the mentally disturbed became keenly sensitive to the sickness of Western civilization as a direct result of their observations in their offices. While Freudian therapists were more or less negativistic and sceptical or indifferent towards Zen because of their libidinal orientation, other psychiatrists or psychotherapists whose minds were not limited by theories but more open to psychic reality, showed their interest in what Suzuki talked about. Among them, Jung was the first one who recognized and appreciated the meaning of Zen experience. In his foreword to Suzuki's *Introduction to Zen Buddhism*, he stated, "The only movement inside of our civilization which has, or should have, some understanding of these endeavours is psychotherapy." He compared Zen experience with the mystic experiences of Meister Eckhart and John Ruysbroeck and interpreted it as a process of individuation, his term for "becoming whole." However, he made an understandable reservation by stating that "Great as is the value of Zen Buddhism for understanding the religious transformation process, its use among Western people is problematic." Whether its use among Western people is problematic or not is a question to be answered in the future. But if Suzuki did not feel the value of its use for the West in respect to "becoming whole," what would be the meaning of his life-work dedicated to Zen's transmission to the West? Personally I would rather like to stress another statement of Jung's: "I have no doubt that the *satori* experience does occur also in the West." Because I believe, so far as the Cosmic Unconscious is concerned in which *satori* takes place, it is all-embracing and boundless beyond the differences of culture. Even though he is conditioned by culture, man has the intrinsic potentiality to make a leap and free himself from his attachment to cultural prejudices, the product of discrimination, by becoming conscious of the Cosmic Unconscious which is universal. Following Jung, Karen Horney, through her personal contact and discussions with Suzuki, became very much interested in Zen.[4] Her holistic approach to man himself and her basic concept of the real self with her stress on the importance of intuition in therapy, all urged her to study and absorb eagerly what Zen had consummated. In her trip to Japan with Suzuki, the memory of which is still vivid in my mind, she met and exchanged opinions with quite a number of Zen masters. Even though she had been considered as one of the leaders of the culturists group, she, as a person, was much greater than her theory. As she felt herself congenial and had so much in common with Zen, she was anxious to develop her ideas by thought stimulation experiences in Japan. Unfortunately due to her sudden death, what she got from this trip became unavailable for us. After her death, Suzuki had a series of lectures and discussions with her group that was led by Harold Kelman.

In 1957, Suzuki was invited to a conference in Mexico by Erich Fromm. Their encounter resulted in the publication of a book, *Zen Buddhism and Psychoanalysis*.[5] It was quite a meaningful event, because while originating in different cultures and at different times, Zen and psychoanalysis had been sharing the same function of restoring man as a whole being in this modern age of split personality and anxiety, and they were brought into direct contact for collaboration to confirm mutually their common end.

Thus, his incessant activities for elucidation and transmitting Zen in the East and West began to bear fruit during the latter part of his life. It is a most outstanding fact that all through the long years of his pioneering activities, he worked practically single-handed. In that sense, he was alone and independent, although he had the helpful assistance and personal care of Miss Mihoko Okamura until his death. The way he opened was followed and cultivated by many others including R.H. Blyth, Alan Watts, R. DeMartino and P. Kapleau.

One evening, when I was staying with him in Ipswich, near Boston, I happened to ask him, while we were seated talking, "What is Hyakujō's 'Sitting alone on the summit of Mt. Dàxióng'?"[6] As a reply, he suddenly raised himself with tremendous agility, and sat cross-legged in the chair. I can never forget my experience that his whole body suddenly looked grander and radiated

---

4. Ed. Karen Horney: psychoanalyst, 1885–1952.
5. Ed. See also the contribution by Erich Fromm below.
6. Ed. Hyakujō Ekai: 百丈懷海 Bǎizhàng Huáihǎi (720–814). The author refers to Hyakujō with Japanese pronunciation, as is common in Zen writings, but switches to Chinese for the name of the mountain: Mt. Dàxióng (Ta-hsiung). Sitting alone on the summit of Dàxióng: 獨坐大雄峰 *dokuzadaiyūhō*.

an enormously overwhelming power at that moment. There I witnessed the forcefulness and dignity of his aloneness.

In 1952, he was still chiefly stressing the importance of *prajñā* in his lectures. But in my view, he was actually teaching us *karuṇā* by his daily conduct. One evening I was telling him of my experience with a patient who had made a radical breakthrough after painful effort and suffering. I was dumbfounded to find him in tears. After a while, he said, "How grateful I feel for what you have done!" Here I felt his great concern with human suffering. From the depth of his heart, he could not help feeling grateful for any help in liberating people from their sufferings. Hence his utterance of gratitude on behalf of my patient who, for him, was not a stranger at all, but a kinsman in the sense that he was also a human being anxiously struggling for the realization of his Buddha-Nature. I was strongly moved at that moment by the effusion of his sincere desire – the expression of *karuṇā* – to free people from their suffering as well as their ignorance. His words penetrated deep into my heart, and his voice is still ringing in my ears awakening me to the real meaning of my work as a doctor.

In the later days of his life, he became more and more explicit in expressing the significance of *karuṇā* in his lectures and writings. Especially after working on the English translation of *Kyō-gyō-shin-shō* ("Teaching, Act, Faith, Enlightenment") by Shinran, one of the most important texts of Pure Land Buddhism, he stressed the meaning of the Great Act, a dynamic expression of *karuṇā* which is really the actual functioning of *prajñā* to enable man to attain rebirth as a whole being.

The words he left on his death bed were, "Don't worry! Thank you! Thank you!" To the last moment in his life, he did not wish to make people suffer for his sake despite the extreme pains he was suffering from his disease, and he never ceased to feel grateful for everything that is given, even death. In that sense, he himself was the example of what he taught us throughout his life, compassion and grand affirmation.

He closed his life here in this world. But, look! For those who can see it, the stone bridge of Jōshū is ever present.

12

The Enlightened Thought

Kobori Sōhaku

I

One of the main achievements of Dr. Suzuki was his success in communicating the incommunicable. The reality of Zen refuses by its nature to be transformed into a Rosetta Stone; it refuses ever to be translated into any kind of conceptual words. It reminds me of Zhuāngzǐ's (Chuang-tze's) story of the three gods:

> The one called Chaos[1] (C. *Húntún*, J. *konton*) ruled the centre of the universe. The one called Shù 儵 (Shuku) was god of the south sea and the third one Hū 忽 (Kotsu) ruled the north sea. As they were close friends, they met one day at the place of Chaos. He entertained his friends so nicely that the gods of the northern and southern seas wished to repay him. They consulted together and came to a conclusion, "While everyone has seven holes through which one sees, hears, eats and breathes, Chaos possesses none of them; let us try to hollow him out." Each day they carved one hole in him and, after a week when they had accomplished the work, Chaos died. (ch. 7.)

It was Dr. Suzuki who attempted to introduce *Húntún*, the reality of Zen, to the Western way of thinking. Without killing *Húntún*, he made him communicable to Westerners to the extent that they came to notice the actuality

---

1. Chaos. This name's signification should not be understood in the sense of the "confusion" after order or system has collapsed, but rather in the earlier sense of "the confused state without form and void of primordial matter before the creation of orderly forms" (*Webster's Dictionary*). Chaos indeed was the most ancient Greek god.

of a well-weathered standpoint in the East. In the West the understanding of such a new standpoint seems really meaningful, particularly in the midst of the trends of modern thought. Erich Fromm, the psychoanalyst, said,

> Taoism and Buddhism had a rationality and realism superior to that of the Western religions. They could see man realistically and objectively, having nobody but the 'awakened' ones to guide him, and being able to be guided because each man has within himself the capacity to awake and be enlightened. This is precisely the reason why Eastern religious thought, Taoism and Buddhism – and their blending in Zen Buddhism – assume such importance for the West today.[2]

In the present world, man, being separated from nature, alienated even from himself, relies only upon the progress of science and technology in order to improve his standard of living and to build a limited heaven on earth. But man, as a matter of fact, is appalled by the idea that, while during the past 200 or 300 years he has increased his scientific knowledge enormously and is adding to it at an ever increasing rate, his wisdom of how to live together with his fellow men appears to have improved little, if at all.

Therefore, man at present must bear the sense of alienation due to the contradiction between individual intelligence in science and group stupidity in war. It is for just such a situation that communication between East and West in regard to finding new bearings has come to be felt necessary – the bearings according to which man could be integrated within himself and at the same time able to live with fellow men in spite of their diversities of situation.

II

Our "mission is to help to construct a cultural bridge between East and West, making it possible for Love to achieve her end." This is a statement by Dr. Suzuki in his editorial of *The Cultural East* magazine:

> Where there is no spiritual vision, there is no culture, for culture reflects one's spiritual attainments. When spirit speaks directly to spirit this is Enlightenment. When the spirit is enlightened, Ignorance ceases to assert itself, and mutual understanding is made possible. An enlightened spirit is always creative, and from it springs culture in its manifold

---

2. *Zen Buddhism and Psychoanalysis* (New York: Grove Press, 1960), 80.

forms. A mutual cultural understanding therefore means an enhancement of one's spirituality.[3]

As he stresses it, mutual understanding is necessary between East and West; for this the spirit of man must be enlightened at its root. This is one of the most important aspects of Dr. Suzuki's thought. And, in order to understand the meaning of the enlightened spirit, I should like to add my view. His thought is not to be classified as similar to other ideologies which are specific notions of thought limited to some nations or people. Rather it presents bearings common to human beings without any exclusive prejudices, making it possible for them to live together in peace. The thought of Dr. Suzuki is not the mere logical outcome of a certain fashion of scientific or metaphysical thinking, but issues directly out of his experience, enlightened to the essential reality of man as well as the world of nature. In other words, he did not approach reality from the outside, but he himself became one with the reality of the "Cosmic Unconscious" (in his terms), which lies at the root of all existence and unites them all in the oneness of being.

He often said of himself, "I am not a scholar," by which he might have been suggesting that an ordinary scholar, so to say, lives in search of a certain reality through logical or objective thinking, setting himself apart from what he is pursuing. When the one who observes or pursues and that which is observed are set apart, the result of the observation will not be an integrating result. At present, for instance, man, without deep reflection, relies only on scientific ways of improving life, unaware of the cogent fact that in his observation of nature, he totally overlooks himself. Einstein, as I understand, affirmed "the four-dimensional universe," that is adding the new dimension – time – to the three physical dimensions theretofore realized. But still, from my view, this four-dimensioned universe is lacking one more dimension, that is the living observer Einstein himself; through him, the rest of the four dimensions are integrated. Was he himself aware of being this fifth dimension which indeed he was? So long as natural science is not aware of the undiscovered dimension which integrates nature and man, the objective world, no matter how much it may be improved, will never be a sufficient condition for bringing man towards his own well-being, towards the world of mutual understanding among enlightened spirits.

---

3. *The Cultural East* 1 (July 1946), 1–2.

III

As I said before, a distinguishing characteristic of Dr. Suzuki's thought is the fact that it is a spontaneous flow of his consciousness deeply rooted in his Zen experience. The consciousness, once culminated in him at its *ne plus ultra*, was then broken through into the infinite Cosmic Unconscious (Chaos) which precedes any of the bifurcations or polarizations necessary to the thinking process. The Cosmic Unconscious as such is the real basis which is common to the vast expanse of nature – space, time, constellations and universes, non-being as well as beings, including animals, plants, and human beings. This Cosmic Unconscious goes beyond the limits of the intellectual realm of human beings heretofore attained, so that sometimes it is likely to be called the "mysterious" or "supernatural" realm. But such terms are limiting notions coming from an un-integrated understanding, unaware of the essence of nature and man.

Fortunately, however, the consciousness of human beings is rooted deeply in the Cosmic Unconscious. At the moment when human consciousness, having gradually submerged into the ocean of the Cosmic Unconscious, suddenly rises up to the surface of that unconscious, it cuts into the level of normal consciousness again. Here, Zen declares that it is human consciousness awakened to the original nature: *satori* (enlightenment).

We must be very careful regarding the process of the awakening experience; we must bear in mind that it by no means is a mere continuation of the conscious state of mind, nor is it a mere submersion into the abyss of the unconscious. But it is the regaining of consciousness after having once "gone through" the Cosmic Unconscious. This "regained" consciousness, however, is never to be mixed with perception or cogitation but, according to Dr. Suzuki's favourite terminology, it is "unconscious consciousness" or "conscious unconsciousness." Unless we understand this process fully, the term "enlightened spirit," affirmed by Dr. Suzuki as the common ground through which men become able to have mutual understanding, may not be clearly communicated.

IV

As a typical example which presents this process of the enlightened spirit, let me introduce a dialogue from the *Hekiganroku* or the Blue Cliff Collection.[4]

---

4. See D.T. Suzuki, "The *Hekiganroku*," *The Eastern Buddhist* New Series 1.1 (September 1965), 5–6. Ed. *Hekiganroku*: Bìyán lù 碧巖 (碧巌録).

Jō Jōza[5] (one of Rinzai's main disciples) once asked Rinzai, "What is the essence of Buddha's teaching?" Rinzai, getting off his meditation seat, seized him, slapped[6] him, and pushed him away. Jō stood there utterly lost. Then a monk standing by said, "Jōza, why not bow?" Jō, just about to make a bow, all of a sudden awakened to the supreme enlightenment (Case No. 32).[7]

Let me note here some of Engo's comments[8] attached to each sentence of Jō's *kōan*. Under the passage "Rinzai, getting off his meditation seat, seized him, slapped him, and pushed him away," Engo commented, "*Today [Rinzai] grasped [his student]. This is the old master's kindness. Even outstanding Zen monks in the world could never escape from it [the grasp].*"

The comment means that Rinzai's treatment of his student, at the moment his student's religious consciousness reached culmination, was really timely, and was backed by deep compassion.

Under the line "Jō stood there utterly lost," Engo commented, "*He has fallen into a dark cave where only dead devils are gathering. Lost all consciousness.*" The comment means: The consciousness of Jō has merged into the Cosmic Unconscious, but it is not yet enlightened, being in a state of darkness. Under "Just about to make a bow, all of a sudden, he awakened to the supreme enlightenment," he puts, "*It is just like the light given in darkness.*" Hakuin adds, "All of a sudden a dead one has revived." Here we can see the darkness of the Cosmic Unconscious suddenly changed into light – the supreme enlightenment. According to Dr. Suzuki, the conscious mind of Jō, which was still on the level of ambivalence, had reached its end; then Rinzai, who was well versed in such a process of consciousness (this is why he was an outstanding Zen master), gave his kind help to his student, a slap! This is indeed the deep, compassionate heart of Zen. But Jō still stood there, submerged in the ocean of unconsciousness, not knowing who he was or what it was that he was doing at that moment, losing all of his previous consciousness in which until that moment he had flowed waveringly during his life in pursuit of truth. At that

---

5. Ed. Jō Jōza 定上座 Dìng shàngzuò.
6. In Western custom, a slap may be insulting and may mean punishment, but from the Zen point of view, it has quite a different connotation. In a sense, it helps the student to get direct insight into reality, removing all wavering consciousness by a timely slap. The slap gives the motivation for getting to reality. Sometimes it connotes a religious negation, not by idea but through total act. The functions of beating by a stick or of slapping by the hand do not differ so much in Zen instruction.
7. Rinzai Gigen (d. 867) was one of the outstanding Zen masters of the Táng Dynasty. He used a method known for its immediateness. Jō Jōza was one of his leading disciples, and succeeded to his master's rough and direct way of Zen teaching – demonstrated with the fullness of his being. This story tells us how Jō came to real *satori* after tremendous effort. Such awakening would not just happen unless one had gone through a long, basic training of Zen meditation. Ed. Rinzai Gigen 臨済義玄 (臨濟義玄 Línjì Yìxuán).
8. "The *Hekiganroku*," 5–6. Ed. Engo Kokugon 圜悟克勤 Yuánwù Kèqín (1063-1135).

moment, one of Rinzai's advanced students, who had been watching, stimulated his fellow monk to make him break through the abyss of unconsciousness. He said, "You! Why not make a bow?," and this voice pushed him into awakening to the essential wisdom. Jō made a bow. Oh! What a new world he is revived in now! See the wonder of this moment depicted in the appreciatory verse of Setchō:[9]

> Korei had no difficulty
> In lifting up his hand:
> Look! in a minute, he clove the piled-up
> Ranges of Mount Ka.[10]

The god Korei suggests Rinzai here. And his slapping of the Jōza clove the piled-up unconsciousness and then, just as the Yellow River flowed between the ranges of the Ka mountains, essential wisdom sprang out the moment the Cosmic Unconscious was broken through.

V

From the case I have introduced above, we might have a glimpse into the process of the experience of enlightenment. In the philosophy of Buddhism, it is spoken of as "the awakening of the great Wisdom (*prajñā*)." This means that an individual spirit, through the experience of a "total-manness," is elevated from the level of discrimination and finitude to the level of non-discrimination and infinity. There one sees that he is no longer enclosed in the limited ego-centric shell which rejects other egos. Now he stands on the basis of "being" which everybody and everything equally share; he is immersed in the fountainhead of eternal life. At the root of individuality, then, one sees the universal and infinite nature of man. From this viewpoint, all human beings can understand and respect each other.

Within the range of Dr. Suzuki's thought, if his idea of the awakening to the great Wisdom (*mahā-prajñā*) may be called the first peak, the next peak must be the idea of the great Compassion which he sometimes compared to Love. He introduced this into the cultural milieu of the West as the principle synthesizing all different ways of thinking and life. I am going to try to make clear the interrelation between the great Wisdom and the great Compassion.

---

9. Ed. Setchō Jūken 雪竇重顯 Xuědoù Chóngxián (980–1052).
10. Korei (巨靈 Chinese: Jùlíng) was the legendary god of the Yellow River, who by one stroke of his hand cleft the mountain ranges of Ka which were hindering the flow of the Yellow River toward the ocean. Rinzai's one slap, which smashed the piled doubts of Jō, is compared to Korei's mighty stroke. Ed. Mount Ka: 華山 (華山) Mount Huá.

The Buddhist technical term *prajñā* is often used in combination with *pāramitā*. We can interpret *pāramitā* in at least two ways. One meaning is "reaching the other shore" (by the transcendental wisdom); the other is "attainment of the transcendental wisdom." In the *Laṅkāvatāra Sūtra*, an important passage runs, "Wisdom is free from the idea of being and non-being, yet a great compassionate heart is awakened in itself."[11] This is the most important passage not only in the philosophy of the *Laṅkāvatāra* but in the whole teaching of Mahāyāna Buddhism. As I noted above, *prajñā-pāramitā* means in one sense the completion of the transcendental wisdom which awakens one to the basis of all beings. But the great wisdom is never to be accomplished by itself alone; the awakening to the basis of all beings should be the common experience of men. As long as it remains on the level of individual experience or limited to a specific group of men isolated from other people, it will be but a limited, relative and, therefore, finite wisdom, though at times it may attain to a solitary, saintly life. It will never be the supreme wisdom shared by all mankind. As all men are living in a mutually related community, the mere individual attainment of the supreme wisdom would never be meaningful; it would never be concerned with the well-being of mankind as a whole. According to Dr. Suzuki, here the conception of a Bodhisattva is inevitable: a Bodhisattva never wishes to become Buddha, the one who has completed the great wisdom, unless all beings in the world, past, present and future, are enlightened as well.

> If he attains to a state of self-realization which he finds so full of peace, bliss, and strength, his natural desire is to impart it to his fellow beings. Technically, when he has finished benefiting himself, his next step is to go out into the world and benefit others. In reality, he cannot do good for himself without letting others share in it.[12]

The great wisdom is sensitive to its own incompleteness; it is not a static intellect; it cannot but work dynamically upon anyone who still remains under delusion. As long as unenlightened spirits remain, the heart of an enlightened one pains continuously. The great wisdom is tormented, suffering its own incompleteness. This innate sensitivity of the great wisdom is compassion. In the inmost depth of Cosmic Unconsciousness, wisdom and compassion are still undifferentiated. When the supreme wisdom is awakened in man, the compassionate heart simultaneously awakens – the completion of the great wisdom – just as it is the nature of light to rush from its source into darkness. The essential framework of Dr. Suzuki's thought, I believe, consists

---

11. The opening stanza recited by Mahamati in the Sòng translation of the *Laṅkāvatāra Sūtra*. See D.T. Suzuki, *Studies in the Laṅkāvatāra Sūtra* (London: Routledge, 1931), 215.
12. *Studies in the Laṅkāvatāra Sūtra*, 214.

in these two main peaks of wisdom and love – or *prajñā* and *karuṇā* – and both issued immediately out of his enlightened spirit. When an enlightened spirit thinks, it creates an enlightened thought.

When the light of enlightenment illuminates a man inwardly, it becomes the great wisdom which cuts off all limited, distorted and ego-centric ideas. When it illuminates outwardly, it becomes the great compassion – love which moves towards the welfare of living beings in the world, enlightening their spirits.

VI

In the history of Western thought, men once stood equally related to God and had no doubts as to the meaning and value of life. However, since all principles that had been dominating man lost their authority, man came to assume that "God is dead." And man began to presume to take the part of the Creator, finding in machines something approximating the creative power of the Creator.

Man believes now in science and technology which should give him a relative heaven on earth. And yet he does not know why he and his fellow men are feeling their life so empty and meaningless. Man, at a loss, looks around himself and comes to feel the solitude of being alienated from the centre of his existence. Man has also become faced with the fear that, by means of scientific products, he will be wiped from the world in a nuclear holocaust. It was not only from such modern trends of thought but also from much deeper and more fundamental reflection upon the being of man that Dr. Suzuki attempted to introduce a new standpoint into the present world. What he wished to contribute, I believe, is the idea of a total man in whom great wisdom and great love are deeply rooted. While wisdom will be able to assume control of scientific knowledge and thus save man from self-destruction, love will provide a basic understanding of men in diverse situations and also a basic harmony of man and nature.

VII

When I met with Dr. Suzuki for the last time, his body was in a room in the cellar of St Luke's Hospital in Tokyo. He was already in the coffin before the altar. It was early morning and I was alone in the room. I stepped forward to him and lit a candle. As I bowed deeply, the scent and smoke of the burning incense enveloped us, making us one. I recited the following verses:

However innumerable sentient beings are,
I vow to save them;

However inexhaustible the passions are,
I vow to extinguish them;
However immeasurable Dharmas are,
I vow to master them;
However incomparable the Buddha-truth is,
I vow to attain it;
Throughout your 96 years, nothing else but this vow,
And look! you have left one more vow;
How *Ya-Fū-Ryū*[13] it is!
Oh, my teacher, my teacher...Kwatz![14]

I offered this Kwatz to him with full strength, out of the bottom of my heart. It involuntarily came out of my inmost gratitude for his love to me. As soon as I finished reciting the verses before the coffin, tears suddenly fell down my cheeks, though I had not any clear conscious of sadness. That was my last farewell to the teacher in bodily form.

On the afternoon of 14 July, his body became a wreath of white smoke in the crematorium in Kita Kamakura. The smoke vanished into the cool breeze blowing from the sea. Where did he go? Look, here he is. He will never die – the vow he made! His great will which communicated the incommunicable and shared it with all human beings, will not vanish forever. The wheel of this vow, which had gone throughout his 96 years, must be driven further and further, generation after generation, as long as human beings exist on the earth.

---

13. *Ya-fūryū* is the name which was given him as a lay student of Zen by his Zen teacher Sōen Shaku. The term *ya-fūryū* is really hard for us to translate into English. *Fūryū* has a subtle meaning similar to that which the Japanese aesthetic principles *wabi* or *sabi* imply. It connotes a refinement of life or a spiritual elegance in life even though life is not rich or plentiful in appearance. The source of this term should be ascribed to the verse made by Hakuun Shutan, a noted Zen master of the Sòng Dynasty. (Ed. Hakuun Shutan 白雲守端 Báiyún Shǒuduān 1025–73.) The verse was composed as the comment on the case in which Rinzai for the first time opened his eye to the reality of Zen under the sixty blows of his teacher Ōbaku. It says: Just where there is no-*fūryū*, there is likewise *fūryū*, too.

"No-*fūryū*" points to the world of the Cosmic Unconsciousness where subject and object are not differentiated. *Ya-fūryū* means that as soon as the undifferentiation – no-*fūryū* – is broken through, an enlightenment takes place, it is the re-gained consciousness. When it flows, it becomes subject or object, joy or sadness...and it becomes the eternal vow of human beings to share enlightenment with each other.

14. Kwatz. We find "Katsu," a shout, not only in old Zen masters' records but in the actuality of Zen discipline even today. It serves at times as a practical means to help toward the comprehension of reality and at times it becomes the living reality of Zen itself.

13

The "Mind-less" Scholar

Alan Watts

I have never had a formal teacher (*guru* or *rōshi*) in the spiritual life – only an exemplar, whose example I have not really followed because no sensitive person likes to be mimicked. That exemplar was Suzuki Daisetz[1] – at once the subtlest and the simplest person I have known. His intellectual and spiritual mood or atmosphere (*fū* 風) I found wholly congenial, although I never knew him really intimately and although I myself am an entirely different kind of person. Suzuki introduced me to Zen when I first read his *Essays in Zen Buddhism* in mid-adolescence, and in the years that followed I read everything he wrote with fascination and delight. For what he said was always unexpected and open-ended. He did not travel in the well-worn ruts of philosophical and religious thought. He rambled, he digressed, he dropped hints, he left you suspended in mid-air, he astonished you with his learning (which was prodigious) and yet charmed you with scholarship handled so lightly and unpretentiously. For I found in the engagingly disorganized maze of his writings the passage to a Garden of Reconciled Opposites.

He showed why Zen is immensely difficult and perfectly easy, why it is at once impenetrable and obvious, why the infinite and eternal is exactly the same as your own nose at this moment, why morals are both essential and irrelevant to the spiritual life, and why *jiriki* (the way of personal effort) comes finally to the same point as *tariki* (the way of liberation through pure faith). The trick in following Suzuki was never to "stay put," as if you had at last got his point and were on firm ground – for the next moment he would show you that you had missed it altogether.

---

1. Ed. Daisetz: an alternative spelling sometimes used for Daisetsu to avoid over-accentuation of the last vowel.

Suzuki was also outside the ordinary ruts in that, without any show of eccentricity, he did not present himself in the stereotype of the usual "Zen personality" which one finds among Japanese monks. Anyone visiting him for the first time, expecting to find an old gentleman with flashing eyes, sitting in a bare *shibui*-type room, and ready to engage you in swift and vigorous repartee, would have been very much surprised. For Suzuki, with his miraculous eyebrows, was more like a Chinese Taoist scholar – a sort of bookish Lǎozǐ – gifted, as all good Taoists are, with what can only be called metaphysical humour. Every so often his eyes twinkled as if he had seen the Ultimate Joke, and as if, out of compassion for those who had not, he were refraining from laughing out loud.

He lived in the Western-style section of his home in Kamakura completely surrounded with piles of books and papers. This scholarly disarray was spread through several rooms, in each of which he was writing a separate book, or separate chapters of one book. He could thus move from room to room without having to clear away all his reference materials when feeling inclined to work upon one project rather than another, but somehow his admirable secretary Miss Okamura (who was actually an *apsara* sent down from the Western Paradise to take care of him in his old age) seemed to know where everything was.

Suzuki spoke slowly, deliberately and gently in excellent English with a slight and, to our ears, very pleasing Japanese accent. In conversation, he almost always explained himself with the aid of pen and paper, drawing diagrams to illustrate his points and Chinese characters to identify his terms. Though a man of wonderful patience, he had a genius for deflating windy argument or academic pedantry without giving offence. I remember a lecture where a member of the audience asked him, "Dr. Suzuki, when you use the word 'reality,' are you referring to the relative reality of the physical world, or to the absolute reality of the transcendental world?" He closed his eyes and went into that characteristic attitude which some of his students call "doing a Suzuki," for no one could tell whether he was in deep meditation or fast asleep. After about a minute's silence, though it seemed longer, he opened his eyes and said, "Yes." During a class on the basic principles of Buddhism:

> This morning we come to Fourth Noble Truth...called Noble Eightfold Path. First step of Noble Eightfold Path is called *shōken*. *Shōken* means Right View. All Buddhism is really summed up in Right View, because Right View is having no special view, no fixed view. Second step of Noble Eightfold Path...(and here there was a long pause). Oh, I forget second step. You look it up in the book.[2]

---

2. Ed. The miscellaneous omission of definite articles is retained in this verbal transcript.

In the same vein, I remember his address to the final meeting of the 1936 World Congress of Faiths at the old Queen's Hall in London. The theme was "The Supreme Spiritual Ideal," and after several speakers had delivered themselves of volumes of hot air, Suzuki's turn came to take the platform and he said,

> When I was first asked to talk about the Supreme Spiritual Ideal I did not exactly know what to answer. Firstly, I am just a simple-minded countryman from a far-away corner of the world suddenly thrust into the midst of this hustling city of London, and I am bewildered and my mind refuses to work in the same way that it does when I am in my own land. Secondly, how can a humble person like myself talk about such a grand thing as the Supreme Spiritual Ideal?... Really I do not know what Spiritual is, what Ideal is, and what Supreme Spiritual Ideal is.

Whereupon he devoted the rest of his speech to a description of his house and garden in Japan, contrasting it with the life of a great city. This from the translator of the Laṅkāvatāra Sūtra! And the audience gave him a standing ovation.

Being well aware of the relativity and inadequacy of all opinions, he would never argue. When a student tried to provoke him into a discussion of certain points upon which the celebrated Buddhist scholar Junjirō Takakusu differed from him, his only comment was, "This is very big world; plenty of room in it for both Professor Takakusu and myself." Well, perhaps there was one argument when the Chinese scholar Hu Shih accused him of obscurantism (in asserting that Zen could not be expressed in rational language) and of lacking a sense of history. But in the course of a very courteous reply Suzuki said, "The Zen master, generally speaking, despises those who indulge in word- or idea-mongering, and in this respect Hu Shih and myself are great sinners, murderers of Buddhas and patriarchs; we are both destined for hell." I have never known a great scholar and intellectual so devoid of conceit. When I first met Suzuki, I was flabbergasted that he asked me (aged 20) how to prepare a certain article, and that when I was brash enough to give my advice he followed it. Academic pomposity and testiness were simply not in him. Thus certain American sinologists, who make a fine art of demolishing one another with acrimonious footnotes, are apt to go into a huff about his rather casual use of documentation and "critical apparatus," and speak of him as a mere "popularizer." They do not realize that he genuinely loved scholarship and thus made no show of "being a scholar." He had no interest in using bibliography as a gimmick for boosting his personality.

Perhaps the real spirit of Suzuki could never be caught from his writings alone; one had to know the man. Many readers complain that his work is so un-Zen-like – verbose, discursive, obscure and cluttered with technicalities. A Zen monk once explained to me that the attitude of *mushin* (the Zen style of unselfconsciousness) was like the Japanese carpenter who can build a house without a blueprint. I asked, "What about the man who draws a blueprint without making a plan for it?" This was, I believe, Suzuki's attitude in scholarship: he thought, he intellectualized, he pored over manuscripts and dictionaries as any Zen monk might sweep floors in the spirit of *mushin*. In his own words,

> Man is a thinking reed but his great works are done when he is not calculating and thinking. "Childlikeness" has to be restored with long years of training in the art of self-forgetfulness. When this is attained, man thinks yet he does not think. He thinks like showers coming down from the sky; he thinks like the waves rolling on the ocean; he thinks like the stars illuminating the nightly heavens; he thinks like the green foliage shooting forth in the relaxing spring breeze. Indeed, he is the showers, the ocean, the stars, the foliage.

14

Memories of Dr. D.T. Suzuki

Erich Fromm

In attempting to write a few words of memories of Dr. Suzuki I am struck by the paradox that it is so difficult to write memories about him precisely because I see him so alive before me. How can one write "memories" about a man who has just left the room for a moment, and whose presence is felt with all vividness?

I write these lines in the garden of our house in Cuernavaca (Mexico) where Dr. Suzuki stayed with us for several months, exactly ten years ago. Here he sat, walked, read, conversed, and although it is ten years ago, the strength and radiance of his personality makes him ever present.

Should I write about his never-failing kindness, about his firmness and truthfulness, his concentration, the absence of vanity and Ego in him? Those who knew him, know all this; and for those who did not know him, words like these cannot mean much. Perhaps I should mention his ever-present interest in everything around him. He was delighted to see a Mexican rug, or piece of pottery, or silverware. It was not only a matter of seeing it, but of touching it, feeling its texture and its form. He gave life to everything by his interest, by his active relatedness; a person, a cat, a tree, a flower – they all came to life through his own aliveness. The following story may illustrate this: when he had been in Mexico two years before, he visited the house of a friend and colleague of mine, Dr. Francisco Garza, and admired the beautiful garden with its many old trees. Two years later, when he returned and visited Dr. Garza's home again, he looked at one of the trees and asked, "What happened to the branch of the tree that was here last time?" Indeed, a branch had been cut off, but Dr. Suzuki remembered that branch and missed it.

Should I give an example of his thoughtfulness? He always wanted to make us a gift of a Japanese stone lantern. But there were many difficulties entailed in packing it, shipping it from Japan to Mexico, and finally in getting it through the Mexican customs without our having to pay the import duties, a point upon which Dr. Suzuki insisted. While all these circumstances delayed the matter, he never forgot it. Just at the beginning of this year I received a letter from Dr. Suzuki stating that the lantern had been shipped, that he had found a way to pay the import duties, and mentioning the kind of place that would be best to place it in our garden. Indeed, the lantern arrived as he had wished – I am looking at it as I write this – but Dr. Suzuki had died before I could confirm the arrival of his gift.

Should I write about the effect his very presence had on me, on my wife and on so many other friends and colleagues? His love for life, his freedom from selfish desires, his inner joy, his strength, all had a deep effect. They tended to make one stronger, more alive, more concentrated. Yet without ever evoking that kind of awe which the great personality so often does. He was always himself, humble, never an "authority"; he never insisted that his views must be followed; he was a man who never aroused fear in anybody; there was nothing of the irrational and mystifying aura of the "great man" about him; there was never a sense of obligation to accept what he said because he said it. He was an authority purely by his being, and never because he promised approval or threatened disapproval.

My wife and I first became acquainted with Zen through his books, and later by attending his seminars at Columbia University in New York; after that, by many conversations here in Mexico. Sometimes we thought we had understood – only to find later that we had not. Yet eventually we believed that the worst misunderstandings had been overcome and that we had understood as much as one can with only the limited experience which is our lot. But undoubtedly whatever understanding of Zen we acquired was greatly helped not only by what Dr. Suzuki said or wrote, but by his being. If one cannot put in words what being "enlightened" is, and if one cannot speak from one's own experience, Dr. Suzuki's person represented it. He himself, his whole being, was "the finger that points to the moon." I told him many Chassidic stories which he enjoyed and appreciated in their close connection with Zen thinking. One of them illustrates what I am trying to say with regard to him: A Chassid is asked why he comes to visit his master; does he want to hear his words of wisdom? "No," he answered, "I just want to see how he ties his shoelaces."

While Dr. Suzuki stayed here in Cuernavaca, he participated in a one-week workshop on Zen Buddhism and Psychoanalysis organized by the Mexican Psychoanalytic Society.[1] About fifty psychoanalysts from the United States and Mexico participated, mainly because this was a unique opportunity to

---

1. Ed. This conference was in 1957, and one of its fruits was the book by Fromm and Suzuki entitled *Zen Buddhism and Psychoanalysis* (New York: Grove Press, 1960). See further in the contributions by Kondō Akihisa and Kobori Sōhaku above.

hear several lectures given by Dr. Suzuki, to hear his remarks in the discussions, and perhaps more than anything else, to be in his presence for a whole week. And indeed, his presence was responsible for a remarkable phenomenon. As one might have expected, the meeting began with the usual distraction due to over-emphasis on thoughts and words. But after two days a change of mood began to be apparent. Everyone became more concentrated and more quiet. At the end of the meeting a visible change had occurred in many of the participants. They had gone through a unique experience; they felt that an important event had happened in their lives, that they had wakened up a little and that they would not lose what they had gained. Dr. Suzuki participated in all the sessions with punctuality and interest. He never made a concession of thought in order to be "better understood," but neither did he insist or argue. He was just himself, his thinking firmly rooted in his being. The hours of the sessions were many, the chairs were hard. All he needed was to be alone from time to time. One day Miss Okamura and my wife were looking for him; they could not find him anywhere, and just as they began to become a little worried they saw him, sitting under a tree, meditating. He was so relaxed that he had become one with the tree, and it was difficult to see "him."

I have often wondered about the unique quality in Dr. Suzuki. Was it his lack of narcissism and selfishness, his kindness, and his love of life? It was all of these, but often I have thought of still another aspect: the childlike quality in him. This needs some comment. The process of living hardens the heart of most people. As children we still have an open and malleable heart; we still have faith in the genuineness of mother's smile, in the reliability of promises, in the unconditional love which is our birthright. But this "original faith" is shattered sooner or later in our childhood. Most of us lose the softness and flexibility of our hearts; to become an adult is often synonymous with becoming hardened. Some escape this fate; they keep their heart open and do not let it harden. But in order to be able to do so, they do not see reality fully as it is. They become as Don Quixote, seeing the noble and the beautiful where they are not; they are dreamers who never awaken fully to see reality including all its ugliness and meanness. There is a third solution, but an exceedingly rare one. The persons who take this road retain the softness of a child's heart, and yet they see reality in all clarity and without illusions. They are children first, then they become adults, and yet they return to being children without ever losing the realism of adulthood. This is a difficult way, and that is why it is so rare. I believe it was this which characterized Dr. Suzuki's personality. He was hard as rock and soft as wax; he was the realistic, mature man, who was able to look at the world with the innocence and faith of the child.

Dr. Suzuki was a "radical," by which I mean that he went to the root. And the root, for him, was man. His humanity shone through the particularity of his national and cultural background. You forgot his nationality, his age, his "persona" when being with him. You spoke to a man, and nothing but a man. It is because of this that he will be present always; a friend and a guide whose physical presence was secondary to the light which radiates from him.

15

A Personal Tribute

Edward Conze

Owing to my sudden move from Britain to the USA, the invitation to contribute to this memorial number of *The Eastern Buddhist* reached me too late to say anything that could do justice to the actual importance of D.T. Suzuki as a religious leader of genius. All I can do is to offer a small autobiographical note.

In 1937, at the age of 33, the bottom had fallen out of what I then thought was my world. My political faith had collapsed under the impact of Stalinism and of what I had observed in Spain, my marriage had failed, my job seemed distinctly bleak, I had even started to consult psychoanalysts, and there seemed nothing left that I could live for. Then one day I happened to look into the window of one of the bookshops opposite the British Museum, my curiosity was aroused, and just on chance I bought the third volume of *Essays in Zen Buddhism*. For weeks thereafter I retired each day into Hampstead Heath, devoured each page of the book again and again, and rapidly acquired all of Suzuki's other works one by one.

What had happened was that D.T. Suzuki had revivified an earlier interest in Buddhism. It had begun with a reading of the Tauchnitz edition of Lafcadio Hearn's *Gleanings in Buddha-Fields* when I was 13. It was renewed again through contact with Buddhist scholars when, at the age of 21, I was a student in Heidelberg. It is noteworthy that I have always been much more attracted by Suzuki's exposition of the metaphysical profundities of the Mahāyāna than by his account of the practicalities of Zen. This is probably due to my German origin and background, for most non-Asian scholars working on *prajñāpāramitā* have so far been Germans.[1] To me it is a measure of the greatness of the man that Suzuki should have made the Mahāyāna equally

---

1. Ed. *Prajñāpāramitā*, the perfection of wisdom (of a bodhisattva), a regular theme in the annotated translations and other writings of Edward Conze.

palatable to two such divergent national mentalities as the German and the Anglo-Saxon. Because, since the Buddha himself was neither a German nor an Englishman, it may well be that both the metaphysical and the practical interpretation are equally near to His original doctrine.

Under the impulse of D.T. Suzuki's message I then withdrew into a private wood belonging to a Quaker friend of mine in the New Forest, and practised as much meditation as can be practised in this evil age. Then I emerged again, went to Oxford, and published a number of books in which I have tried to transmit the understanding of the Mahāyāna, and particularly of the *prajñāpāramitā*, which D.T. Suzuki had first conveyed to me. His assurance, once by word of mouth and once by letter, to the effect that he thought that I had actually "understood Buddhism," has given me great happiness and encouragement. For me, therefore, Daisetz Teitaro Suzuki will always remain a charismatic figure who raised me from a living death and has enabled me to lead a meaningful life for nearly three decades. And what he has done for me, that he has done for many others also.

16

Zen and Philology: On Ui Hakuju and Suzuki Daisetsu

Ueda Yoshifumi

Buddhist tradition is taken as an object of study in a number of academic fields, including history, anthropology, psychology, philosophy, art, sociology, religion and literature, but surely these cannot all be viewed as disciplines directed to probing its essential nature.[1] If there is indeed a discipline that may be called Buddhist studies in this sense – not merely because it takes Buddhist tradition as an object – then there must be a methodology that distinguishes it from other fields treating Buddhism.

The predominant methodology in modern Indian Buddhist studies is philological. It is not the only approach being applied, but it may be said that focus on literary remains and research through the study of texts forms the mainstream of Buddhist scholarship both in Japan and elsewhere. Such study is, of course, an important tool, but I wonder if greater reflection on its limitations as a means of illuminating the core of Buddhism is not necessary. The fundamental problem inherent in such an approach may be seen by examining the prefatory verse to the *Mūlamadhyamakakārikā*:

> I pay homage to the perfectly enlightened one – the Buddha, who is supreme among teachers of the *dharma* – who has taught co-dependent origination characterized by no ceasing, no arising, no discontinuance, no permanence, no oneness, no many-ness, no coming, and no depart-

---

1. This is a translation of "Ui Hakuju to Suzuki Daisetz," which appeared in *Suzuki Daisetz zenshū geppō* 21 (June 1982), 1–5, and 22 (July 1982), 1–10. Readers are also referred to "Bukkyōgaku no hōhōron ni tsuite," in *Daijō bukkyō no shisō* (Tokyo: Kokusho Kankōkai, 1977), 63–86. The longer original title of the translation was "Reflections on the Study of Buddhism: Notes on the Approaches of Ui Hakuju and D.T. Suzuki."

ing, in which all discriminative discourse is quiescent, and which is blissful.

The central concept of the *Mūlamadhyamakakārikā* is emptiness (*śūnyatā*) or co-dependent origination (*pratītyasamutpāda*) (these two terms are said to be synonymous). This verse states that co-dependent origination is characterized by the extinction of all discriminative discourse (*prapañca*), all verbal expression based on false discrimination. Similarly, it is later stated that in emptiness, all discriminative discourse dies away (ch. 18, v. 5). In Candrakīrti's commentary, this discriminative discourse is taken to indicate simply "words" (*vāc*). If this is the case, however, then emptiness or co-dependent origination cannot be explained in words. The question therefore arises, for Buddhist scholarship, how a philological method, which deals with words, can illuminate what cannot be verbally expressed.

Looking again to the prefatory verse, however, we must consider the phrase, "the perfectly enlightened one – the Buddha, who is supreme among teachers of the *dharma* – who has taught (*deśayāmāsa*) co-dependent origination...in which all discriminative discourse is quiescent." Here, the words of the Buddha are spoken of as teaching (*deśanā*). Co-dependent origination, which is inexplicable, nevertheless can be taught through the words termed *deśanā*. The question concerning methodology, then, is whether the words dealt with in philological study are *prapañca* or *deśanā*. If they are *prapañca*, then they may be amenable to a philological approach, but they are totally useless for leading to a grasp of emptiness or co-dependent origination. If they are *deśanā*, then the question arises whether scholarly training can enable one to deal with them even though one is not enlightened. It is widely assumed that if we think along the lines indicated by Buddhist texts, our thoughts and expressions will naturally be *deśanā*. But it is because the Buddha is enlightened that he can preach Dharma. How is it possible for us, in our research, to select our words so that they are free of *prapañca* and become *deśanā*? Must not such a consideration form part of our methodological self-awareness if we are to have a field of research that may genuinely be called "Buddhist studies"?

If research in Buddhism is to advance not merely in quantity – in the number of texts taken into the domain of linguistic study – but qualitatively also, new approaches must be formulated. It is impossible to outline such an approach here, but as one step toward such effort, I would like to reflect on the limitations of a strictly philological method, and on the danger of inadvertently overstepping those limitations, by comparing the approaches to several basic concepts of two modern Japanese figures, Ui Hakuju and D.T. Suzuki.

Suzuki's work is of course well known and widely read, but his influence on methods of academic Buddhist studies has not been great, and the depth and originality of his contribution to our knowledge of Buddhism is not as well recognized as it should be. As a scholar, Ui's position is much more firmly established. He was one of the pioneers of modern Buddhist studies in Japan, and his monumental research in Buddhist thought, based on meticulous textual study, continues to wield a dominating influence. In such research, however, there is a tendency to assume that Buddhism is fully open to exploration through these methods. Thus, there is a constant danger of falling into error by attempting to grasp through a philological methodology what lies beyond its limits. Below, I will consider several examples.

SUBJECTIVITY-ONLY AS DISCRIMINATION OF NONDISCRIMINATION

The understanding of the term "subjectivity-only" (*vijñaptimātratā*) is a central problem in the study of Yogācāra Buddhism.[2] Subjectivity (*vijñapti*) basically signifies all mental activity of perception, thought and feeling – the seeing subject that knows by discriminating objects. Through practice, the bodhisattva eliminates discrimination and realizes suchness or true reality, which is free of the subject–object dichotomy. The suchness that is attained, however, is termed subjectivity-only. Why should the realization that the bodhisattva attains through the elimination of the discriminating subject be called "subjectivity-only"? In his study of the *Mahāyānasaṃgraha*, Ui comments on this problem:

> What is it like when one has reached the true and real subjectivity-only in which both object and subject are eradicated? In Paramārtha's exposition, it is called "undefiled subjectivity, the mind pure in its nature"; the term for it includes the word "subjectivity." Since he has employed "subjectivity" in such compounds as "subjectivity-only with no object" and "subjectivity-only as means," he adopts the term here also. Strictly speaking, however, the term "subjectivity" should have been abandoned.   (*Shōdaijōron kenkyū*, 72)

In the stage of "subjectivity-only as means," all objects have been made empty but the perceiving subject has not; it is therefore understandable that

---

2. The Yogācāra term *vijñapti* holds two opposing meanings. Fundamentally, it is synonymous with *vijñāna*, the knowing (*jānāti*) of things by division (*vi-*) into subject and object. At the beginning of the *Viṃśatikā*, Vasubandhu states that *citta, manas, vijñāna* and *vijñapti* are all synonyms. That is they all indicate the active knower. Thus, the Chinese translation of *vijñapti* is almost always the same as that of *vijñāna*: zhí 識 shiki (to know). In addition, when used together with *pratibhāsa* (*ābhāsa* etc.), "to appear as," *vijñapti* implies that which is known. Without losing the significance it shares with *vijñāna* (what perceives and knows), it is said to appear as form (*rūpa*) etc.

this stage should be called "subjectivity-only with no object." In the stage of "true and real subjectivity-only," however, both subject and object are made empty and abandoned. The question arises, then, why it should be labelled "subjectivity," as in "undefiled subjectivity." Why even the term "true and real subjectivity-only" to indicate a state in which the perceiving subject has already been eradicated? Ui reasons that because the term "subjectivity" has been used up to this point, it continues to be employed. This, however, is not persuasive. If "subjectivity-only as means" is an appropriate term for the stage in which there is a perceiving subject but no object, then when there is neither subject nor object – when the subject–object dichotomy has been eradicated – it would be natural *not* to use "subjectivity." Why is a term that should, "strictly speaking," be abandoned still used? Unless this is explained, Ui's interpretation is inadequate.

Ui's understanding of the use of the term "subjectivity" in subjectivity-only is representative of the interpretation that dominates the world of Indian and Buddhist studies in Japan at present. According to this understanding, "subjectivity" in such compounds as "undefiled subjectivity," "true and real subjectivity-only," and "pure subjectivity" is a misnomer. Ui states that "In the case of the eradication of object and subject as 'true and real subjectivity-only' the term 'mind' [as in 'Buddha-mind'] should be used; it should certainly not be called 'subjectivity'" (*Shōdaijōron kenkyū*, 72). From the stance of philological research, however, once one has ascertained that the term "subjectivity" appears in the texts, one must interpret its meaning. To claim, because its usage does not agree with one's own interpretation, that it should not have been used and to try to do away with it, must surely be called a violation of one's own methodology.

The question that Ui raises is not simply a problem of Paramārtha's translations. In the *Triṃśikā* verses 25 and 26 and Sthiramati's commentary, subjectivity-only is identified with thusness of mind (*cittadharmatā*), suchness, and the nonexistence of both grasped object and grasping mind. If one takes Vasubandhu, Sthiramati and Paramārtha literally, in non-discriminative wisdom, suchness or thusness, that there is no subjectivity and that there is only subjectivity are both established simultaneously. The intellect that works in philological research, however, cannot accept this self-contradiction, and ways to overcome or neutralize it are sought. Ui's explanation quoted above was born in this way, and it must be said to be an error arising from failure to recognize the limits of philological methods. Unless we have methods by which we can grasp the inherent self-contradiction in non-discriminative wisdom or suchness, not by rationalizing or effacing it, but as it is, we will not be able to understand the Buddhist texts.

Suzuki offers a viable alternative interpretation. He explains, concerning the *Treatise on No-Mind* (*Mushinron*) attributed to Bodhidharma, "Precisely because it is no-mind, it is able to see, hear, think, and know."³ This is diametrically opposed to Ui's understanding quoted above. To perceive or know is for the perceiving subject (i.e. grasping, *upalabdhi*) to be functioning; thus, according to Ui, if there is seeing or knowing, then there is subjectivity (mental activity), not no-mind. However, non-discriminative wisdom or suchness in which there is neither subject nor object is in fact called subjectivity-only; this means that subjectivity (false discrimination) has been transformed into non-discriminative wisdom and that in this wisdom (Vasubandhu calls it "no-mind"),⁴ there is subjectivity (seeing, hearing, thinking, knowing). This corresponds to the thought of Treatise on No-mind as explained by Suzuki. "No-mind" here does not mean simply that there is no mental activity, but indicates the non-duality of nonexistence of mind (both object and mind are eradicated) and its existence (seeing, hearing, thinking, knowing). This is expressed in the Treatise, "Where should there be no-mind apart from seeing, hearing, thinking and knowing?" Thus, Suzuki explains no-mind as the "mind of no-mind" and "discrimination of nondiscrimination," indicating the simultaneous establishment as a single whole of absence of discriminative perceiving and knowing (no-mind) together with perceiving and knowing.

Subjectivity-only as used by Vasubandhu and Sthiramati has, in its ontological aspect, this same meaning. "Only" implies the nonexistence of objects and also of the subject. On the one hand, it means that a thing known or perceived is not known as it is; though seen as an existing object, it does not really exist. The seer that stands opposite the object in the relationship of knowing is designated false discrimination (*vikalpa*), for it takes an object that does not exist as existing. This nonexisting object is discriminated nature (*parikalpita-svabhāva*). The seer itself exists, for it is other-dependent nature (*paratantra-svabhāva*), meaning that it arises from causes and conditions.⁵ Since the object does not actually exist, there is only the seer.

On the other hand, however, if there is no object grasped, neither can there be a subject that grasps. This is expressed, "Through [grasped objects being] discriminated nature (i.e., nonexistent), other-dependent nature (subjectivity) is empty."⁶ Subjectivity, then, exists, for it arises through causes and conditions, and at the same time it is empty or nonexistent through the nonexistence of its object. This emptiness differs from the nonexistence of perceived objects in relation to the existence of the subject. The emptiness of the subject embraces other-dependent nature (existence of subjectivity or *vikalpa*) itself, so there is no existence that stands relative to it. This nothingness or non-being (*abhāva*) signifies the emptiness of all *dharmas* taught in

---

3. *Zen shisōshi kenkyū*, in *Suzuki Daisetz zenshū* (Tokyo: Iwanami Shoten, 1982), vol. II, 230.
4. *Acitta*, in *Triṃśikā* v. 29.
5. *Triṃśikā* v. 21.
6. Sthiramati's commentary on *Triṃśikā* v. 22.

the Prajñāpāramitā Sūtras; it is absolute nothingness, and is termed fulfilled nature (pariniṣpanna-svabhāva).

Thus, the "subjectivity" of subjectivity-only affirms the existence of the perceiving subject precisely where subject and object have been eradicated. With both subjectivity-only and no-mind, where there is no mind or discriminative thinking, there is mind, and this mind (discrimination) is always thoroughly pervaded by the nonexistence of mind (nondiscrimination). Maitreya's *Madhyāntavibhāga* states, "It is established that grasping (*upalabdhi*, i.e. subjectivity) has the self-nature of no-grasping (*nopalabdhi*, no-subjectivity). No-grasping and grasping are therefore the same" (I, 7). Here, existence and nonexistence or affirmation and negation are identified.

We see, then, that in subjectivity-only, the three natures discussed in Yogācāra are all included. The nonexistent object is termed discriminated nature, and the existence of the subject is other-dependent nature. Further, through the nonexistence termed discriminated nature, other-dependent nature is also empty. The emptiness in which discriminated nature and other-dependent nature are one is fulfilled nature.[7] Other-dependent nature (subjectivity) and fulfilled nature (emptiness) are therefore both different and nondifferent.

Fulfilled nature is thusness (*tathatā*), the object of supreme wisdom (*paramārtha*). Since supreme wisdom is non-discriminative, it is always nondual with its object; hence, fulfilled nature indicates both thusness or suchness (the seen) and non-discriminative wisdom (the seer). The expression "subjectivity-only" does not include a term indicating wisdom such as *jñāna* or *prajñā*, but since it signifies suchness[8] and is nondifferent from fulfilled nature, it must be seen to indicate non-discriminative wisdom also.

Since subjectivity-only is a term for the wisdom or suchness realized by the bodhisattva, its two aspects of existence and nonexistence reflect the fundamental nondualistic structure of reality in Mahāyāna thought. Other-dependent nature is the essence (*ātmaka*) of all things, which arise from causes and conditions and are thus karma-created (*saṃskṛta*) and existent. Fulfilled nature is the thusness of all things and, as we have seen, has the nature of absolute nothingness. Since other-dependent and fulfilled nature are both different and non-different, the relationship of all things (*dharma*) and thusness (*dharmatā*) is also one of both difference and non-difference.[9] This is also the relationship of the karma-created and the uncreated. In subjectivity-only, the "subjectivity" is karma-created, and "only" points to the nonexistence of subjectivity implied by the nonexistence of objects, that is to fulfilled nature or the uncreated.

---

7. *Triṃśikā* v. 22.
8. *Triṃśikā* v. 25.
9. Sthiramati's commentary on *Triṃśikā* v. 25.

SUBJECTIVITY-ONLY WITH NO OBJECT

The basic structure of subjectivity-only also has an epistemological aspect. That other-dependent nature (karma-created) and fulfilled nature (uncreated) are both different and non-different means that subjectivity and no-subjectivity or nondiscrimination (*avijñapti*) are also so related. Subjectivity-only refers to discriminative thought and perception that occurs without departing from nondiscrimination (non-duality of wisdom and object); this is the discrimination of non-discrimination. In the thought of Asaṅga and Vasubandhu as seen in *Mahāyānasaṃgraha* and *Triṃśikā*, subjectivity refers basically to the seer in contrast to the seen. Hence, "subjectivity-only" is seeing and knowing without any object. This is subjectivity where both subject and object have been eradicated; it is, as we have seen above, both non-discriminative wisdom and suchness.

Perception without any object, however, presents a paradox that cannot be dealt with through a philological methodology; hence, subjectivity-only cannot be understood literally, and it comes to be understood conceptually. Throughout most of the history of Yogācāra thought in China and Japan, it has been interpreted to mean that things regarded as existing objectively, independent of the subject, actually exist only within the subjectivity. In this interpretation, Yogācāra thought is clearly a kind of idealism. Further, Dharmapāla's commentary on *Triṃśikā*[10] provides a basis for just such an understanding in its concept of the "evolving of subjectivity" into seeing and seen parts. A close reading of *Triṃśikā* and *Mahāyānasaṃgraha*, however, shows that subjectivity-only means not that subjectivity evolves a seen-part but rather that it is the perceiving subject without any object that is seen. Discriminated nature (nonexistent object) and other-dependent nature (perceiving subject) therefore stand in an ontological relationship of nonexistence and existence, and also in the epistemological relationship of object and subject. When object and subject are brought into these relationships, subjectivity-only is attained. This is the meaning of subjectivity-only in Asaṅga, Vasubandhu, Sthiramati and Paramārtha.

Earlier we were confronted with the self-contradiction that in no-mind (the eradication of both subject and object) there is perceiving and knowing. Here, in the concept of subjectivity without any object, the intellect is again blocked by something alien to our world of experience, but this is the literal explanation of subjectivity-only in *Mahāyānasaṃgraha* and *Triṃśikā*. These two self-contradictions are two faces of non-discriminative wisdom, or suchness, or subjectivity-only. Suzuki explains the aspect of seeing and knowing

---

10. *Chéngwéshí lùn* as translated by Xuánzàng.

in no-mind as "mind of no-mind" or "discrimination of nondiscrimination." How does he treat the aspect of subjectivity without any object?

Suzuki poured a great deal of thought into finding an English equivalent for *prajñā*, which is another term for non-discriminative wisdom, and devised the compound "*prajñā*-intuition." Late in life, however, he came to feel that there was a sharp distinction between *prajñā* and intuition:

> In intuition, there is still an object, but *satori* is self-realization without any object. In other words, it is unmediated; it is perception by the whole that is established where subject and object are not yet divided. *Prajñā*-philosophy states "Form is emptiness, emptiness is form." It is perception characterized by self-identity that arises from within form itself, or from within emptiness itself. It is not ordinary perception. It is not a perception limited to one faculty like vision or hearing, not perception with subject and object, or mediation.   (*Tōyō no kokoro*, 94)

Suzuki deeply probed *prajñāpāramitā* and Huáyán thought, but in the area of Yogācāra, he seems to have been familiar chiefly with the *Awakening of Faith* and the *Laṅkāvatāra-sūtra*, and not to have read such writings as *Mahāyānasaṃgraha*. Thus, he seems to have been unacquainted with the meaning of the term subjectivity-only outlined above. Further, this structure of subjectivity-only had not yet been discussed in scholarly studies. Thus, the expression "*satori* (*prajñā*) is self-realization without any object" was not derived from Buddhist texts or secondary sources, nor can it be traced to Zen literature. It was probably a spark born from the contact of Suzuki, who had deeply experienced *satori*, with western Europe.

According to Suzuki, *satori*, *prajñā*, or non-discriminative wisdom is self-realization without any object, and perception by the whole. "Whole" (*zentaisei*) includes subject and object. Since it is the perception that arises from this whole, it is not a bifurcating mode of perception like vision or hearing; "subject and object are not yet divided." To borrow the Yogācāra expression, "seen and seer are same, same." "Same" is used twice here: on the one hand, the wisdom that sees is non-discriminative and does not differentiate among *dharma*s, for it does not stand in dualistic opposition to objects. On the other hand, the suchness that is the seen, the object, is nondiscriminated, and there is no discrimination as *dharma*s. Non-discriminative wisdom is the subject and suchness is the seen, but they are the "same," that is "not yet divided" into seer and seen. Suzuki calls this "perception." It is not our usual perception, but direct knowing, without any mediation of thought or word. It is also "self-realization" (*jikaku*), meaning that wisdom and object are not divided as subject and object, for wisdom to know an object is none other than for wisdom to know itself. "Wisdom without any object" means that this wisdom does not grasp by objectifying in any way. When, for example, wisdom sees a form (*rūpa*), in that form wisdom is "subject and object not yet divided," and seer and seen are the same; hence, "seeing" has the character of "self-identity."

Because of this "self-identity," in Yogācāra thought, subjectivity (*vijñapti*) is used to signify both the seer and the seen. As the seen, it is "subjectivity that has appeared as form, etc." (*rūpa-ādi-pratibhāsā vijñapti*). This seen is not simply an object, but simultaneously is itself subject or seer. However, since seer and seen stand as opposite poles in the relationship of perceiving and knowing, it is impossible for one to be the other at the same time. Hence, where there is discrimination (seer and seen divided), the seen is at the same time seer, but that seer is negated in the seen; the non-difference of seen and seer is not mere identity, but possesses a self-contradictory structure of mutual negation simultaneous with identity. In the same way, the seer that occurs in discriminative thought and perception also stands in an identity with the seen that is characterized by self-contradiction. Therefore, when "subjectivity that has appeared as form" is the seen, the seer is negated and, at the same time, is identical with the seen; here, things are known from within, through subjectivity becoming them. Further, when subjectivity as form is established in the standpoint of the seer, the seen is negated and, at the same time, is identical with the seer; here, subjectivity knows itself without objectifying itself.

The first aspect – subjectivity knowing things by becoming them – is expressed by Suzuki as "perception characterized by self-identity that arises from within form itself." "Self-identity" denotes the state of "subject and object not yet divided," in which the subject has become one with things. That this seeing "arises from within form itself" means that "subject and object not yet divided" is established in things. Things are seen through the perception at work in this "subject and object not yet divided" or "self-identity."

In the second aspect – subjectivity knowing itself without objectifying itself – this same perception functioning where "subject and object are not yet divided" is further established in the standpoint of the subject; hence, subjectivity knows itself directly, without objectifying itself and without any mediation. Suzuki's expression, "self-realization without any object," signifies the entirety of both aspects – subjectivity knowing things by becoming them and knowing itself without objectification – from the side of the latter. Without knowing things by becoming them, it is impossible for the subjectivity to know itself without objectifying itself, just as it is impossible for the finger to point to itself. The realization that is self-knowledge without self-objectification is achieved precisely because, at the same time, one knows things by becoming them. To know things by becoming them is none other than to know oneself without objectifying oneself. Hence, as Nishitani Keiji states, "The stance of being submerged (*maibotsu*) in things is the stance of self-realization."[11] There is only subjectivity without any object, and since this subjectivity submerges itself in a thing (form) – becomes empty and the same as no-subjectivity – it is seen as form.

In "subjectivity appearing as form" in this way, knowing things and knowing oneself are both established freely and without hindrance, and the bodhisattva carries on a life characterized by both.

Thus we find that the basic structure of *prajñā* as set forth by Suzuki matches that of non-discriminative wisdom taught in Indian Buddhism. Here, we can draw two conclusions. First, although Zen is often asserted to be a highly specialized offshoot of Buddhism, developed under the influence of Chinese thought and culture, at its roots it draws upon the central current of Indian Mahāyāna Buddhism. Second, we see that Suzuki's explanation of Zen is not an exclusively personal and idiosyncratic view, but an exposition that articulates the character of Zen at its fundamental level.

FORM IS EMPTINESS, EMPTINESS IS FORM

Nāgārjuna asserts that "the reality of all things" is synonymous both with emptiness and with wisdom. In other words, in it object and wisdom are nondual. On the side of wisdom, it is *prajñāpāramitā*; on the side of object, it is emptiness, suchness, formlessness, *dharma*-realm, and *paramārtha* (object of supreme wisdom). In that it is "wisdom that has attained the other shore" (*prajñāpāramitā*), it is highest perfect enlightenment. That emptiness or *prajñāpāramitā* are two faces of the same reality is expressed in Asaṅga and Vasubandhu as the nonduality of suchness and non-discriminative wisdom, and as "seen and seer are same, same."

Since the *prajñāpāramitā* discussed in the preceding section forms the basis of Nāgārjuna's thought, its structure of simultaneous identity and mutual negation should be manifest in his concepts of emptiness and co-dependent origination. These have both ontological and epistemological aspects. The ontological aspect is expressed "form is emptiness, emptiness is form." "Form" is a thing with colour and shape; it can be grasped by perception and is one part of existence. "Emptiness" means that there is nothing. "Is" indicates the identity or nondifference of form (existence) and emptiness (nonexistence), and thus clearly involves a self-contradiction. In a purely philological

---

11. With Yoshikawa Kōjirō, *Kono eien naru mono* (Kyōto: Yūkonsha, 1967), 198. This concept is also expressed in the Zen phrase, "No-thing in mind, no-mind in things." "No-thing in mind" corresponds to subjectivity-only with no object; "no-mind in things" is subjectivity as no-subjectivity, appearing as form. It is the mutual conformity of these two opposing aspects that is true reality. See Ueda Shizuteru, *Zen bukkyō* (Tokyo: Chikuma Shobō, 1973), 38–40.

methodology, however, self-contradiction is unacceptable. In order to avoid self-contradiction, Ui asserts that what is negated by the term emptiness is not form itself, but rather form that is conceived as "existing independently" and not as "existing together with other things in mutual interrelation and interdependence." Further, the "form" whose existence is affirmed in "emptiness is form" is also not the form itself, but form "that exists together with other things in mutual interrelation and interdependence." Here, "form" is understood to have two different meanings: (1) form that exists and stands in a relation of mutual interdependence with other things, and (2) form that is conceptualized as independent and not interrelated, but that does not really exist. Since what is affirmed and what is negated are not the same, the original self-contradiction is dissolved.

Suzuki, however, states, "Where the finite form merges into the infinite that is emptiness, at the same time emptiness reflects itself in the finite form. Here, the unmediated perception that is *satori* becomes possible" (*Tōyō no kokoro*, 94). Suzuki makes no distinction in the meaning of "form"; it is always the identical form. One form – with a certain coloration and shape – completely melts and merges into the vast and unlimited nothingness and becomes the infinite void. Thus, form becomes one with emptiness. At the same time, infinite emptiness takes the limitedness of form and becomes manifest; here, emptiness becomes form. In this way, a self-contradictory relation in which form and emptiness, existence and nothingness, finite and infinite are one and at the same time different is established.

Comparing the understandings of Ui and Suzuki outlined above, we find that Ui's can be easily grasped, but Suzuki's presents a number of difficulties. What does it mean that the limited form melts and merges into the infinite? Provisionally, we can take this to describe a mystical experience in which form enters into the formless and becomes one with it. But then what are we to make of the reverse, where indeterminate formlessness reflects itself in finite form? How is it possible for the infinite to enter the finite? Does "reflect" mean that the infinite transfers its own reflection into the finite? If so, since it has then become finite, is it not impossible to speak of the infinite *itself*? "Reflect" implies something that sees, but is it the infinite, or something else? None of these questions are answered. Probably a good number of Suzuki's readers have felt that his explanation expresses a special understanding that cannot be grasped without the experience of Zen. Further, many may assume that the emptiness of general Mahāyāna thought taught in Prajñāpāramitā Sūtras should instead be understood as Ui does. The general inclination among Buddhist scholars – though with many variations – is to follow an understanding like Ui's. In my opinion, however, it is Suzuki's interpretation that clarifies emptiness.

Emptiness is taught in the Prajñāpāramitā Sūtras, whose central theme is the *practice* of *prajñāpāramitā*, that is how the bodhisattva should perform *prajñāpāramitā*. In other words, *prajñāpāramitā* is at the same time wisdom and practice. *The Heart Sūtra* begins, "When Avalokiteśvara Bodhisattva was deeply practising *prajñāpāramitā*, he clearly saw that the five aggregates were all empty..." It goes on, "Form is itself emptiness, emptiness is form." This emptiness is the content of the practice of *prajñāpāramitā*.

The other Prajñāpāramitā Sūtras are similar. That "all things are empty" or "ungraspable" is taught in relation to the contemplative practice of bodhisattvas. Edward Conze, in the introduction to his translation, *The Perfection of Wisdom in Eight Thousand Lines*, speaks of the great repetitiveness of the sūtra as though it were a stylistic failing. In fact, the sūtra is not a treatise meant to develop doctrine or thought but rather was written to give guidance in practice, and practice is repetitive performance (*bhāvanā*). Jízàng (549–623) termed the emptiness of the Sānlùn "emptiness-contemplation," for emptiness is inseparable from the contemplative practice called *prajñāpāramitā*.

We see, then, that emptiness in the Prajñāpāramitā Sūtras is inseparable from practice. When we review Ui's interpretation with this in mind, unacceptable features come to light, for he gives inadequate attention to the practice of *prajñāpāramitā*. He states,

> Emptiness indicates the ungraspability of the definite substance of things that unenlightened beings and those of other teachings consider real, and of the everlasting, existent *dharma*-substance that followers of Hīnayāna Buddhism speak of. It is, in other words, the absence of a self-nature as real substance. (*Indotetsugakushi*, 271)

As we have seen, that "form is empty...sensation, thought, feeling and consciousness are empty" is taught in relation to how the bodhisattva should view the five aggregates when performing *prajñāpāramitā*. Thus, it refers to the emptiness of form seen by the bodhisattva. If the form negated by emptiness in the statement "form is empty" is the form seen by the bodhisattva in the practice of *prajñāpāramitā*, then clearly the form affirmed in the reverse expression, "emptiness is form, emptiness is sensation, thought, feeling, consciousness," also refers to the form seen by the bodhisattva in practice. Emptiness-contemplation holds a logical structure in which form is both negated and affirmed; this is precisely expressed in Suzuki's words, "Where the finite form merges into the infinite that is emptiness, at the same time emptiness reflects itself in the finite form."

According to Ui's interpretation, unenlightened people and followers of other teachings or of Hīnayāna Buddhism see things as possessing a definite substance or as an everlasting *dharma*-substance. The Mahāyāna bodhisattva does not see form as real substance, but rather as "being mutually interrelated with all other things and existing as itself for the first time on the basis of this relationship." This mode of existence implies, according to Ui, that things are characterized by co-dependent origination. That form is emptiness and that form is co-dependent origination are completely identical in meaning. Thus, what is negated by the word emptiness, which means "There is no...," is the form that is not co-dependent origination, that is the form conceived as having real substance. It is the form seen by the unenlightened and followers of other teachings or Hīnayāna, who have nothing to do with the practice of *prajñāpāramitā*, not the form seen by bodhisattvas. Earlier I remarked that Ui grasps the "form" in "form is emptiness, emptiness is form," which originally has a self-contradictory structure, as two kinds of form – negated and affirmed – and in this way dissolves the original contradiction. As we see here, the negated form and the affirmed form are seen by completely different persons. Moreover, whether form is taken as co-dependent origination or as conceptualized substance, this understanding of emptiness cannot produce a plausible interpretation of the entire expression "form is emptiness, emptiness is form." If form is co-dependent origination, it is not negated by emptiness; hence, even when "form is emptiness" is reversed as "emptiness is form," no new meaning emerges. If "form is emptiness" is taken to mean that form as substance is emptied and abandoned, it is not without meaning, but the reverse, "emptiness is form," becomes completely meaningless. In this case, emptiness indicates the negation of form as real substance and not the emptiness as co-dependent origination; hence, it is impossible to go from emptiness to form.

By contrast, Suzuki's interpretation well expresses the structure of non-discriminative wisdom or *prajñāpāramitā*. That the finite and limited form fuses and merges into the infinite emptiness means that in the practice of *prajñāpāramitā*, the form seen by false discrimination is eradicated (false discrimination comes not to discriminate form) and becomes non-discriminative wisdom or true *prajñāpāramitā* (wisdom that has attained the other shore). This is no-mind, or the eradication of both object and subjectivity, or "all things are empty" (object and wisdom both empty). At the same time, however, in this non-discriminative wisdom (no-mind), discrimination (seeing, hearing, perceiving, knowing) functions; hence, it sees form. That emptiness reflects itself in the finite form means that this non-discriminative *prajñā*, in which both object and wisdom are empty, sees form through its discrimination of nondiscrimination (mind of no-mind); hence the word "reflect." Further, emptiness reflects itself because emptiness is suchness or *dharma-realm*, characterized by the nonduality of object and wisdom. Thus, the form seen by the mind of no-mind is identical with the mind that sees it. Here, both mind and object are none other than emptiness, that is suchness or *dharma-realm*; hence, for the seeing mind, the object seen is itself. "Discrimination of nondiscrimination" and "form is emptiness, emptiness is form" share the identical self-contradictory structure and are two aspects of the same reality. The former expresses the side of mind or wisdom, and the latter, the side of the seen object.

CONCLUSION

What is seen by *prajñā* or known by non-discriminative wisdom – whether called thusness (*tathatā*) or emptiness or subjectivity-only – is fundamentally inexpressible in words, and yet somehow expressed. Here, self-contradictory verbal structures are unavoidable. If this is the case, unless we devise ways by which we can accept those words as they are with their self-contradictions, we will not be able to grasp accurately the world of religious experience that Buddhist texts seek to transmit to us and will fall into misunderstandings. Suzuki was able, through Zen, to penetrate to the depths of Mahāyāna Buddhism. Concerning his understanding of the *Heart Sūtra* he states, "The *Heart Sūtra* should not be approached through the intellect, though at first it may appear to suggest that. It should be approached by following the lines of religious experience" (*Hannyakyō no tetsugaku to shūkyō*, 144). The religious experience mentioned here is, of course, not limited to Zen. Suzuki had a great interest in the *myōkōnin* – "wondrous, excellent people" – of Shin Buddhism and sought to depict their inner lives, for he saw that the world they attained through the *nenbutsu* and that which he had reached through Zen were fundamentally one. Following the lines of religious experience is surely not limited to the areas to which Suzuki directed his attention. Future scholarship in Buddhism must awaken to the necessity of devising such paths and direct efforts in this direction.

(Translated by Dennis Hirota)

17

D.T. Suzuki and Pure Land Buddhism

Bandō Shōjun

Dr. D.T. Suzuki (1870–1966) was born in the province of Kaga (the present Ishikawa Prefecture) in the north-western part of Japan, a famous stronghold of Shin Buddhism. As a child, he is said to have often accompanied his mother to hear sermons at Shin Buddhist temples. This exposure to ardent Nembutsu devotees through his mother's intermediation must have left its imprint on the young Suzuki, for he was later to turn with increasing frequency to deal with Pure Land, and particularly Shin Buddhist themes, especially that of the *myōkōnin*.

The *myōkōnin* were paragons of devotion in Pure Land Buddhist history about whom biographies developed into a genre of literature inspiring faith in a life of Nembutsu devotion. The term *myōkōnin* is derived originally from the Chinese Pure Land Buddhist Patriarch Shàndǎo's 善導 (613–81) commentary on the *Meditation Sūtra*. In one passage of this sūtra the Buddha tells Ānanda, "They who practise the Nembutsu shall be known as the blooming white lotus (*puṇḍarīka*) among human beings." Shàndǎo interprets this passage in his *Commentary on the Meditation Sūtra* (*Gūanwúliàngshòu jīngshù*) as follows:

> How rare are those who constantly devote themselves to the Nembutsu. So rare are they that to them there is nothing comparable. For this reason, a simile is sought among the *puṇḍarīka* of human beings. The *puṇḍarīka* is a rare flower. Thus are these devotees to be called the most wonderful flowers of humanity. In China these flowers are traditionally associated with the sacred tortoise. The Nembutsu devotees are really the finest specimens of humanity (*nin*, people); they are wondrously good (*myōkō*); they are the best of the best; they are the rarest; they are the most excellent of people.

During the Edo period (1603–1868) in Japan, a number of biographies of *myōkōnin* were compiled. Because of the political pressure imposed by the feudal government at the time, most of these accounts depicted them to be illiterate people of little means who were subservient to the feudal system. While portrayed as warm-hearted and compassionate people steadfast in their Nembutsu faith, they were at the same time cast in the role of strictly observing the Confucian ethics of the feudal society, such as maintaining loyalty to the feudal lord (*shōgun*) and obeying their parents and elders.

Dr. Suzuki recognized that the *myōkōnin*s had a "deep significance in the general field of religious experience" and applied himself to a study of this matter. In the 1924 issue of *The Eastern Buddhist*, he translates the sayings of the Shin teacher *myōkōnin* Shichiri Gōjun (1835–1900) under the title, "Sayings of a Tariki Mystic."[1] While touching on the subject in *Jōdokei Shisōron* (*Studies in Pure Land Thought*, 1942), he deals at length with the *myōkōnin*s Shōma (1799–1871) of Sanuki (present Kagawa Prefecture on the island of Shikoku) and Monodane Kichibei (1803–80). In *Nihonteki Reisei* (*Japanese Spirituality*, 1944), he deals with the early *myōkōnin* Dōshū (d. 1501) of Akao (present Toyama Prefecture) and Asahara Saichi (d. 1933). The latter, "one of the most remarkable modern examples," is taken up again in the book *Myōkōnin* (1948). In the "*myōkōnin*" chapter of *A Miscellany on the Shin Teaching of Buddhism* (1949), he discusses the woman *myōkōnin* Mrs Hina Mori (no dates) as well as Saichi. The latter he again discusses in *Mysticism: Christian and Buddhist* (1957) and in his posthumously published edition of *Myōkōnin Asahara Saichi-shū* (1967). In his numerous writings and lectures, Dr. Suzuki often referred to Shin Buddhism, especially in his later years. For example, in his preface to *Myōkōnin Monodane Kichibei* (ed. Kyō Kusunoki, 1948), Dr. Suzuki at the age of 78 remarks,

> Religious devotion of a solely passive nature considerably reflects the colour of feudalism. Although it may well have been appropriate for the time, if it means conformity to each and every thing, it is not in accord with the present-day social condition. We must positively initiate a movement toward eliminating detrimental factors in the political and social welfare spheres. Shin Buddhists in the future, while pursuing a spiritual life embodying Other Power, must affirm what might be called Self Power within Other Power.

In another passage he states, "Under the feudal political system, the Great Compassion worked in the individuals alone. It was no more than an isolated faculty without organization. With regard to this, deep reflection is required of those devoted to Other Power." In the *Myōkōnin* he continues,

---

1. *The Eastern Buddhist* 2.2 (July – September 1924), 93–116.

> Their [the *myōkōnin's*] lives are consistently characterized by feelings expressed as "Thank Amida!" "What a blessing!" and "I am more than grateful!" Not only is their way of life characterized by non-resistance and *ahiṃsā* (non-violence), we might even say that this attitude was for them a source of great delight. Though certainly demonstrating a certain level of spiritual maturity in a personal context, how much more would we appreciate this attitude in the context of the life of the whole community? This may well merit room for further reflection.

In this connection he also has this to say:

> I cannot help wishing that they (Nembutsu devotees) take the step from mere passivity to constructive and general activity to deliver sentient beings.... My special wishes go to those people devoted to Other Power that they may enter the "Samādhi of the Lion's Invincible Charge" (*siṃhavijṛmbhito nāma samādhi*).

At this point, Dr. Suzuki appears to be observing that of the polarities of "self-benefiting" and "other-benefiting" or "self" and "society," *myōkōnins* and Nembutsu devotees in general are inclined to be "self-benefiting" and oriented to the self rather than to society. He does not, however, fail to elaborate:

> The two directions from the world of *mayoi* (delusion)[2] to the world of *satori* (Enlightenment), and from the world of *satori* to the world of *mayoi*, should not be regarded as distinct from each other. The deliverance of myself, as it is, is the deliverance of others. If so, "to commiserate with, to share sufferings with, and to care for sentient beings" which characterizes the Compassion of the Path of the Sages should be regarded as no different from the Compassion of the Path of the Pure Land.

His remarks considered in total, it becomes apparent that he never made issue of the priority of either of the two polarities of self and other. Rather were his observations of duality based upon non-duality. That is to say, while it is true that he cautioned *myōkōnin* and Nembutsu devotees against settling at ease in self-benefiting activity, he did not indiscriminately attempt to inculcate a positive attitude toward other-benefiting activity at the expense of the self-benefiting aspect.

---

2. Ed. Verbal noun *mayoi* 迷い from the verb *mayou* 迷う, to lose one's way.

Dr. Suzuki's non-dualistic perspective of *myōkōnin*s has been expressed in a number of lectures and writings in both his home country as well as abroad. I am reminded of a public lecture he gave during the Fourth East-West Philosophers' Conference held at the University of Hawaii in 1964. He was 94 at this, his third occasion to participate in the Conference. The title of his lecture was "The Person in Zen Buddhism," and though not addressed directly in regard to *myōkōnin*s, a passage he quoted in the lecture strikes me as typifying Dr. Suzuki's ultimate view regarding them. The passage comes from *The Eternal Smile*, a novel by Per Lagerqvist, a Nobel Prize winner in the field of literature. The passage in summary is as follows:

> When a group of people who had renounced the world congregated one day discussing various topics, the question was raised, "For what reason did God create the world with such an amount of suffering and inequality?" As there was none among them who could properly answer the question, they all agreed to go on a journey to seek God that he might answer the question in person. After walking on and on a great distance, they saw in front of them a bright, open space, a clearing in the woods. There they saw an old woodcutter with a white, saintly beard, silently at work. Seeing him, the children in the party immediately approached him and started to clamber about him out of friendliness. Everyone instantly recognized him as God himself. When they addressed their important question to Him, He simply said, "I have done my best," and continued his work in silence. It was not long before an unaccountable transformation took place in their minds. Their long-cherished doubt had completely dissipated they knew not when. Being satisfied with the answer of no-answer, and full of indescribable joy, they took to their return journey with peaceful minds, infused with an unfathomable sense of solidarity.

I cannot help but think that in this passage is couched the essence of Dr. Suzuki's view of *myōkōnin*s for it clearly reveals the Bodhisattva state of the "*samādhi* of Genuine Play," in which benefiting the self and benefiting others are harmoniously merged. In this way was it beautifully expressed that the true other-benefiting activity is performed beyond words and self-consciousness. Ultimately, Dr. Suzuki's view of *myōkōnin*s regards their self-benefiting activity, as it is, as benefiting others, that their seemingly personal life of joy and happiness in the Dharma has a far-reaching, though invisible, social extension, and that this activity is none other than the actual expression of the ever-functioning Great Compassion of Amida Buddha.

Especially because he is generally thought of as an expounder of Mahāyāna Buddhist thought, Zen and Kegon philosophy in particular, Dr. Suzuki's writings on Pure Land Buddhism published in juxtaposition with other seemingly incongruous themes have perplexed not a small number of people. For example, Mr Christmas Humphreys, President of the London Buddhist Society, once frankly told me that among Dr. Suzuki's writings, those on Pure Land Buddhist themes were beyond his understanding. The reason for this may have been that Amida Buddha who has an aspect of personality (technically it is called Dharmakāya as *upāya* or skilful means)[3] possibly reminds people of the Christian God. Dr. Suzuki, however, repeatedly emphasized that while Amida can be regarded as a dear parent (*oyasama*), in this respect Amida is different in nature from God the Father in Christianity. The heart of Pure Land Buddhism thus appears to be beyond the comprehension of those, especially Westerners, who are accustomed to thinking in terms of theism and atheism, favouring one to the exclusion of the other. There is a persistent inclination in the Western mind to identify Amida Buddha in Pure Land Buddhism with God in Christianity, thereby regarding Pure Land Buddhism as a kind of theism. This leads to their dismissing this form of Buddhism as alien to authentic Buddhist thought which is "nontheistic" in nature. For this reason, the nature of Amida Buddha as "Dharmakāya as skilful means" is a unique feature of Mahāyāna Buddhism which needs to be clarified all the more in the future for a better understanding of Pure Land Buddhism.

Dr. Suzuki often admired Shinran Shōnin's (1173–1262) *Kyōgyōshinshō* ("Teaching, Living, Faith, and Realization"), the chapter on Realization in particular. I presume he felt a special familiarity with what is expressed in this chapter, since all passages contained therein are dominated by Tánluán's (476–542) thought which emphasizes the non-duality of Dharmakāya in its Suchness and in its manifested form. This chapter is concluded by the following quotation, "It is like the Harp of Asura. There is nobody playing it; yet the melody comes out of it in the way of just-so-ness." He also loved to recite the passage preceding it:

> The Bodhisattva sees all beings as if they were ultimately non-existent. He liberates an innumerable number of beings; yet in reality there are no beings who attain liberation. The Bodhisattva liberates all beings as if he were engaged in play.

It is said that the Bodhisattvas of pure heart who show advanced levels of attainment have no consciousness of saving anyone while in actuality saving numberless beings; they are like children absorbed in playing in the garden. There is no doubt that Dr. Suzuki saw the essence of the "true man of no rank" in Zen Buddhism and of the *myōkōnin*s of Pure Land Buddhism as

---

3. Ed. This refers to the concept of *hōben hosshin* 方便法身, the "Dharma-body as skilful means," i.e. the provisional form of the true body of the Buddha, his Dharma-body.

attaining this state of genuine play. Nor is there any doubt that Dr. Suzuki, who never tired of admiring this quality throughout his life, was himself already an embodiment of it.

Part IV

Thinking about the Pure land

18

The Concept of the Pure Land

Kaneko Daiei

THE PURE LAND THAT EMERGES IN THE AWAKENING TO SELF

I have been asked to speak on the topic of the Pure Land, an issue that has riveted my attention these past several years, and although I have devoted much thought and research to it I cannot say I have done enough research to reach any definite conclusions.[1] I plan to speak, however, on an aspect I feel confident I have understood. At the same time I should also ask your consideration since I shall in the course of my talk also touch on points about which I still have doubts. As you may know I was born to a Shin temple family, and so from the time I was a child I heard talks about a place called the Pure Land, recited the *nenbutsu* and did the Pure Land rituals. But at the same time I could not understand what the Pure Land was all about. I thought all the talk about the Pure Land and hell was some kind of pedagogic device conjured up by the ancients to instruct us on certain matters, a view I held for quite some time. As the discussion of faith among those around me became more intense, my thoughts, too, began to dwell on this question, but my thoughts were centred around the Buddha, who to my mind was an ambiguous figure though I felt he must exist in some way.

As to the Pure Land, well, I must admit this was still unclear to me. Further, as far as my religious life was concerned, the question of the Pure Land was not an important one at all; what was important was the Buddha. As long

---

1. This is an adapted translation of the first chapter of Kaneko Daiei, *Jōdo no kannen* 浄土の観念, "The Concept of the Pure Land" (Kyōto: Bun'eidō, 1925), 1–25. Ed. The text was originally "a talk" and the translator, Wayne S. Yokoyama, added a number of phrases in square brackets to smooth it out. In this edition the square brackets have been removed for ease of reading.

as we could understand what the Buddha was, that was enough (or so I told myself), and my thoughts hinged on my belief centred around the Tathāgata. To me, a faith centred around Pure Land rituals was a mistaken belief, a mere expediency, for the truth was that it was the Buddha, not the Pure Land, that took priority; anything else was just not good enough. Someone told me what Rennyo (1415-99) had said about the Land of Bliss being a place we should look forward to with anticipation; those who wanted to go there needed only to make their request to Amida who, though he was not a Buddha himself, would turn them into Buddhas.

As I listened to this story I thought to myself that this Pure Land teaching was a belief in the compassion of the Buddha. But it also inclined me to think it didn't matter whether or not one understood what the Pure Land was. But that Pure Land has, on the basis of my belief, come to be reactivated in me. It seems nowadays there is a growing tendency for people to think that religion and religious belief can do without such thoughts associated with the Pure Land. As for myself, I found this situation unsatisfactory, and so my thinking placed priority on determining what possible meaning the Pure Land holds for us. This desire for us to determine what possible meaning the Pure Land holds for us, pushed one step further onto a broader plane, is for us to grasp what possible basis there is for our existence in the nation, in society, in the religious world. This led me to conjecture that, if there is such a basis in the background, then it is one to which man cannot fail to aspire should he perceive it. I felt that these were matters we must bring ourselves to consider in a complete and satisfactory way; these were the thoughts governing my heart. These points taken together, the question of the Pure Land, as I mentioned above, is one that in recent years has gripped me heart and soul, and so on the present occasion I would like to share some of my thoughts with you, ordinary though they may be.

The talk I will now give, to reiterate what I have just said, is firstly to explore in simple terms the dimension of what meaning the Pure Land - through our Awakening to self as individuals - holds for us. Actually I had first thought of relating my personal impressions in detail, remarks as I opened my talk with, for there are a great many things I ought to clarify about myself, but what happens when one does that is one ends up relating all sorts of personal events to no purpose, so I will limit those remarks to what I have already mentioned, and instead focus in detail on the concept of the Pure Land in the Mahāyāna sūtras. Originally I had intended to talk simply on the Pure Land as a theme, but a postcard message from our friend Mr Fujinami suggested the present theme, and that is how I came to settle on it. Now, as to the theme of the concept of the Pure Land in the Mahāyāna *sūtras*, we must ask what meaning the Pure Land has come to hold. As with my earlier discussion focused on the theme of religious bodies as far as the Buddhist world and congregation are concerned, I intend to focus the discussion on how the

Pure Land was understood in the Mahāyāna teachings. Here my views will border on the subjective rather than the objective (*kyakkanteki*),² and I should say "necessarily subjective" as I intend to speak out of my own Awakening to self, that is my own spiritual understanding (*etoku*) of matters, outside of which I cannot utter even a single word. First, as to the meaning held by the so-called Pure Land in terms of the contents of an Awakening to self, I wish to discuss how the following passage from the Mahāyāna canon is explained.

THE CONFESSION FOUND IN VASUBANDHU'S *TREATISE ON THE PURE LAND*

First, standing on the basis of my Awakening to self, I will begin the discussion by exploring the meaning of the Pure Land as seen in this extremely simple expression that opens Vasubandhu's *Treatise on the Pure Land*:

O World-honoured One, I with One mind
Take refuge in the Tathāgata of unimpeded Light
Filling [the universe] in every direction,
And I pray to be born in the Land of peace and happiness.³

Vasubandhu's confession appears at the very beginning of the *Treatise on the Pure Land*. Expressed in the simplest of terms, while predating us by some two thousand years, it expresses perfectly our feelings, expresses what we ought be saying. To analyse this simple statement, there are three terms we must look at closely: first, the "I" [the Self, i.e. the seeker], second, the "Tathāgata" [the Buddha] and third, the "Land" [the Pure Land]. In my discussion I will refer to these as the Three Principles. The Land, called the Land of peace and happiness, is the Pure Land. Though there is meaning to the confessional appeal to the World-honoured One, we will have to pass this over for the time being. And so, starting with our first term, "I" or the Self, this appears as the I with One mind that takes refuge in the Buddha of unimpeded Light filling the universe in every direction; herein also our next term, "Tathāgata," for the Buddha, appears; and finally, in the desire to be born in

---

2. Ed. This is slightly revised from the original publication, because *kyakkanteki* means "objective."
3. Vasubandhu's *Treatise on the Pure Land* (J. *Jōdoron*; T. 1524), with a well-known commentary by Tánluán (T. 1819), that figures importantly in Shin theology. For a translation of the former, see Vasubandhu's "Gatha on a Birth [in the Pure Land]" (*Ganshōge*), in D.T. Suzuki, "A Preface to the *Kyōgyōshinshō*," *The Eastern Buddhist* NS 6.1 (1973), 1–24, where the present passage of which is rendered, "O World-honoured One, I pay homage singlemindedly to the Tathāgata whose Light reaches unimpededly to the end of the ten quarters. I pray to be born in the Land of Peace and Happiness" (v. 21).

the Land of peace and happiness, or the Pure Land, we find our third term, "Land." Thus, from this we can surmise that unless we have all three – the Self, the Buddha and the Pure Land – then we cannot establish a true religion. From the perspective of the Self as the believing constituent, the Self is what believes and the Buddha is what is believed in; the Self takes refuge in the Buddha and so proceeds to the Land of that Buddha. All three elements appear at the very beginning of the confession. Now if any one of the three did not exist, then it would seem as if this magnificent edifice would all come tumbling down, and so if we consider it from that sort of perspective, whether there is a Pure Land or not lies beyond our knowing. Our thinking there is a Pure Land would seem to derive from the emotive powers of what our spiritual ancestors have thought, but actually it would seem to us the Pure Land so called does not exist. Here, first of all, although the Pure Land crumbles away, we tend to feel, as I said before, the Buddha somehow exists. But when we start to ponder the question as to where that Buddha exists, since we have already decided that the existence of the Pure Land is inconclusive, then the existence of the Buddha also becomes inconclusive. Thus, if we do away with the Pure Land, we do away with the Tathāgata, and what we are left with is the Self. While the vast majority of people give not a thought to whether this Self exists or not, Buddhism takes this issue as its very starting point. And so we are left completely in the dark as to what is knowable.

But there is another set of terms of which we should also take notice: the Taking of refuge and the Desire for birth. I take refuge in the Buddha of unimpeded Light pervading every direction, hence there is a Buddha and a Self, and the Self takes refuge in the Buddha. Logically speaking, unless the Buddha and the Self exist as two independent entities, this would make the movement of one taking refuge in the other an impossibility. But, if the Taking of refuge were to emerge at the point where we arrive at an Awakening to self as to the lives we pursue, through that praxis of taking refuge we would be standing at the very nexus where on the one hand the Self so called presents itself to us and on the other the Buddha so called presents itself. I will explain these matters as we go along, but when we are in that defining situation where we feel compelled to bow our heads in complete humility, it is at this juncture that the Taking of refuge emerges. The praxis of taking refuge then is a further entering of the depths [where the Self and the Buddha emerge simultaneously]. Since at this juncture there emerges the Self in the act of taking refuge and the Buddha in the act of being taken refuge in, the Taking of refuge assumes the form of a single praxis. On the basis of that single praxis we can sense the presence of the Self and at the same time we can sense the presence of the Buddha. The same would apply to the heart expressing the Desire for birth. Different from the heart or mind as we ordinarily understand it, it is the praxis of heart or the mind of praxis. Can we not say this praxis of heart and mind, known as the Desire for birth, is what brings the Self and the Land to presence themselves simultaneously? In my discussion, when speaking of the Taking of refuge and the Desire for birth, I will refer to them as the Two Praxes.

THREE PRINCIPLES–TWO PRAXES–ONE MIND; ONE MIND–TWO PRAXES–THREE PRINCIPLES

Now, while the Taking of refuge and the Desire for birth are completely different praxes, were we to go one step further and peer truly into the hearts of our own Selves, our hearts of taking refuge would be borne toward the Desire for birth. Were we to shift the direction of that heart with which we turn to the Buddha, with which we take refuge in the Buddha, it would as such be transformed into the Desire for birth. When that happens, do not the praxis we designate as the Taking of refuge and the praxis we designate as the Desire for birth come to be governed by the so-called one mind? It is at this juncture that there emerges the configuration described in Vasubandhu's treatise: the Three principles–Two practices–One mind, or the One mind–Two practices–Three principles. Were we capable of understanding the configuration the One mind–Two practices–Three principles assumes, were we capable of understanding clearly the mode in which it emerges into our lives, we would naturally come to an understanding of the so-called Pure Land. The unhindered Light filling the universe in every direction is descriptive of the Tathāgata; peace and happiness is descriptive of the Land; when deprived of these descriptive designations, we tend to regard the "I," the "Tathāgata" and the "Land" – that is the Self, the Buddha, and the Pure Land – as three separate entities that have to be linked by the praxis of taking refuge or by the praxis of desiring for birth. But this heart of ours, ruled as it is by our fact-filled heads, is not like this, for it proceeds – does it not? – by ascertaining matters from the beginning, from the One mind and then on to the Two praxes; from the Two praxes and then on to the Three principles; and peering dimly in that direction, seeks to pursue the way it perceives.

And so, from the harmoniously commingled "O World-honoured One, I with One mind," we can derive the Self and the Tathāgata and the Land. Placing the one most familiar to us – the Self – at centre and juxtaposing the others to this Self, we proceed to ask: what is the Taking of refuge, what meaning does the Buddha hold? Yet, what in the world is it we are referring to as the Self? As I mentioned above, we may have doubts about the Pure Land or about the Buddha, but the vast majority of people never entertain any doubts about the Self; they assume the so-called Self exists. But the truth is that the Self is an extremely complex issue. To explain what it is, let us suppose the Self is the same as Man. If so, then what is this we call Man? If we proceed from this point, all of us, however vaguely, hold to some ideal concept of

Man. There are the words of a plainsong that has been around for ages that goes, "Even among crowds of men, there is a Man unlike other men; aspire to become that Man and other men will aspire to be a man like you." In this song the word Man appears many times, saying, as if to contradict itself, that while there are many people yet there is no one. But, when you understand the meaning of the poem, it is simply saying that when you are just another face in the crowd, you are just another person indistinguishable from other people; but when you become a man uncommon among men, you become a person unlike the rest; you become a model human being. What is intended by a model human being I cannot tell, but this is the person all people aspire to become. In Vasubandhu's *Treatise on Buddha-nature*,[4] he discusses the question of Man. Actually he employs a Buddhist term, "sentient beings," that has broader and deeper implications than Man, but I will, for the present purposes, render it simply as Man. We may ask: Is Man just one who possesses the faculties of sight and hearing and so on? Or is Man one who is in possession of Buddha-nature? Merely to be a limited being with the ordinary human faculties, with eyes horizontal and nose vertical, does not necessarily make him Man: the distinguishing characteristic is to possess the qualities of buddhas called Buddha-nature. This ideal concept, says the Treatise, is what defines Man, as set forth, in effect, in the plainsong above. The "crowds of men" refers to Man possessed of the human faculties, the uncommon man refers to Man possessed of the qualities a Buddha possesses. If we think about this concept of Man, although we may not be asked to state it at this very moment, all of us hold to an active concept of Man in our minds. At a preliminary stage in life when this concept is not operative, a person knows nothing of the matter of reflecting on oneself. But, at some point, this concept becomes active at the very centre of one's being, and one gradually becomes able to reflect on oneself. Once informed of our self-worth, we come to ask ourselves whether we are doing our part in life or not. As such reflection gradually deepens, we become conscious of the sorrowful nature of life and the evil karma of living. In that phrase, "O World-honoured One, I," what is that "I," or Self, that is awakened to? It is Vasubandhu himself gaining a true insight into the actualities of the Self. Here I always recall the words, "As for me, Shinran," in *Notes Lamenting Differences*, section two. Whenever I read this passage, I insert my own name, "As for me, Kaneko," to give it stronger impact – for, what others think I know not, but as for me.... Though it might just have been a conventional phrase for him to express himself in that way, in that phrase, "As for me, Shinran," I feel he did not wish to dispense with the topic so simply. In that one phrase he is bringing forth his Self in its entirety. As he sits before an audience of serious-minded fellow seekers who, to inquire

---

4. Vasubandhu's *Treatise on Buddha-nature* (J. *Busshōron*; T. 1610).

about the Way, have had to journey across the barriers of twenty provinces, he discloses himself, bringing forth his Self in its totality in this one phrase, "As for me, Shinran," with all the various kinds of sorrow and evil that burden his soul. The "I" of "O World-honoured One, I" is not the first-person singular of grammar. Reflected here, rather, is the totality of Vasubandhu's Awakening to self, here revealing itself is the sorrow and evil of the Self – all in this term "I" or Self.

THE TRANSITION FROM DISTRESS TO TAKING REFUGE

With the disclosure of this Self burdened with evil and sorrow, there emerges a praxis; this is none other than the praxis of Taking refuge. Here, setting aside the academic question of whether or not there is an ego-self, we encounter what Buddhism calls the Impediments and the Delusions in the form of various kinds of sorrow and evil. On first impression, we may make light of the Impediments and the Delusions as so much mind-dust or uncleanliness of the heart. There are some religions that think it only necessary to remove this uncleanliness of the heart and to eradicate the mind-dust and all will be well.[5] When we hear such an opinion, we are at first inclined to agree with it, but Buddhism does not take such a light view of these matters and points out to the seeker in strong terms that a round of suffering in hell or as hungry ghosts are the fates that await those who dally in self-complacency. It is not as if some dust or grime is dripping onto something beautiful; in the internal environment of the heart, Hate, Lust, Jealousy, Malice wear down what little is left of this part of ourselves. In other words, it is as though our Self had been thrown headlong into the clutches of these malevolent forces, where it is left to their caprices. Here, where this part of ourselves is tormented by Malice, Jealousy and so on, one might aptly describe the situation by use of the Buddhist terms *hell* and *hungry* ghosts.

What Śākyamuni called *suffering* and, as the cause of suffering, attachment, I have referred to with the words evil and sorrow, but whatever the difference in terms the reality that *evil* and *sorrow* define makes its presence felt. When I truly confront this Self in reality, the thought of taking refuge emerges in me, I bow my head naturally in true humility, placing my palms together in prayerful repose. When I do this, in response to my experience of taking refuge, what we call the Buddha presences itself to me. Thus, as I stated above, in my experience of taking refuge, there appears to me on the one hand the

---

5. Ed. This may be a reference to Tenrikyō, a religion quite well represented in Kyōto as well as at the headquarters at Tenri City, and in which emphasis is placed on the sweeping away of karmic dust to make way for the shared experience of "joyous life" (*yōkigurashi*).

Self sunk in evil and sorrow, and on the other hand there appears the Buddha of unimpeded Light who sheds his light on me.

That is to say, it is not that we know from the first that the Buddha is there and so we take refuge in him; in my experience of taking refuge there emerges in me a certain attitude, and at the same time, in the experience of this experiencing subject, the Buddha makes its presence felt in me. This being the case, as far as we are concerned, when we come to a pure understanding of Self, when in our own experience we carry out the praxis of taking refuge, there is no question of whether or not the Buddha exists, or approaching the problem from the other side, the very terms by which we express whether the Buddha exists or not become problematic. When we say that the Buddha exists, what do we normally mean? It usually means that from out of somewhere there arises to our mind the image of a great humanlike figure who, seeing our suffering, takes pity on us and rescues us, and so we take refuge in this Buddha. This is clearly an irreproachable sentiment, and it of course allows no room for the possibility that the Buddha does not exist. If the Buddha exists, then we can believe in him; if the Buddha does not exist, then it would be ridiculous to think we could believe in him. But, in this attitude of wanting to confirm first the existence of the Buddha and then believing in him, there enters a sort of impureness of spirit. When, in true cognizance of the Self, we put our palms together in our experience of taking refuge, the Buddha that appears to us at that point is not what we ordinarily refer to as "existing"; not stopping with the question of existing or not-existing, it transcends the duality of being and not-being to assume its being. I use the term *pure subjectivity* to describe this situation, and the reason is that our always insisting on the existence of the Buddha does not manifest a pure subjectivity. In the word for "existing" as conceived by our human mind, in which connection we need not be reminded here of Kantian philosophy, the concept of our existence, as where we are, is comprised of numerous factors such as time–space and cause–result. While these go to determine the Self, what is determined in this way can never be a pure subjectivity. A pure subjectivity is the transcending of our thinking in terms of existing and not-existing, and it is there, as we place our palms together in the experience of taking refuge, that the Buddha reveals itself.

And so, the question of whether or not the Buddha exists is, to me, one of rather secondary importance. Of greater importance is whether one has gained a true insight into this part of ourselves. Or, if there is as yet no understanding of the Self at the outset, what is important is to know that this is what I have come to be, to know why this has come about as a prelude to self-reflection, and to become cognizant that the one engaged in self-reflection is sunk in evil and sorrow. When one's mental outlook matures to the point of taking refuge, for the first time the Self presents itself, in response to which the Buddha, shedding its light, comes to the rescue out of deep concern for one's welfare. In this sense the Buddha is what discloses itself in the paradisiacal realm of my Awakening to self.

Is the Buddha what transcends us, or is it what is immanent, lying within us? – this is a question that has long been discussed [among Buddhist thinkers]. But these words *transcendence* and *immanence* are tricky, for people are often remiss in their usage of these terms and will go about declaring out of hand that this is transcendent or that is immanent. For those of us who have had the pure experience of taking refuge, though, when we think of the emergent Buddha, the Buddha is both transcendent and emergent. To be both immanent *and* transcendent is not necessarily as contradictory as it sounds. From the standpoint of the pure subject I transcend myself, but in my transcendence of myself I am all the same descending into myself. That is when I pray to the Buddha, the more earnestly I pray, in a sense the further afield the Buddha moves from me, and as the awareness of the great distance between the Buddha and myself grows all the stronger, all the same I am in the end assimilated into the Buddha. When I think the Buddha is standing before me, suddenly he appears from behind; when I think the Buddha is standing behind me, suddenly he appears before. In regard to this unexpected nature of the Buddha the great teacher Tánluán, among others, has an extremely interesting explanation, which I will present here in brief outline. In his gloss on the invocatory phrase, "O World-honoured One, I with One mind take refuge in the Tathāgata of unimpeded Light filling the universe in every direction," he says its correct understanding turns on the words, "I, with One [mind]." As long as I truly experience the Awakening to self, the Taking of refuge in the Tathāgata of unimpeded Light filling the universe in every direction is an event that comes about naturally.

Now, when we inquire about the significance of the Desire for birth in the Land of peace and happiness, here too the Self becomes problematic. Up to now the Self immersed in evil and sorrow was explained as a completely individual affair, but by the term "individual" it is not as if we were simply talking about some complete stranger when discussing this part of ourselves. At the same time, this part of ourselves is actually operating in abundance in the background of the lives of many people. I have parents, brothers and sisters, and friends, and all these various people around me are the ones who, taken together, make up my age and generation. And so when I speak of the Self, I am speaking collectively of those around me, those who make up my age and generation. In Buddhist terminology, this collective Self would be expressed as the sentient beings everywhere that populate the real world. Prior to this real world is the Self. Since the Self is of this nature, when the Self takes refuge in the Tathāgata, at that very moment we are forced to recognize the existence of a sort of paradisiacal realm, the world of that Land of peace and happiness transcending the real world. Thus, when we discern the real world – behind which lies this part of ourselves – where the many beings comprising sentient beings live, at precisely this moment there appears the Buddha who discerns this "I" of ours, and in the same way there appears his Land, his world of the Other shore, the Land of peace and happiness that shines its Light on this real world. It is from this experience that the desire arises in us to proceed to that Country.

And so, if we think in terms of the One mind or the Self, the Tathāgata is the Light that shines on the reality of the individual Self, the Land of peace and happiness is a dimension or realm of sorts that shines its light on the real world represented by those surrounding the Self, hence, brought to expression by the Self. Seen from the other perspective, when we become truly conscious of the reality of the Self, at that point emerges the Tathāgata to be taken refuge in; if we can truly discern the way of being of this world, and wish to proceed to that Land, it is only natural that the desire arises in us to be born in that Land of peace and happiness. As regards this point, then, the matter of our taking refuge in the Buddha and desiring to proceed to the world of the Other shore arises of itself, as long as we can attain to that Awakening of self in which we become truly conscious of our ego-self. Thus, it is not a matter of first determining whether or not there exists a Land of peace and happiness or a Buddha; rather, it exists on the basis of the fact that, as I pray to the Buddha, in my person the desire to go to the Pure Land arises in me directly.

In that I have merely reiterated here what I have said on other occasions, I am afraid my talk may have been difficult for many of you to sit through, but I wished to clarify in simple terms the significance the Pure Land holds in relation to the content of my Awakening to self.

I have explained these matters at the outset in simple terms, since I think it will affect how you understand my explanation of the topic of the Pure Land in the Mahāyāna *sūtras*. There may be those among you who will feel I have been overly intuitive in describing my case, but this is not so, and what I wanted to point out in the course of my talk was that here lies a great Way.

As I stated before, there is a wondrous place where we enter the depths, but how is this explained in the *sūtras*? And as we read the *sūtras* why must we perceive it in that way? These are matters I hope to clarify in another talk on the Pure Land as understood in the Mahāyāna *sūtras*.

(Translated by Wayne S. Yokoyama)

19

The Pure Land of Beauty

Yanagi Sōetsu
(adapted by Bernard Leach)

Rereading this work I am gripped by the fact that despite his failing health, Yanagi uses up his whole being in expressing his thoughts. Because he lived so much with beauty, exploring it from every direction, he opened for us a number of gateways, to the point where none remained. It would almost seem as if he were impatient to tell us that in fact we were already living in the midst of Heaven. Although I have so often heard him enunciate these thoughts, the fresh impact impresses me once again.   From the Foreword by Hamada Shōji (1962)

PREFACE

I write this book from a bed of sickness.[1] During a long illness [his last], there has been suffering, but a great depth of understanding has come and for that I am thankful. As I lie in bed I have had pots and pictures brought into my room for me to look at. I have got into the habit during long sleepless nights of allowing my thoughts to ponder over the strange miracle of the quiet beauty of each object. On arousing myself I would make the effort to put down my thoughts before they vanished. When I think backwards, I feel that it was the consequence of this process, during my illness, which helped my concept of

---

1. Original note by the Editors of *The Eastern Buddhist*: This English adaptation of Yanagi Sōetsu's (1889–1961) *Bi no Jōdo*, which was first published in Japanese in 1962, was made by the renowned British potter Bernard Leach, friend of Mr Yanagi for fifty years. Mr Leach's original title was "*Heaven of Beauty.*" Some editorial revisions have been made. For reasons of cost, a small number of illustrations have been omitted, but the thought of Yanagi Sōetsu is clear as it stands.

beauty to mature. This gave rise to my wish to put these conclusions together in writing. The content is one aspect of the thought which I have finally reached, and, humble as it may be, yet at long last it is the outcome of four attempts. Now that my body is disabled I cannot do as I wish. Upon rereading what I have written it seems to me that I would have done better to have set down the essentials yet more simply, but to rewrite is too much for my weariness. Thus I decided to have my thoughts printed for the time being in this little booklet.[2] In conclusion, I would like to have the opportunity to go more thoroughly into my concept of beauty here presented, and one day to construct a Buddhist aesthetic.

I

To write about "Heaven" (the Pure Land) in this era of the intellect may cause some people to smile. Be that as it may, I cannot help thinking about a "Pure Land of Beauty," and I want to set myself to write down what has occupied my mind of late. If from the outset, anyone doubts the existence of such a place, it would be all right if for the time being he just assumed that such a place did exist. It is upon this hypothesis that I would like to proceed to speculate with the reader.

Even then, however, if you feel doubtful about this expression, "Pure Land of Beauty," you may simply think of it as "the Utopia of Beauty" and that also will do. If furthermore you substitute "the Land of Non-duality" in place of it that will be even better; but the significance of that I shall come to later. Ultimately, then, the "Pure Land of Beauty" is a Land of Non-duality, and I would like to go step by step and explain its meaning. There will be those, I am sure, who will question whether a Utopia of Beauty (i.e. the Land of Non-duality) exists, even question whether we have to assume such a thing. Why do we have to discuss such a problem?

In fact it is deeply interesting to note that in the two thousand years or so of Buddhist history during which the Pure Land has been spoken of, there never has been any question as to its existence. Words almost to excess describing the Pure Land there are, but never did its existence pose a serious question. The reason for that was that "the Pure Land" was here-and-now and in no far place. Of course, we have such expressions as "the Pure Land billions of miles away" (10 × 10,000 × 100,000,000). That is only to show the contrast between this defiled world and the Pure Land. In other words, it is distant in proportion to the enormity of our sins. But just when we become deeply aware of our sin, at this instant the Land of Salvation is felt. I think one may

---

2. Ed. The present article: *Bi no Jōdo* ("The Pure Land of Beauty").

say, therefore, that "the Pure Land" is not far off, that the "Heaven of Beauty" becomes a reality in the midst of one's awareness of ugliness. Again, I am not saying that the Pure Land and the defiled world are identical. It is when you loathe and leave this defiled world in earnest that it transforms itself and becomes directly connected with the Pure Land. So far as this defiled world is our present actuality, "the Pure Land" becomes an actual place.

From ancient times people have said, "Loathe and leave this defiled world; gladly take refuge in the Pure Land." Because these two are one and the same, ultimately, the more acutely you feel this defilement, the more you come to feel the Pure Land. That is why, in a religious experience of such immediacy, it may be more correct to say that there was no time to question the existence or non-existence of the Pure Land.

In Christianity, generally speaking, the problem of the existence of God was central throughout its history and the result of a dualistic way of thinking – of God (the Creator) and man (the created); of God (the Judge) and man (the judged) – which will always result in opposition. But rather than to divide in such a way, Buddhists see truth in that which precedes division. Thus Buddha is not a Judge or a Law-giver, but is all-embracing Absolute Compassion itself. There is no one who falls into eternal Hell, and even the greatest sinner is not excluded from deliverance. Such an all-embracing place is the meaning of "the Pure Land of Non-dualism." Thus when I speak of a Pure Land of Beauty it is to be understood as a place where all things without exception are accepted within Beauty. I would like to explain this matter step by step.

Again that is why, fundamentally, man and the Pure Land are not separated by a great gap. As I explained above, the statement that the Pure Land (Jōdo or Heaven) is a vast distance away is equivalent to saying that man has, a posteriori, ceased being man. But when one returns to one's original nature "the far is the near." This may be the reason Buddhists did not call into question whether the Pure Land existed or not. Only when they perceived it they described its radiant eloquence with every conceivable adjective of praise. Fundamentally, Buddhism does not divide man from Buddha. This is because the Buddha is no other than "an awakened person." In like manner, it is when the light falls upon this defiled world that it is the site of the Pure Land (Heaven). Light turns night into day. Just as night and day are not different worlds, this place defiled by human passions and the Pure Land are not different. It is like the persimmon which when unripe is astringent, yet left as it is becomes sweet. In other words this heavy, sin-laden body as long as it exists is the place where the Compassionate Heart is most moved to action. Thus the Pure Land being inseparable from the world of defilement is an idea peculiar to Buddhism. In the Jōdo school the statements, "Loathe the defiled world" and "Seek joyously the Pure Land," are always used together. This is because the mind which abominates defilement is the very same mind which welcomes the Pure Land. The beauty of the Pure Land of which I speak is to be found in that very mind which hates the ugliness surrounding us.

II

Now I would like to write about the Beauty of the Pure Land. First, I shall describe what takes place therein, its astonishing design. Second, I shall relate how this is not merely a figment of the imagination, but a demonstrable fact.

When we speak of "a Pure Land of Beauty" what is conjured up in most people's minds is probably some imaginary place as in a dream. But that is misleading because we can see the evidences of this Land everywhere around us. In Buddhism we have such expressions as *shari* ("here") and *sokkon* ("this very moment"). Since it is possible for me to speak of "the Pure Land of Beauty present here at this very moment," not as an abstract concept but as the concrete reality right before my eyes, how could I fail to be captivated by such a subject?

Jōdo (Heaven), then, can be seen in objects themselves. Moreover, not necessarily in lofty or special things, but in the quite ordinary and humble. For this reason I am going to write about the Pure Land of Beauty that is expressed in normal crafts. First let me deal with what takes place in this Heaven. On examination one begins to see many strange happenings; but chiefly this is so for the dualistic minded. In actuality the apparent strangeness is no other than lucid fact. This enigma will gradually resolve itself as I proceed.

III

The first thing that one discovers is the curiosity that in this land there is no choosing between upper and lower. This upper and lower can be understood from various points of view – rich and poor, noble and ignoble, intelligent and stupid, gifted and ungifted. In this world of ours it is impossible to escape from the higher and the lower, however in the Pure Land of Beauty we begin to learn that such discrimination has no meaning.

Now when we consider art, that which comes to mind immediately is the issue of talent or lack of talent, or, genius and the average man, the chosen or the un-chosen. According to the generally accepted idea it is almost unthinkable for one to participate in the arts without special talent. However, it becomes apparent that in the Land of Beauty there is hardly any meaning in such distinctions. This is because in the Pure Land the possibility is present of the ordinary man performing the miracle of creating things of great, even greater beauty. Indeed, it is this which I would like to call "the Pure Land."

Are we not surrounded by overwhelming numbers of unsigned, anonymous objects in testimony to this miracle?

Example

Everyone knows the marvellously decorated Cízhōu pots of the Chinese Sòng dynasty, but the astonishing fact is that it was the custom of the potters of that time and locality to employ children of around ten years of age to paint those pots. We cannot suppose that children who could not read or write could have received high instruction in art, or that they possessed special sensibility. To crown this, as far as their work is concerned, there was no great difference between one child and another; they all painted beautifully. When thinking of these examples, rather than conclude that the beauty of the work was determined by talent or lack of talent, it would be truer to understand it as the outcome of constant repetition and hard work.

Therefore, in this field the question of above and below, of talent and non-talent does not apply. When we see this lovely brushwork we might imagine that some genius of an artist must have done it, but such a conclusion would

Figure 1 Cízhōu ware, Sòng Dynasty, China.

be due to the cramped and conventional habit of thinking that only famous or highly gifted painters can produce such outstanding work. When we grasp the real state of things, we begin to understand that those wonderful Sòng pots were produced in a world where oppositions such as talent or lack of talent, wisdom or stupidity, almost entirely vanish. The reason why I draw attention to Sòng ware is because in it one sees almost the ultimate beauty of pots. In this world, so to speak, we can catch a glimpse of Heaven, the Pure Land. Is it not true that among Sòng pots examples of ugliness are rare? This demonstrates the feature of all things being saved in the Pure Land.

IV

Another pair of opposites in the consideration of beauty is the difference between skill and clumsiness. But this kind of discrimination vanishes in the Pure Land, leaving almost no trace of meaning. Usually, technical skill enhances the beauty, yet there are instances in art in which clumsiness contributes to beauty, adding strength. In the Pure Land we may see again and again examples where the very clumsiness is allied to beauty.

The apparent advantages and disadvantages of skill or un-skill are beside the point, for these qualities are not determinants in this land. Rather, we can even state that there are all too many instances of excessive skill leading to ugliness, and it is frequently the case, in reverse, that clumsiness gives rise to friendliness of feeling; the truth of this can be seen everywhere. It is due to the fact that skilfulness easily becomes clever contrivance, whereas clumsiness is more often combined with innocent simplicity.

Example

In the National Japanese Folk Craft Museum there is a very beautiful Korean folk landscape painting. It shows an elementary line and the method of representation is childlike, and yet as such it has great beauty. Looking at such a painting, we have before us the proof that it was done in a world where skill was not essential. This assures us that in the Pure Land skill is not indispensable. We may even say skill by itself would be an obstacle to achieving such innocent and artless beauty. Furthermore, we may conclude that once we have been entrapped by skilful knowledge it may be too late for us to reach the Pure Land, perhaps impossible.

Originally, there are no doubt examples of clumsiness standing in the way of the expression of beauty, and, therefore, it cannot be said that clumsiness is essential to artistic expression. But at the same time we may conclude that skill is not indispensable either. In fact, when we weigh which of the two is most blameworthy, we find the greater danger lies in skill. With skill comes all kinds of temptations. How many works of art have stumbled and fallen because of this?

Figure 2 Korean folk painting.

V

Next, we come to understand that just as there is no distinction between higher and lower in the Pure Land of Beauty, there is equally no higher or lower in objects. Let us take the distinction between noble and ignoble, rich and poor. It is not the aristocratic or ornate objects which are most highly valued. We find many examples of things which are humble and liable to be disregarded because they are common folk-utensils being accorded a high place in this Heaven. In the Pure Land all oppositions between aristocratic and plebeian, rich or poor, are erased for us. Thankfully, the Pure Land seems to be so made that humble objects, just as they are, are allowed to become bound to great beauty. The vast quantity of such things puts this beyond doubt, and enables us to see how the very sumptuousness of wealth or aristocracy often contains less of truth and beauty.

Example

The most suitable examples which come to mind are the various old and famous Tea utensils, the tea-bowls and so on revered in Japan today as masterpieces and National Treasures. But when we reflect on the fact that most of them were originally cheap, ordinary day-to-day articles (e.g. Korean rice-bowls) do we not perceive that in our Heaven of Beauty distinctions of nobility have little significance? At any rate, from the undeniable fact that these originally modest folkcraft utensils made in great quantity have achieved the highest rank in the world of Tea, we can conclude that in the Pure Land the distinction between noble and humble is almost obliterated. When we carry the thought further we see that those articles which are over-decorated with aristocratic intention lean towards unhealthy decadence. We can no longer state that merely being aristocratic can ensure a high place in Heaven. Coloured Nabeshima porcelain is a good example of this, particularly the red enamelled variety, because it was made for the use of the feudal ruling clan, and was finely finished in the choicest material. These Nabeshima porcelains were certainly refined, but from the point of view of art can we describe them as of the highest standard? Their lack of vitality and freedom and the feeling of constraint they give is due to the restricted state of mind in the makers when they were being made, which tended to suppress creative freedom. Some people consider that coloured Nabeshima ware is the finest of red enamelled porcelain, but this is because they merely confirm the prevailing conventional thinking which regards aristocratic objects as of the first order, and things made for the masses of a low order. We certainly cannot call this Nabeshima ware the best of red enamelled porcelain. If only you can see an object in its naked reality then you can understand how baseless the judgment is that all aristocratic things are best.

To summarize, we can now realize that those folkcrafts which have hitherto been disdained in fact quite often are accorded a high rank in the Pure Land of Beauty. The proof of this may be seen most directly in the evidence of the genuine Tea Wares of Japan. As one can see from the coloured enamels of Nabeshima, aristocratic wares, contrary to general opinion, are not necessarily examples of a free and creative spirit. It is thus clear to us that differences in worldly rank do not apply here, for it is not rare for articles of humble origin to express beauty of a high order.

VI

To this point I have discussed the marvels which take place both in man and in the things he makes. Now I wish to consider the appearance of the same marvel in the ways in which the things are made. I have encountered countless instances of the miraculous manner in which objects, howsoever made, are embraced by beauty. It is just such a world I want to describe as the Heaven of Beauty, a land in which all is included and embraced in beauty. It is also the place in which ugliness cannot occur. Here we come to comprehend the way in which the who, the how, and the what all become beautiful. This is the exquisite work of the Pure Land. Ultimately, the footprints of ugliness disappear; all traces vanish; the duality comes to an end. In the *Sūtra of Eternal Life*, there is reference to the "non-existence of duality of beauty–ugliness." This is indeed a laudable description of what takes place. Again we have the phrase "neither purity nor defilement," and indeed in this Heaven the roots of all such dualities are severed.

Since ultimately the Pure Land of Beauty does not belong to relativity, it is the place of non-duality, the land of non-dualistic beauty. Here the slate is wiped clean of all relativity.

This beauty, therefore, is not what remains after the negation of ugliness. It is an absolute with no antonym. It is thus not the antithesis of ugliness, it clearly belongs to a world where the dichotomy of "beauty–ugliness" has died out. This beauty of the Pure Land, then, expresses an aspect of beauty which has no antonyms. "Beauty" or "good" are but provisional names. Compelled to express it, I can only say it is "that which is not-two." Even then, that does not mean "something of the nature of not-two-ness"; it would be better to say that "not-two" is itself beauty.

Ultimate beauty thus becomes impossible apart from non-duality. Since being non-dual it cannot but be beautiful, ugliness, on the other hand, disappears as a matter of course. In short, the absence of duality is, per se, beauty, but not by overcoming or rejecting ugliness. If I must add anything further, perhaps I can call this the beauty of Beauty itself, or autonomous beauty. Therefore, conversely, it is beauty without ugliness, beauty which has no antonym. Finally, I would like to call this ultimate beauty "the beauty of the Pure Land." Once entered, ugliness has no place, "all things become beautiful." This is why Buddhists could not help arriving at the idea that "everything without exception is Buddha." Therefore, in the Pure Land of Beauty there is nothing that does not gain salvation. All things are accepted in this aspect of beauty. Do such things really occur, or is this a dream? To prove it is no fantasy I would like to cite the following examples.

Examples

It is probable that on both sides, East and West, let us say before the twelfth century or earlier, it was almost impossible to find anything which was ugly. This implies that in those earlier times this miraculous phenomenon of ubiquitous beauty prevailed. If we examine the matter closely, even in less ancient times, we are able to see the concept "everything without exception is Buddha" at work in art.

Again, as examples, just as one can rarely find any specimens of ugly Coptic or Inca weaving, so also in more recent time, there is not a single piece of Okinawa textile which could really be described as ugly. This miraculous world where ugliness becomes impossible is what I call "the Pure Land of Beauty."

In this age of overwhelming ugliness, we cannot help feeling a strong yearning for this Heaven where ugliness is not possible. Since it is an actuality that time, space and man really can be embraced without exception by the blessings of beauty, would it not be well to give this consideration as an aesthetical problem of the utmost urgency? In view of the fact there is not a single example of ugliness among Coptic, Inca or Okinawan textiles, and also recollecting they were done by very simple and humble people, it is a certainty that this marvel, "everything without exception is Buddha," is actually taking place in the Pure Land of Beauty. Wonderful as it may seem, this is the place where distinctions between good and bad, high or low, or beauty and ugliness, both in men and or in objects, vanish.

VII

Now we come to the third marvel that takes place in this Pure Land. As an inevitable result of this wondrous working, in those places and periods where ugliness did not prevail, all men from the rulers down to the humblest used only genuinely good things from morning to night. This means these ordinary articles made in perhaps large quantity by ordinary people, are by the very property of number closely allied to beauty. In this way even the poorest people lived amongst superb artefacts. Today, if we think of this it seems a dream, but in those times and places people were unable to live in ugliness, in fact the articles used by the poor were the most beautiful – a truly wonderful spectacle to be seen in the Heaven of Beauty, is it not?

Even from an economical standpoint this was ideal, not only because the goods were inexpensive but because they remained excellent. The cheaper they were the greater was the guarantee of beauty. What a fortunate phenomenon! Here we find the happy unity of beauty and frugality. Beauty and low cost were not opposed, whereas our constant experience in our own age is the reverse. In "the Land of Beauty" there is not the slightest discrepancy between them. In some cases, beauty is even enhanced because of low cost. Could we imagine a happier state of affairs? This is because today in our present environment troubles originating in the conflict between beauty and low cost occur all too frequently.

Example

I shall take a very simple example and try to describe the way in which the miracle of beauty actually took place. Amongst Japanese ways of weaving there was one type of indigo-dyed *kasuri*[3] that prospered in several centres from the close of the Feudal Period into the early Meiji Restoration (from the mid-nineteenth century to the turn of the century). It was traded from port to port and was used by the fairly upper class on down to the lower-class population. Hardly any chest of drawers would have failed to contain one or two garments made of this *kasuri*. In those days it was a very ordinary cotton cloth for clothing. It was not expensive, except for one kind in which the pattern was minute, but the cost of the ordinary kind could not have troubled anyone's purse and everyone employed it for normal daily use. Yet considered from our viewpoint today this indigo *kasuri*, cheap and for daily use, is of a remarkable beauty, particularly when used and frequently washed. This commonly used cloth is in its very unpretentiousness refreshingly beautiful, and in it we can see before our eyes the identity of beauty and thrift.

Kasuri represents the most highly developed technique in Japan. It may be called the characteristic Japanese cloth. To Japanese themselves it is a common cloth seen everywhere, but when foreigners see it they are surprised by its fresh loveliness. Not only foreigners, anyone who can see its authentic

---

3. Note by Bernard Leach: *Kasuri* is a unique kind of textile, originating in India, in which either the thread of warp, or of the weft, or both, are dyed in calculated lengths before weaving to form pattern.

beauty will come to realize what a fine textile has been evolved on these shores. Can we not see by this the astonishing fact that the Japanese have been in the habit of commonly using something of great beauty without taking any particular notice of it – one more actual example of the harmony between beauty and economy?

So far, I have said nothing about the beauty of the colour. In the unsurpassed loveliness of the indigo dye we can see the identity of thrift and beauty. Today, the situation is degenerating. True indigo and the colours produced from it have risen greatly in cost. But we cannot escape blame. It is we ourselves who have allowed this state of affairs to develop.

We human beings, without even a sense of regret or any reflection have permitted the loss of this beautiful colour. We have allowed ourselves to be driven into this inescapable situation. It is because of this stupidity that now ugly colours have become so widespread.

VIII

Next, in the Pure Land it is so arranged that everyone is saved by the hand of beauty. This means that in our fundamental state we are all, without exception, saved. Put more simply, man is originally made so as to make and use beautiful things. Hence originally things are arranged rather that the making of ugly things is impossible. If at any time man finds himself dispossessed of this happy state, the cause may no doubt be laid on acts which disturb and defile this natural order. This would be like a child who is given by his parents a ticket for a trip, and throws it away, making the gift useless, and finally being unable to go on the expedition.

When we look at nature which surrounds us, for example, grass and stones, not to speak of flowers or butterflies, we discover there is not a thing which is ugly. There all things are beautiful in their true state. Although some of us might consider certain things less beautiful than others, such judgment is based on self-centred human ideas. In nature itself "ugliness" is inconceivable. It is from human convenience that man discriminates, but in nature the difference between the high and the low, beauty and ugliness has no meaning.

Example

The clays of Swankolok in Thailand and of Tamba in Japan which people might call poor raw material, are from a man-centred viewpoint said to be bad, or, not being white, too ordinary. Judged from nature itself, however, there is no such thing as bad or ugly material. We can see this as a fact before

Figure 3 Swankolok ware, Thailand.

our eyes when we look at Swankolok or old Tamba wares, which cannot be imagined apart from these so-called bad materials.

Such clays in their very poorness of quality are given life by the way in which they are employed in fine pots. Used in a suitable way, one sees that the so-called bad clays come to life. We may learn from this that the birth of beauty of this sort is paradoxically dependent on what has been called poor clay. In the same way, man, if he is able to live in his original nature, will make nothing which ever goes wrong. Should anything be amiss it would be more reasonable to think that the cause was on the human side. Where does such error arise? All said and done, all mistakes arise due to our attachment to the discriminating mind, dividing I and thou, beauty and ugliness, skilfulness and unskilfulness, upper and lower.

IX

When we come to think in this way, all that man makes, if left to itself, should tread the "path of non-error." The reason why we do fall into error is simply because something happens which impairs our original nature. We are all inclined to conclude that in order to create something beautiful, some kind of special gift is necessary, but that is not so, for left in our pure state, all of us are in possession of the ability to create something beautiful. This is a truer way to grasp the situation.

Example

The best example and proof is found in those objects made by primitive peoples so wonderfully that often they are emulated even by modern artists. This is not because every primitive craftsman is an outstanding genius but because such people live a life truer to their original nature than civilized people. In a similar way we find beautiful paintings done by children. This too is because more often than adults, children dwell in their original nature. When children become educated, or sophisticated, they lose their capacity to draw freely and beautifully. Even by this evidence we may judge what is happening to us. If only a man is capable of living in his original state, ugliness in his work will cease. Primitive people, looked down upon as "underdeveloped," create free and lovely things because their life has not been affected by artificiality as has the life of so-called cultured man. For this reason they are able to give effortless freedom to their work. We know such primitives do not receive a high level of education, also that any attempt to educate them immediately results in their handwork becoming lifeless. Thanks to the very fact that they are not equipped with knowledge and discrimination, they have no attachments and are therefore free. Thus they can express freedom both in their hearts and in their work, with resulting beauty.

Neither does this necessarily mean that we should return to primitive life. Once we understand how intellectual culture restricts our freedom, we should then be able to perceive with great wisdom just where the shortcomings inherent in the nature of the intellect lie. Our "knowledge" should be inclusive of this perception. Because we cultured people lack this wisdom, we have become less able to express ourselves freely in work. "Primitive beauty," then, may be called "original beauty." In Buddhism they often say "Show me your original face." The word "original" is profoundly significant as it points to "that which we are before the awakening of the intellect, when dualism commences." Buddhists have employed various words to give expression to this: *hongu* ("that with which we are provided from the outset"); *hon'u* ("original being"); *honbun* ("man's fundamental calling in life"); *honrai* ("that which we are, undivided"); *honshō* ("original nature") and so forth. There is an old Chinese saying, "Back to our native home, forthwith!" This can be interpreted as an expression of man's desire to return to his original being. His desire for the Pure Land, then, may be taken as nostalgia. If, for the moment, we call this innate nature of ours the Buddha-nature, we may say that beings as well as things are all naturally endowed with this Buddha-nature. If, for the moment, we replace the term "Buddha-nature" with "Beauty-nature," we can then see that all things are from the very beginning endowed with beauty. Affirmation of this truth is taking place endlessly in the Pure Land of Beauty.

Above, I have stated that if we return to our original nature we can steer clear of the path of error. This means also that when we become one and flow with the things before us, we enter the path of non-error. Take, for instance, weaving, which is determined by a numerical law (threads in the warp and weft). If we recall that as long as this law is obeyed the road is safe and beauty is definitely assured, then I think the truth of what I have said about textile beauty becomes self-apparent. Should we not pay more heed to the fact that this path of non-error opens for each and every one of us as a way to the Pure Land?

Suppose we are about to decorate a pot. Do you realize that it is possible for anyone at all to produce beauty each time the attempt is made without blunder? I am sure that to many people this must seem like wishful thinking. But this is no dream. I shall give an actual example. Recently, I saw a Korean bottle of the Yi Dynasty on which an incredible pattern was painted with effortless freedom. You would think that only a child could have achieved such innocent simplicity and directness. The pattern itself was so unusual and extraordinary that one would have difficulty in imagining how the painting could express such beauty, but the fact remains that, just as it is, its beauty was such that it could not have been improved upon. Here we are shown that a world does exist in which all things, however drawn, are lovely. At this point the fact is demonstrated that there is a situation in which such things as above and below, skill and clumsiness, concept or lack of concept in men are all without any difficulty, just as they are, completely embraced by beauty. From this we can see that in the world of art there is, without question, a pathway of non-error lying in readiness. I myself have set eyes on the beauty which appears in this realm, and so I cannot help bearing witness to manifestations of this Pure Land of Beauty. The reason for this is that in this World of Beauty unskilfulness, lack of intelligence, whosoever the maker, whatever is drawn, all is given life, and there is nothing at all to prevent this from taking place. The Yi Dynasty bottle teaches us the truth so clearly. But it is no isolated case. The world contains countless examples which reveal it to us. How can we doubt then the actual existence of the Pure Land of Beauty?

X

The reader may have perceived already that what I mean is that the Pure Land is, ultimately, no other than Free Beauty. Briefly, this means release from humanly contrived bondage and a return to the original nature which is the Beauty-nature. Since this means a liberation from attachment to things, it also means the free mind. In Buddhism, becoming free-minded is returning to the "non-abiding Mind." This "non-abiding mind" is the "mind of non-obstruction" inherent in the Buddhist way of life. Shinran pointed to this very mind with his words, "Nembutsu is the single path of non-obstructiveness." Again the Zen master Daie was asserting the same idea when he said, "Non-abiding is the Buddha-mind." To conclude, if a man lives a life of free-mindedness, then whatever he makes will avoid ugliness. Therefore, as long as a man can remain in a state where his free mind is not obstructed, no matter who he is, or what he makes, he cannot help creating something of beauty. In this sense in all things of beauty may be found effortlessness and naturalness. In other words, they have the inevitability of something that comes about of itself.

Freedom here means the unobstructed expression of one's own innate character, and objects made with such a natural mind are free of any particular human interference; put another way, it may be described as the ordinary and undisturbed state of affairs. In this the most commonplace things are inevitably related to beauty. In contrast, that which is abnormal has something unnatural which takes us far from the Pure Land of Beauty. It does not hold out the promise of happiness. In our own time there is an increase of the sensational, abnormal and sometimes perverse in objects of art. I can see in this trend no secure abode for art.

In this way, the "Beauty of the Pure Land" finally comes to mean beauty which is free of anxiety, a quiet beauty which is disturbing to no mind. When free beauty is disturbed, ugliness results. Ugliness finally is a representation of an unfree state, and therefore is an indication of bondage. To lose freedom is to become ugly. Recently many works of art have appeared which profess "freedom." But as long as this remains within the confines of an "ism," what they profess is no longer true freedom. Instead it becomes enslaved to the thought of freedom. Real freedom must be free even from the "ism" of freedom.

Example

What was it that made those men of Tea gather together apparently inferior ordinary articles and praise them as masterpieces? I think it was because they were able to see a quality of quiet settled beauty in these unobtrusive things. In their commonplaceness they discovered a deep and modest quality of beauty (*shibusa*) which is found in nature itself, and they were able to appreciate that the things which they selected were produced from a free or "non-abiding" mind which was not attached even to the thought of beauty. It was a mind free from fixed ideas. The character of those masterpieces was something born of such a mind. That which made the Tea masters unique was their perceptive desire to live with such things as their companions. The whole sense of Tea-life is the savouring of peace of body and mind through beauty. For this reason the Cult of Tea has flourished for centuries as a Way of Life, because in it is a spiritual fulfilment of the heart's desire.

XI

We have so far discussed Free Beauty as being equivalent to the "Pure Land of Beauty." In Free Beauty there are two conspicuous characteristics. Negatively stated, there are two forces which may restrain freedom. The first to be mentioned is the self, or "ego." We are all prone to stick tenaciously to our self and to become self-imprisoned. When we become imprisoned by the clinging ego, we immediately part company with freedom and bind ourselves to un-freedom. This is because the ego (the attached mind) obstinately clings to man and will not let him go. So, when we want to be accepted into the "Pure Land of Free Beauty" it becomes necessary for us to cut somehow our ties with the "ego." If any trace is left, attaining this Land is extremely difficult.

How does the setting up of this "ego" of ours come to bind us? Once we set up an "ego" this implies setting a "self" against an "other," a duality. Moreover, once this dualism is established man becomes involved in discrimination, and to extricate himself from this is not an easy matter. The "Pure Land" is a place of non-duality which does not allow any kind of dualism, so, as I have already explained, all such differences as talent or lack thereof, cleverness or stupidity, skill or lack of it, aristocracy or humility, have been done away with. Ultimately to slide into dualism is to draw further away from Heaven and back into the impure world. And as this is also what causes ugliness to come about, it becomes impossible without getting free of dualism to express beauty. A word of warning here, however: Jōdo (Heaven)[4] must not be taken dualistically, that is as opposed to the mundane world; it must be seen as being in duality yet not bound to duality. It is not in the nature of Jōdo to repulse duality. To work in the very midst of dualism is what makes Jōdo what it is. To transcend and to reject duality are two entirely different things.

So far what I have stated is that it is the ego which gets us ensnared in dualism. The most serious aspect of this is that the "ego" invariably sets about judging everything with self at the centre of judgment. Just as the pictorial construction of the written Chinese characters for "discriminate" (*funbetsu* 分別) shows, we divide and set apart when we judge. To put this more pointedly, the working of our knowing mind is a devil that enslaves us day and night. Although the discriminating mind as such admittedly has its value,

---

4. Ed. Jōdo: literally "Pure Land."

nevertheless at root it is discrimination which takes us out into the dual world, and it is a power to be feared because it takes us further and further from the Pure Land.

Example

Modern art, in general, advocates the new, the latest, and makes an "ism" the point of departure. If this position is stubbornly defended in accordance with the law of dualism, something newer is quickly bound to emerge in its place. Such newness is merely transient. In due course it will be pushed aside as old-fashioned and will be unable to stand the test of time. Why must it be so attached to a duality of the new versus the old? One view of history asserts that this very opposition is that which brings about progress. For instance, in the dialectic of Hegel's philosophy, thesis, antithesis and synthesis go through unending cycles. This may be progress from the historical standpoint, but it also means unending conflict without any promise of final peace.

    The world as we see it is full of continuous conflict. This confused state of affairs exists because our minds are unable to transcend the duality of the new and the old, of left and right, East and West and so on. It is for this reason that Buddhists never cease to expound the way in which men can shake themselves free from the dualistic world. As we have already been warned, there are two things which bind us to duality, the first being the "ego," and the second, "discrimination" prompted by the "ego." The root division between self and other causes all oppositional confusion. Therefore, Buddhism continually urges us to release ourselves from the suffering inherent in duality. Similarly, we may consider that all the pain of ugliness results from the same cause.

XII

We acknowledge that the great difference between man and other sentient beings lies in the fact that man is the master of intellect. The intellect may have reached a summit in man, yet, unfortunately, it is this "discriminating intellect" which drags everything down into dualism. What is even worse, we become proud of this intellect of ours, become convinced that by exercising it we are thereby some superior order of being. The overworking of this faculty shuts man's mind off from freedom, and it develops into a new and formidable adversary. Discrimination always proceeds by a process of dividing, and all man's sufferings, ignorance and ugliness arise from his being caught in this trap of dualistic reasoning. Unless we remove the dualistic hoops from the barrel, so to speak, we cannot regain that freedom which is our original nature. As long as we refuse to do so, we must go on experiencing the un-free state. Ugliness is no other than a manifestation of this subjection. When free beauty is restrained by the "ego," or by the intellect, it can never show us its true and normal nature, or, at the very least, it would become difficult. When I reflect on all the ugly articles I have seen, it seems to me they all show traces of the "ego" and vestiges of the intellect – signs of the un-free state. We may learn much by keeping in mind the vast quantity of things of true beauty to be found amongst the utensils of folk life.

Example

When we examine the kind of beauty in folkcrafts we find that it emanates from the innocent mind [leaping from the heart to the hand]. In contrast, luxurious, pretentious things contain much that is false because of the very effort to express beauty – all too often the intellect is overworked. Do we not find from daily experience that it is intellect which is thus the seed of ignorance?[5]

Take the many examples of great beauty to be found in Takasago weavings. I think once we come to know this has no relation at all to an "ego" and its discriminations, we thereby learn something concerning the character of its beauty.

XIII

Folkcrafts are first of all made by quite ordinary people; secondly, the articles made are nothing out of the common. These basic conditions are such that there is no opportunity to assert the "ego," or to scheme with the intellect in the actual work. The minds of the makers together with the quality of the articles made are thereby free and peaceful. Things born in such peace and freeness of mind are thus naturally embraced or accepted by beauty.

I have used the expression "acceptance," a word implying passivity. In truth if we enter this life of acceptance the chance of our being saved is great, and this we can see as evident in the vast number of actual examples of common folkcrafts which are, as such, things of inherent beauty. This beauty then can be described as the "beauty of acceptance," or the beauty which comes from being saved by the "Other Power." Can we not see from this how inevitably the concept of the "Other Power" is related to that of the Pure Land? Therefore in Buddhism, too, the Other Power school was the Pure

---

5. Note by Bernard Leach: A state brought about by losing sight of our original nature.

Land school. One need only to see a few good examples of folk utensils to be convinced of the truth of this.

Example

In the potter's craft there are two types of glaze effect, *yōhen* (a change in local colours due to intermittent clear-burning and smoky atmosphere in the kiln) and *haikazuki* (changes in local colour due to wood ashes falling upon melting glazes). In these effects we often find an indescribable beauty. It is a quality that belongs altogether to the Other Power. For here we see how much the fallen ash, fire and kiln are to be thanked, and how all is but a blessing of the Other Power. This, then, is the kind of beauty I describe tentatively as the "Beauty of the Pure Land."

XIV

Here I wish to restate that in the "Heaven of Beauty" three great oppositions disappear. In fact, that place in which antonyms have vanished is itself the Pure Land.

The first opposition, distinction between intelligence and stupidity, disappears; the second, the difference between skill and lack of skill, the aristocratic and the humble, becomes invalid; and finally the third, the difference between beauty and ugliness, dies out too. This does not imply that all must become geniuses or great personalities in order to enter this Pure Land. Nor does it mean that we must all become intelligent or skilful. Neither does it imply that in the Pure Land all things acquire the same level of beauty. In this Heaven the common remains common, the stupid, the unskilled, the poor, each person remains as he is, and yet each and every one has his place in Heaven.

Similarly, it is not that the ugly must be transmuted into beauty to attain Heaven, but that even the ugly when light falls on it comes to life and is accepted by Heaven. As I have explained earlier, what takes place can be likened to the changing of night to day; the day comes, but not because we have dispensed with night. Therefore to the Eye of Heaven the dichotomy of day and night, beauty and ugliness, loses its meaning. In the Pure Land school of Buddhism this aspiration for the Pure Land has been expressed as the "Prayer of non-differentiation between beauty and ugliness." This statement must not be understood to mean that all things become beautiful in an identical form. Each and every distinction, remaining uniquely itself, is embraced in the Beauty of Heaven. To conclude, it is not that ugliness alters itself into beauty in order to enter the Pure Land, but remaining what it is, it takes on its own true life and merges into beauty.

Examples

Perhaps the best examples to show what I have been describing are the carvings of Buddhist figures by the itinerant monks Mokujiki and Enkū. These figures are chiselled with rough and almost careless strokes.

As may be seen, this summary treatment does not stand in the way of beauty. By this very means they come to life, in fact the expression of life is all the more enhanced. If we were to smooth out the chisel strokes and

Figure 4 Wood-carving by Mokujiki.

sharp-hewn facets these wooden figures would immediately lose most of their vitality. But the point is that these so-called defects, considered ugly by most people, proceed of themselves to be a guarantee of beauty. When we come across work of this sort it is clear to us that it was done in a state in which the thought of beauty and ugliness had not entered. The idea that something finely carved is good and anything roughly carved is ugly loses its meaning. Every single stroke in its real form is alive and merges into beauty. As a consequence when one looks at such Buddhist figures one may regard them as liberators of true beauty. Does it not astonish us to find that beauty is possible even in such areas?

Thus it is not only genius or intelligence which is necessary for good work, nor does it follow that if the work is clumsy or rough the Pure Land is forever closed. All things, without exception, are taken into that Heaven. In our dualistic world we cannot hope for such a miracle, but, fortunately, we are endowed with the Pure Land of non-dualism in which all persons as well as all things are given refuge.

Why is it that human beings hanker for the Pure Land? Because today there is a vast increase in the ugliness surrounding us and to that extent the Land of Beauty has become far off. This predicament also means that by our own attached minds we are robbed of freedom and have placed ourselves in bondage. The owner of this attached mind may be the artist, or the self-interested patron, or the trend of the times; whatever it may be it is the loss of freedom resulting from self-centredness. Then, whether in the person or in his work, beauty attenuates and vanishes.

Since in our day we have come to believe the man of genius is an exceptional and chosen person, the rest of mankind is neglected and placed in a lower category. We have created a disparity between the ordinary man and genius, and this I believe to be the cause of the great increase of the unbeautiful in the world around us. In the same way we are all made to believe that without skill we cannot give birth to beauty in things, and that the road has been completely closed for the clumsy. This again has been a great factor in the spread of ugliness. This is the reason why I am driven by the desire to deeply relate the common, the stupid, the poor and the clumsy to beauty and see them welcomed into its Heaven. As Buddhists reiterate, "Loathe and leave the defiled world; seek joyously the Pure Land." To save the mass of humanity from deprivation, we cannot but earnestly desire an ideal land of beauty. As I have explained earlier, this "Pure Land" is not in some distant time and place. It is in the very desire for the "Pure Land"; the Pure Land of Beauty, especially, must be found here-and-now, in the "present." Fortunately, we have the simple crafts made by humble people to show us the truth of this. One reason why I have for so long been drawn to folk utensils is because I glimpsed in them the beauty of Heaven on earth. I observed how in just such things the Pure Land is most brightly reflected.

XV

So far I have stated that the "Pure Land of Beauty" is the land which embraces all things and that the folkcrafts are concrete proof of it. In making this contention I do not mean to exclude other forms of art. It goes without saying that both gifted men and articles of high quality and refinement should be securely related to beauty. But what seems to me most interesting is the phenomenon before my eyes of ungifted people and their poor-quality material showing an even surer contact with beauty. This is closely comparable to the relation between eminent and learned and saintly monks who have nursed and nurtured the world of spiritual life in depth, and the simple, humble and unlearned believers who live by pure and profound faith. In Buddhism such simple men of faith are called *myōkōnin* ("wondrously good men"). From the point of view of learning, the difference between them is obviously vast, but from the viewpoint of the life of faith no such distinction can be made. On the contrary, often the words and actions of these simple-hearted devotees remind us of great and holy monks. I can well believe that, should there be ranks in Heaven, we would be likely to find the humble, who in this world are without rank, highly placed. Is there not a hidden providence in their very ranklessness among their fellow men?

The beauty found in folkcrafts may be closely compared to the "rankless rank" of the *myōkōnin* 妙好人. It may thus be permissible to call the work of their hands *myōkōhin* 妙好品 (wondrous work).[6] As is self-evident from actual examples, the status which may be given to *myōkōhin* in the "Land of Beauty" is never low. The Zen master Rinzai employed the expression, "the True Man of no-rank." The *myōkōnin* and *myōkōhin*, I am convinced, radiate something of this "True Man of no-rank," and it is in this very radiance that we can have a glimpse into the "Pure Land of Beauty." This is the truth upon which I have fixed my gaze.

I have described how simple country crafts are analogous with the humble, unlettered *myōkōnin*, and how this may be seen in the handwork of such people. I have also said that as far as the spiritual life of *myōkōnin* is concerned, it is often no less than that of their erudite brethren, if not superior. Are we not shown the truth of this by the great number of examples of folkcrafts which hold their own when compared with the works of famous artists? Is it true that the Tea-bowls made by Chōjirō were always as good as the Korean "Ido" bowls made by unknown peasants? Can we assert that the highly regarded pots of Ninsei were always as good as those made by the Folk artisans? When we examine the matter in this way, there can be no doubt I think that the

---

6. Note by Bernard Leach: Or, craft objects which are the counterpart of simple men of faith, *myōkōnin*. Ed. Note the rhyming play of the characters for *-nin* and *-hin*. The characters have been added here.

folkcrafts, regarded as *myōkōhin*, hold a worthy place in the "Pure Land of Beauty."

Example

In the history of Japanese pottery it will be found that among the artist-potters, Kenzan and Ninsei are regarded as holding the highest position. But can one assert that they always achieved the quality of decoration to be found in some of the oil dishes (*abura zara*) made in Seto for the commonest daily use in Japanese households? I could never believe this.

It is not my intention to depreciate Kenzan and others, but to plead for fairness and a revaluation of those folkcrafts which were born of a selfless way of life. This is just like the need for the re-estimation of the humble *myōkōnin* in relation to erudite and holy priests. Ought we not see with great surprise how these lowly crafts hold their own in company with outstanding examples of beauty?

Just as it would be a great oversight to omit the simple men of pure faith when considering religion, so also it would be only a partial view to leave out crafts of a corresponding nature in recording the history of art. I feel it is my special mission regarding the "Pure Land of Beauty" to cause folkcrafts, already accepted into Heaven and thereby "*myōkōhin*," to be more deeply, more properly considered. It is because I feel this so strongly that I have taken up my pen and put together these thoughts, though lying on a sickbed.

Appendix 1
Synoptic List of Text Titles

What follows is a consolidated list of mainly Buddhist texts which are directly referred to in this volume or in the two preceding volumes of the series Eastern Buddhist Voices. These include not only underlying Buddhist scriptures but also commentaries and further texts by various thinkers and teachers, whether Indian, Chinese or Japanese. As far as Japanese Buddhists are concerned, the normative texts of Buddhist tradition are those of the Chinese Buddhist Canon. This includes material with parallels to the Theravāda Canon, the major texts of Mahāyāna Buddhism, and much else besides which originated either in India or in China. Later writings by Japanese exponents such as Hōnen, Shinran, Rennyo and others took on an authoritative aura of their own and are also included here.

In the early twentieth century the manner of referring to all such texts varied considerably. Japanese writers were usually thinking of the older ones in a Chinese form, which may not be exactly the same as a corresponding Sanskrit or Pāli text, if indeed there is one. But by then it had also become fashionable in modern scholarship to use Sanskrit titles as a kind of *lingua franca*, even to the extent of reconstituting or in effect inventing such titles retrospectively. A classic example (already mentioned in the Conventions on Names, Titles and Scripts) is *The Awakening of Faith in the Mahāyāna* (大乘起信論 *Dàshèng qǐxìn lùn*, Japanese: *Daijōkishinron*). Even though modern scholarship agrees that this has only ever existed in Chinese, it was provided with a Sanskrit title on the grounds of a pious ascription to Aśvaghoṣa. The present list is set up in such a way that cross-references from the various authors, though in some cases misleading in isolation, lead to the reliable information which students need today.

Our Japanese authors also took quite varied decisions about how to refer to other texts in Chinese and Japanese which underlie many of their thoughts.

The titles are sometimes translated, sometimes provided with the original characters and so on. It was early days in the global presentation of these important strands in modern Buddhist thought, so there was a certain amount of experimentation. Out of respect to the authors, the policy adopted in these volumes has been to leave the references in the various articles basically as they were. Where confusion might arise, there may be an indication in square brackets or in an editorial footnote. One important reform has been carried out however: the Pāli and Sanskrit transliterations have been standardized in accordance with modern practice.

The main purpose of this integrated list of texts is to facilitate cross-checking. In most cases the cross-references first point to the Japanese pronunciation of the title, even for Chinese texts. This leads to the main entry which shows the main variants in the relevant languages.[1] Since many title variations are just alternative attempts at translation made in those early days, they are not all repeated in the main entries. In some cases it would be misleading to go from Pāli or Sanskrit titles to Chinese or Japanese ones. In such cases there is no main Japanese entry, and the other languages remain as main entries by default. In the case of Pāli texts (P) is added to distinguish them from Sanskrit ones. It should be remembered that Pāli texts did not usually form the basis of Chinese versions.

The listing of a Sanskrit title in a main entry does indicate that there is a corresponding Sanskrit text, but it should be remembered that such titles are often generic, referring to various manuscripts of varying length. They do not identify a specific original text for any particular Chinese version. In cases where an identification is particularly imprecise, or was even simply invented retrospectively, a Sanskrit form will only be shown in square brackets.

When no Chinese pronunciation is given the implication is that, although a suitably educated Chinese person could imagine a Chinese pronunciation for the title, the text is in fact a Japanese composition in classical Chinese.

There is a general problem about how to separate the component elements of Chinese and Japanese titles when they appear in an English language work such as this, because in the original languages no such separations are made. The characters just follow on each other without interruption. Here the following conventions are adopted. In Japanese titles, endings such as -ron (treatise), -kyō (sūtra), -ge (verses) or -san (hymn) are normally thought of, when spoken aloud, as being an integral part of the title, and so are left unseparated. The same is true in principle for the pronunciation of Chinese, but

---

1. This corresponds to the method for multilingual lists devised by the present editor and first presented in Christoph Kleine, Li Xuetao and Michael Pye (eds), *A Multilingual Dictionary of Chinese Buddhism. Mehrsprachiges Wörterbuch des chinesischen Buddhismus*, with appendix and corrections (Munich and Düsseldorf: Iudicium Verlag and Haus der japanischen Kultur [EKŌ], 1999). However in this case the "home language" is Japanese.

as a concession to wide usage some endings such as *lùn* and *jīng* are separated. By analogy, this will also help students to understand the Japanese readings. Again, although there is no such practice in the original languages, Sanskrit and Pāli endings such as -*nikāya*, -*śāstra*, -*sūtra* and -*sutta* are hyphenated for the reader's convenience.

Sino-Japanese characters shown in brackets are alternative forms for the same characters. In general, older forms such as 佛 and 經 (for Buddha and *sūtra*) are shown for texts found in the printed Chinese canon. The simplified forms for these (仏 and 経) may occur when variations in other characters also need to be shown, for example 阿彌陀經 (阿弥陀経). But 般若心經 (Hannyashingyō) is not also shown as 般若心経. Alternatives for single characters are sometimes shown within a title, as in 攝(摂)阿毘達磨義論, to avoid repeating the whole. Character forms for texts by Japanese authors are updated, for example Kangyōhiketsushū 観経秘訣集 (originally 觀経秘訣集). Minor typographical variations which pre-date modern Japanese are very numerous, but are disregarded here. At the same time, although *pīnyīn* has been adopted as the norm for the transcription of Chinese, the modern simplified characters of mainland China are also not used here.

In sum, the pattern for the main entries is as follows:

Romanized Japanese/characters/romanized Chinese (for Chinese texts)
    Title in English (by...*author's name*...)
    Correct Sanskrit form of title if any
    [non-standard, presumed or invented Sanskrit; or comment thereon]
    [other non-standard or abbreviated form, comment, etc.]

***

Abhidhammattha-saṅgaha (P)
    Treatise on the Essential Meaning of the Abhidhamma (by Anuruddha)
    [Equivalent to Shōabidatsumagiron 攝(摂)阿毘達磨義論 Shèāpídámóyì lùn]

Abidatsumashutara 阿毘達磨修多羅 Āpídámó xīudūolúo
    [Abhidharma Sūtra]
    [Known only from citations in the Shōdaijōron]

Abidatsumakusharon 阿毘達磨倶舎論 Āpídámójùshě lùn
    Abhidharmakośa (by Vasubandhu)

Abhidharmakośa > Abidatsumakusharon
Āgama > Agon

Agon 阿含 Āhán
    Āgama
    [General term for Chinese equivalents to the Āgamas; cf. Zōagon, Zōitsuagon]

Aikuōkyō 阿育王經 Āyùwáng jīng
    Aśoka Sūtra

Amidakyō 阿彌陀經 (阿弥陀経) Āmítuó jīng
    Amida Sūtra
    Sukhāvatīvyūha-sūtra
    [N.B. in Sanskrit this sūtra bears the same name as the "larger" one]
    [Smaller Sukhāvatīvyūha-sūtra]
    [Amitāyus Sūtra; this title may also refer to the Muryōjukyō]

Amitāyurdhyāna-sūtra > Kanmuryōjukyō
Amitāyus Sūtra > Amidakyō

Aṅguttara-nikāya (P)
    The Gradual Sayings
    [See also Zōitsuagonkyō]

Anjinketsujōshō 安心決定鈔
    Settled Mind and Determined Mind in Summary
    (Anonymous Shin Buddhist text)

Ariyapariyesana-sutta > Honjikyō
Aśoka Sūtra > Aikuōkyō
Avataṃsaka-sūtra > Kegonkyō
Awakening of Faith in the Mahāyāna > Daijōkishinron
Āyùwáng jīng > Aikuōkyō

Banshūmondōshū 播州問答集
    Collection of Questions and Answers from Banshū (by a disciple of Ippen)

Betsuganwasan 別願和讚
    Hymn of the Special Vow (by Ippen)

Bìyánlù > Hekiganroku

Bonmōkyō 梵網經 Fànwǎn jīng
    Brahma's Net Sūtra
    [Brahmajāla Sūtra]

Bosatsukaikyō 菩薩戒經 Púsàjiè jīng
    The Sūtra of Bodhisattva Precepts
    [= 10th chapter of the Brahmajāla, T1484]

Book of Five Chapters > Godanshō

Bosatsuhonjōmanron 菩薩本生鬘論 Púsà běnshěngmàn lùn
    Treatise on the Original Life of the Bodhisattva
    [N.B. relating approximately to the Jātakamālā]

SYNOPTIC LIST OF TEXT TITLES

Bosatsuyōrakuhongōkyō 菩薩瓔珞本業經 （菩薩瓔珞本業経） Púsà yīngluòběnyè jīng
    Sūtra on the Necklace of the Bodhisattva's Former Deeds

Brahmajāla Sūtra > Bonmōkyō

Brahmaparipṛcchā-sūtra

Bṛhadāraṇyaka Upaniṣad

Buddhacarita > Busshogyōsan

Busshogyōsan 佛所行讚 Fósuǒxíng zàn
    In Praise of the Deeds of the Buddha
    Buddhacarita

Busshōron 佛性論 Fóxìng lùn
    Treatise on Buddha-nature (by Vasubandhu)

Butchikyōron 佛地經論 Fódìjīng lùn
    Treatise on the Sūtra of Buddha Realms
    [Discourse on the Stages of Buddhahood]
    [Treatise on the Sūtra on the Stages of Buddhahood]

Chāndogya Upaniṣad

Chéngwéishí lùn > Jōyuishikiron
Chinese Āgama > Zōagon

Chinkan'yōjin 鎮勸用心
    Cautions and Recommendations to be kept in Mind (by Shōkū)

Chūron 中論 Zhōng lùn
    Middle Treatise
    [I.e. a commentary on the "Middle Stanzas," verses by Nāgārjuna, referred to in Sanskrit as Madhyamakakārikā or on the basis of Tibetan sources as Mūlamadhyamakakārikā, the latter being rendered Konponchūronge in Japanese]
    [Madhyamika-śāstra: if, then, correctly Madhyamaka-śāstra may refer to Chūron (not in Sanskrit) or to Prasannapadā, a similar, later commentary by Candrakīrti]

Commentary on the Amitāyus Sūtra > Jōdoron
Commentary on the Meditation Sūtra > Kanmuryōjukyōsho
Commentary on the Prajñāpāramitā Sūtra > Daichidoron
Commentary on the Treatise on the Pure Land > Ōjōronchū
Commentary on [Vasubandhu's] Treatise on the Pure Land > Ōjōronchū
Dàchéng qǐxìn lùn > Daijōkishinron

Daibibasharon 大毘婆沙論 Dàpípóshā lùn
   Treatise on the Great Compendium
   [Mahāvibhāṣā-śāstra, no known Sanskrit text]

Daichidoron 大智度論 Dàzhìdù lùn
   Treatise on the Perfection of Great Insight
   [Great Treatise on the Perfection of Wisdom]
   [Great Treatise]
   [Mahāprajñāpāramitā-śāstra, no known Sanskrit text]

Daihannyaharamitakyō > Daihannyakyō

Daihannyakyō 大般若經 Dàbōrě jīng
   Great Prajñā Sūtra
   Great Wisdom Sūtra
   [Full title: Dàbōrě bōluómìduō jīng 大般若波羅蜜多經 Daihannyaharamitakyō]
   [Mahāprajñāpāramitā-sūtra]

Daihatsunehangyō 大般涅槃經 Dàbōnièpán jīng
   The Great Parinirvāṇa Sūtra
   [Mahāparinirvāṇa-sūtra]
   [Cf. Pāli: Mahāparinibbāna-sutta]

Daijōdōshōkyō 大乘同性經 (大乗同性経) Dàshèng tóngxìng jīng
   Sūtra on the Clear Grasp of the Great Vehicle
   [Mahāyānābhisamaya-sūtra, no known Sanskrit text]

Daijōhonjōshinjikangyō 大乘本生心地觀經 (大乗本生心地観経) Dàshèng běnshēng xīndìguān jīng
   Sūtra on Meditation on the Stage of Consciousness in the Original Life
   [Meditation on the Stage of Consciousness]
   [Meditation on the Ground of Mind]
   [N.B. "Original life" refers to the life of the Buddha]

Daijōkishinron 大乘起信論 (大乗起信論) Dàshèng qǐxìn lùn (or Dàchéng qǐxìn lùn)
   Awakening of Faith in the Mahāyāna

Daikyō > Daimuryōjukyō

Daimuryōjukyō 大無量壽經 (大無量寿経) Dàwúliàngshòu jīng
   Larger Sūtra on Unlimited Life
   [I.e. on the Buddha of Unlimited Life-span, Amitāyus. Also Larger Amitāyus, Larger Sūtra of Infinite Life, Larger Sūtra on the Buddha of Eternal Life, The Larger Sūtra etc. English titles for this sūtra are often imprecise and vary when drawn from Chinese or Sanskrit respectively.]
   Sukhāvatīvyūha-sūtra

[The Sanskrit title has the divergent meaning of "Sūtra on the Adornment of the Land of Bliss." For a different *sutra* with the same Sanskrit name, see Amidakyō.]

Daishōgonron 大莊嚴論（大荘厳論）Dàzhuāngyán lùn
 Treatise on Great Adornment
 [Dṛṣṭāntapaṅkti]

Daitōsaiikiki 大唐西域記 Dà Táng Xīyùjì
 Record of Western Lands of the Great Tang (by Xuánzàng)
 [Full title of Saiikiki 西域記 Xīyùjì]

Darumadaishiketsumyakuron 達磨大師血脈論 Dámó dàshī xiěmài lùn
 Bodhidharma's Treatise on Lineage (attributed to Bodhidharma)
 [Discourse on the Direct Lineage of the Dharma]

Dámó dàshī xiěmài lùn > Darumadaishiketsumyakuron
Dankyō > Hōbōdankyō
Daśabhūmikā > Jūjūbibasharon
Daśabhūmikavibhāṣā-śāstra > Jūjūbibasharon
Daśabhūmivibhāṣā-śāstra > Jūjūbibasharon
Dàshèng qǐxìn lùn > Daijōkishinron

Denshinhōyō 傳心法要（伝心法要）Chuánxīn fǎyào
 The Key Point of Mind Transmission (by Huángpò Xīyùn)
 [The Pivotal Point of Mind to Mind Transmission]

Dhammapada (P)

Diamond Sūtra > Kongōkyō

Dīrgha-āgama

Dīgha-nikāya (P)

Discourse on the Direct Lineage of the Dharma > Dámó dàshī xiěmài lùn
Discourse on the Pure Land > Jōdoron
Discourse on the Stages of Buddhahood > Butchikyōron
Discourse on the Ten Stages > Jutchikyōron

Divyāvadāna

Doctrine, Practice, Faith, and Attainment > Kyōgyōshinshō
Doctrine-Work-Faith-Attainment > Kyōgyōshinshō
Dṛṣṭāntapaṅkti > Daishōgonron

Ekottara-āgama

Engakukyō 圓覺經（円覚経）Yuánjüé jīng
    Sūtra of Perfect Enlightenment
    [Full title: Dàfāngguǎng yuánjüé xiūduōluó liǎoyì jīng
        大方廣圓覺修多羅了義經. Translation attributed to Buddhatara at the White
        Horse Temple in Luòyáng but possibly apocryphal.]

Essentials > Yuishinshōmon'i
Essentials of Faith Alone > Yuishinshōmon'i
Fànwǎn jīng > Bonmōkyō
Flower Garland Sūtra > Kegonkyō

Gejinmikkyō 解深密經 Jǐeshēnmì jīng
    Sūtra on the Unlocking of Profound Mysteries
    Saṃdhinirmocana-sūtra

Ganganshō 願々鈔
    A Brief Account of the Vows (by Kakunyo)

Ganshōge 願生偈 Yùanshēng jì
    Verse on Birth (by Vasubandhu)
    [Gātha on a Birth (in the Pure Land)]
    [Full title: Wúliàngshòu jīng yōupótíshè yùanshēng jì
        無量壽經優婆提舍願生偈]

Gobunshō 御文章
    Letters of Rennyo (by Rennyo)
    [Gobunshō is the preferred title in the Honganji-ha; see also Ofumi]

Godanshō 五段鈔
    Book of Five Chapters (by Shōkū)

Godenshō > Honganjishōninden'e
Goichidaikikikigaki > Rennyoshōningoichidaikikikigaki

Goshōsokushū 御消息集
    A Collection of Letters (by Shinran)

Guānwúliàngshòu jīngshù > Kanmuryōjukyōsho
Guānjīngshù > Kanmuryōjukyōsho

Gutokuhitanjukkai 愚禿悲歎述懐
    Gutoku's Lament and Reflection (by Shinran)
    [Part of Shōzōmatsuwasan]
    [Gutoku is a nickname meaning "simpleton" which Shinran applied to himself]

Gutoku-shō 愚禿鈔
    Notes by a Simpleton (by Shinran)

[Gutoku is a nickname meaning "simpleton" which Shinran applied to himself]
[The Writing of a Bald-headed Ignoramus]

Great Sūtra > Daimuryōjukyō

Hanjusan > Hanjuzanmaigyōdōōjōsan
Hanjusanmai > Hanjuzanmaigyōdōōjōsan
Hanjuzanmai > Hanjuzanmaigyōdōōjōsan

Hanjuzanmaigyōdōōjōsan 般舟三昧行道往生讚 Bózhōu sānmèi xíngdào wǎngshēng zàn
    Hymns on Rebirth by Continuous Samādhi (by Shàndǎo/Zendō)
    [Pratyutpanna-samādhi: an imprecise equivalent emphasizing immediateness]
    [Hymn to Rebirth (in the Pure Land) by Continuous Samādhi]

Hannyakyō 般若經
    [Collective term for various sutras of the *prajñāpāramitā* group]
    [Wisdom Sūtra]
    [Prajñāpāramitā Sūtra]

Hannyashingyō 般若心經 Bōrě xīngjīng
    Heart of Wisdom Sūtra
    [Heart Sūtra]
    Prajñāpāramitāhṛdaya-sūtra

Hekiganroku 碧巖錄（碧巖録）Bìyán lù
    Blue Cliff Records (by Línjì)

Hōbōdankyō 法寶壇經（法宝壇経）Fǎbǎotánjīng
    Dharma-Treasure-Platform Sūtra (of the Sixth Patriarch)
    [I.e. of Liùzǔ dàshī 六祖大師 (the sixth patriarch), or Huìnéng (Enō)]
    [Short title: Dankyō 壇經 Tánjīng; Platform Sūtra]

Hōjisan 法事讚 Fǎshì zàn
    Hymns on the Religious Rite (by Shàndǎo/Zendō)

Hokekyō > Myōhōrengekyō

Honganjishōninden'e 本願寺聖人伝絵
    The Honganji Illustrated Scroll of the Shōnin's Life (by Kakunyo)
    [Godenshō 御伝鈔 is an abbreviated title]

Honganshō 本願鈔
    Exposition of the Original Vow (by Kakunyo)

Honjikyō 本事經 Běnshì jīng
    Sūtra on Foundational Matters
    [Approximately = Ariyapariyesana-sutta]

APPENDIX 1

Honjōmankyō 本生鬘經 Běnshēngmàn jīng
  [Approximately = Jātakamālā]

Hōonkōshiki 報恩講私記
  Thoughts on the Memorial Ceremony (by Kakunyo)

Hsüang-tsang's Travels to Western Lands > Saiikiki
Húayán jīng > Kegonkyō
Hymns of the Universe > Sanhokkaiju
Hymns of Dharmadhātu > Sanhokkaiju
Hymns on the Last Age > Shōzōmatsuwasan
Hymns on the Three Dharma-Ages > Shōzōmatsuwasan

Ibushūrinron 異部宗輪論 Yībù zōnglún lùn
  Treatise on the Wheel Following Various Schools (by Vasumitra)
  [Treatise on the Wheel of Buddhism as Interpreted by Various Schools]

Ichimaikishōmon 一枚起請文
  One-Sheet Document (by Hōnen)

Ichinentanenmon'i 一念多念文意
  The Meaning of Once-Calling and Many-Calling (by Shinran)

Ichinentanenshōmon 一念多念証文
  Notes on Once-Calling and Many-Calling (by Shinran)

Inscriptions > Songō shinzō meimon

Ippengoroku 一遍語録
  Ippen's Sermons

Ippenhijirie 一遍聖絵
  Pictures of the Wandering Priest Ippen (pictures by En'i)
  (=Ippenshōninerokujōengi)

Ippenshōninerokujōengi 一遍聖人絵六条縁起
  Pictorial Record of Ippen Shōnin in Six Sections (text by Jōkai, pictures by En'i)

Ippen's Sermons > Ippengoroku
Itokuki > Rennyoshōnin'itokuki
Jātakamālā > Honjōmankyō

Jihitsushō 自筆鈔
  Notes Penned by Oneself (by Shōkū)
  [Cf. Tahitsushō]

Jinenhōnishō 自然法爾章
  Clarification of *Jinenhōni* (by Shinran)

216

SYNOPTIC LIST OF TEXT TITLES

Jīngāng jīng > Kongōkyō

Jizōhonganbosatsukyō 地藏菩薩本願經 (地蔵菩薩本願経) Dìzàngpúsàběnyùan jīng
　　Sūtra on the Original Vow of the Bodhisattva Jizō
　　Kṣitigarbhapraṇidhāna-sūtra
　　[Abbreviation: Jizōhongankyō 地藏本願經 (地蔵本願経)]

Jōdoron 浄土論 Jìngtǔ lùn
　　Treatise on the Pure Land (by Vasubandhu)
　　[Discourse on the Pure Land]
　　[Commentary on the Amitāyus Sūtra]

Jōdoronchū 浄土論註 Jìngtǔlùn zhù
　　Commentary on the Treatise on the Pure Land (by Tánluán)
　　[The treatise itself is by Vasubandhu. Also called Ōjōronchū
　　往生論註 Wǎngshēnglùn zhù. Full name: 無量壽經優婆提舍願生偈註
　　Wúliàngshòu jīng yōupótíshè yùanshēng jìzhù]

Jōdoshinyōshō 浄土真要鈔
　　Comment on the Essentials of the Pure Land (by Zonkaku)

Jōdowasan 浄土和讃
　　Songs on the Pure Land (by Shinran)

Jōshūroku 趙州録 Zhàozhōulù
　　Sayings of Zhàozhōu

Jōyuishikiron 成唯識論 Chéngwéishí lùn
　　Treatise on Consciousness Only
　　[Vijñānamātrasiddhi-śāstra, no known Sanskrit text]

Jūjūbibasharon 十住毘婆沙論 Shízhù pípóshā lùn
　　Treatise on the Explanation of the Ten Stages
　　[Daśabhūmi(ka)vibhāṣā-śāstra, no known Sanskrit text]

Jūnimonron 十二門論 Shíèrmén lùn
　　Twelve Gate Treatise
　　[Dvādaśāmukha-śāstra, no known Sanskrit text]

Jutchikyōron 十地經論 Shídìjīng lùn
　　Discourse on the Sūtra of the Ten Stages
　　[Abbreviation: Jutchiron 十地論 Shídì lùn]

Jutchiron > Jutchikyōron

Kangyōhiketsushū 観経秘訣集

APPENDIX 1

Selections on the Key to the Meditation Sūtra (by Shōkū)

Kangyōsho > Kanmuryōjukyōsho

Kangyōshoshiki 観経疏私記
    Private Notes on the Commentary on the Meditation Sūtra (by Shōkū)
    [I.e. Shōkū's notes on Shàndǎo's commentary]

Kanmonyōgishō 観門要義鈔
    Notes on the Essential Meaning of the Gate of Visualization (by Shōkū)

Kanmuryōjukyō 觀無量壽經 (観無量寿経) Guānwúliàngshòu jīng
    The Sūtra on Visualising [the Buddha of] Immeasurable Life
    [The Meditation Sūtra]
    [The Sūtra of Meditation on Amida]
    [Amitāyurdhyāna-sūtra. N.B. no known Sanskrit text]

Kanmuryōjukyōsho 觀無量壽經疏 (観無量寿経疏) Guānwúliàngshòu jīngshù
    The Sūtra on Visualizing [the Buddha of] Immeasurable Life (by Shàndǎo/Zendō)
    [Commentary on the Meditation Sūtra]
    [Abbreviation: Kangyōsho]

Kannenbōmon 觀念法門 (観念法門) Guānniàn fǎmén
    The Dharma Gate of Visualization and Calling to Mind (by Shàndǎo/Zendō)
    [On the Ways of Meditating on Amida]

Kegonkyō 華嚴經 (華厳経) Húayán jīng
    Flower Garland Sūtra
    Avataṃsaka-sūtra

Kegongokyōshō 華嚴五教章 (華厳五教章) Húayán wǔjiàozhāng
    Chapters on the five teachings of Kegon (Húayán) (by Fǎzàng)
    [Full name Húayán yīshèng jiàoyì fēnqí zhāng 華嚴一乘教義分齊章]

Kegongokyōshōtsūroki 華嚴五教章通路記
    Sketch of the chapters on the five teachings of Kegon (by Gyōnen)
    [Abbreviated title: Tsūroki]

Kenjōdoshinjitsukyōgyōshōmonrui 顯浄土真実教行証文類
    Collection of Passages Revealing the True teaching, Practice and Enlightenment of the Pure Land (by Shinran)
    [Full title of Kyōgyōshinshō]

Kishinron > Daijōkishinron

Kōfukujisōjō 興福寺奏状

SYNOPTIC LIST OF TEXT TITLES

Document of Protest by Kōfukuji
[Submitted to the Imperial Court]

Kongōhōkaihiketsushō 金剛宝戒秘訣章
Chapter on the Secret of Diamond-Treasure Precepts (attributed to Hōnen)

Kongōkyō 金剛經 Jīngāng jīng
The Diamond Sūtra
Vajracchedikā-sūtra

Kongōshinron 金剛針論
[Diamond Needle Tract] (attributed to Aśvaghoṣa)

Konkōmyōkyō 金光明經 Jīnguāngmíng jīng
The Sūtra of Brilliant Golden Light
Suvarṇaprabhāsottama-sūtra
Suvarṇaprabhāsa-sūtra

Kōsōwasan 高僧和讃
Hymns on the Patriarchs (by Shinran)

Kṣitigarbhapraṇidhāna-sūtra > Jizōbosatsuhongankyō

Kudenshō 口伝鈔
Record of Oral Tranmission (by Kakunyo)

Kusharon 俱舍論 Jùshě lùn
Abhidharmakośa
Treatise on the Compendium [of the Abhidharma] (by Vasubandhu)

Kyakuhaimōki 却廃妄記
Notes to Avoid Falling into Oblivion (by Jakue-bō Chōen)

Kyōgyōshinshō 教行信証
Teaching, Practice, Faith and Enlightenment (by Shinran)
[Doctrine, Practice, Faith and Attainment]
[Doctrine–Work–Faith–Attainment]
[Teaching, Practice, Faith and Realizing of the Pure Land]
[For full title > Kenjōdoshinjitsukyōgyōshōmonrui]

Laṅkāvatāra-sūtra > Ryōgakyō
Larger Amitāyus > Daimuryōjukyō
Larger Sukhāvatīvyūha-sūtra > Daimuryōjukyō
Larger Sūtra > Daimuryōjukyō
Larger Sūtra on Amitābha > Daimuryōjukyō
Larger Sūtra of Infinite Life > Daimuryōjukyō
Larger Sūtra of Eternal Life > Daimuryōjukyō
Letters of Rennyo > Ofumi

Línjìlù > Rinzairoku
Lotus Sūtra > Myōhōrengekyō
Lotus of the Good Law > Myōhōrengekyō
Madhyamakakārikā > Chūron
Madhyamika-śāstra > Chūron

Madhyāntavibhāgakārikā

Madhyāntavibhāga

Mūlamadhyamakakārikā > Chūron
Mahālaṃkāra-sūtra > Daishōgonron

Mahāparinibbāna-sutta (P)
    The Sutta of the Great Decease
    [Cf. Daihatsunehangyō]

Mahāparinirvāṇa-sūtra > Daihatsunehangyō
Mahāprajñāpāramitā-śāstra > Daichidoron
Mahāprajñāpāramitā-śūtra > Daihannyakyō

Mahāprajñāpāramitā-upadeśa

Mahāvagga (P)

Mahāvastu

Mahāvibhāṣā-śāstra > Daibibasharon
Mahāyānābhisamaya-sūtra > Daijōdōshōkyō
Mahāyānasaṃgraha > Shōdaijōron

Mahāyānasūtrālaṃkāra

Maitreya Upaniṣad

Majjhima-nikāya (P)

Makashikan 摩訶止觀 (摩訶止観) Móhē zhǐguān
    The Great Calming and Contemplation (by Zhìyǐ)

Mandarachūki 曼荼羅注記
    Explanation of the Maṇḍala (by Shōkū)
    [N.B. referring to the Taimamandara]

Mattōshō 末灯鈔 (末燈鈔)
    Lamp for the Latter Ages (by Shinran)

Meditation on the Ground of Mind > Daijōhonjōshinjikangyō

Meditation Sūtra > Kanmuryōjukyō
Miàofǎ liánhuā jīng > Myōhōrengekyō

Milindapañha (P)
    Questions of King Milinda

Mukanshōsōki 夢感聖相記
    Record of Perceiving Holy Appearances in a Dream (ascribed to Hōnen)

Mūlamadhyamakakārikā > Chūron

Mumonkan 無門關（無門関）Wúménguān
    The Gateless Gate

Muryōjukyō > Daimuryōjukyō

Mushinron 無心論 Wúxīn lùn
    Treatise on No-mind (attributed to Bodhidharma)

Myōgishingyōshū 明義進行集
    Collection to Clarify the Meaning and Advance the Practice [of the Nenbutsu] (by Shinzui)

Myōhōrengekyō 妙法蓮華經 Miàofǎ liánhuā jīng
    The Sūtra of the Lotus Blossom of the Wonderful Dharma
    [The Lotus Sūtra, The Lotus of the Good Law]
    Saddharmapuṇḍarīka-sūtra
    [Hokekyō 法華経: widely used shorter name for the Lotus Sūtra]

Myōhōrengekyō-ubadaisha 妙法蓮華經優婆提舍 Miàofǎ liánhúa jīng yōpótíshè
    Exposition of the Lotus Sūtra (ascribed to Vasubandhu)
    Saddharmapuṇḍarīkasūtra-upadeśa

Myōkōninden 妙好人伝
    Biographies of Myōkōnin (compiled by Kōsei and Sōjun)
    [Published by Sōjun in five volumes, 1842–58]

Myōkōninden zokuhen 妙好人伝続編
    Further Biographies of Myōkōnin (compiled by Zō-ō)
    [Published by Zō-ō in 1850]

Nankaikikinaihōden 南海寄歸内法傳 Nánhǎi jìguī neìfǎ zhuàn
    Record of the Journey across the Southern Sea to Seek the Dharma (by Yìjìng)

Nehangyō > Daihatsunehangyō
Nirvana Sūtra > see Daihatsunehangyō
Notes Lamenting Differences > Tannishō

APPENDIX 1

Nyoingosho 女院御書
   Letters to the Cloistered Dowager (by Shōkū)

Nyūshutsunimonge 入出二門偈
   Gāthas on the Two Gates of Entering and Leaving the Pure Land (by Shinran)

Ofumi 御文
   Letters of Rennyo (by Rennyo)
   [Ofumi is the preferred title in the Ōtani-ha; see also Gobunshō]

Ōjōjōdoron 往生浄土論
   [=Jōdoron]

Ōjōraisan 往生禮讚 (往生礼讚) Wǎngshēng lǐzàn
   Hymns in Adoration of Rebirth (by Shàndǎo/Zendō)

Ōjōraisange 往生禮讚偈 (往生礼讚偈) Wǎngshēng lǐzàn jì
   Hymns in Adoration of Rebirth (by Shàndǎo/Zendō)
   [=Ōjōraisan]

Ōjōronchū 往生論註 Wǎngshēnglùn zhù
   Commentary on the Treatise on Rebirth (by Tánluán)
   [The treatise is by Vasubandhu. Also called Jōdoronchū 浄土論註. Full name: 無量壽經優婆提舍願生偈註 Wúliàngshòu jīng yōpótíshè yuànshēng jìzhù]

Ōjōyōshū 往生要集
   Teachings Essential for Rebirth (by Genshin)
   [A Collection of Essentials on Rebirth in the Pure Land]

Once Calling > Ichinentanenmon'i
Once-calling and Many-calling > Ichinentanenmon'i
One Sheet Document > Ichimaikishōmon
On the Ways of Meditating on Amida > Kannenbōmon
Platform Sūtra > Fǎbǎotánjīng
Prajñāpāramitāhṛdaya-sūtra > Hannyashingyō
Prajñāpāramitā-śāstra > Daichidoron
Prajñāpāramitā Sūtra > Hannyakyō
Pratyutpannasamādhi > Hanjuzanmaigyōdōōjōsan
Puṇḍarīka-sūtra > Myōhōrengekyō
Púsàjiè jīng > Bosatsukaikyō
Questions of King Milinda > Milindapañha

Rennyoshōningoichidaikikikigaki 蓮如上人御一代記聞書
   Sayings and Doings of the Great Life of Rennyo Shōnin (author unknown)
   [Record of Sayings from Rennyo's Life]

Rennyoshōningyōjōki 蓮如上人行状記
   A Record of the Activities of Rennyo Shōnin (compiled 1716)

Rennyoshōnin'itokuki 蓮如上人遺徳記
   Record of the Virtues Bequeathed by Rennyo Shōnin
   [Short title: Itokuki]

Rinzairoku 臨濟錄 (臨済録) Línjìlù
   Sayings of Línjì (Rinzai)

Rokujōengi > Ippenshōninerokujōengi

Ryōgakyō 楞伽經 Léngqié jīng
   The Laṅkāvatāra-sūtra

Ryōgonkyō > Shuryōgonkyō
Saddharmapuṇḍarīka-sūtra > Myōhōrengekyō

Saiikiki 西域記 Xīyùjì
   Record of Western Lands (by Xuánzàng)
   [Record of Travels to Western Lands]
   [Hsüang-tsang's Travels to Western Lands]
   [Full title (little used): Daitōsaiikiki 大唐西域記]

Saiyōshō 最要鈔
   Summary of the Essentials (by Kakunyo)

Sāmaññaphala-sutta (P)

Saṃdhinirmocana-sūtra

Saṃyukta-āgama

Saṁyutta-nikāya (P)

Sankashū 山家集
   Collections from a Mountain Retreat (by Saigyō)
   [N.B. also pronounced Sangashū]

Sanhokkaiju 讚法界頌 Zànfǎjiè sòng
   Hymns on the Realm of Dharma
   [Hymns on Dharmadhātu]
   [Hymns of the Universe]

Sanjōwasan 三帖和讚
   Threefold Wasan (by Shinran)

Sanmaihottokuki 三昧発得記
   Record of Receiving Revelation during Samādhi (ascribed to Hōnen)

Sanshinbonsan 三身梵讃　Sānshēn fànzàn
　　Sanskrit Hymns on the Triple Body

Senchakushū > Senjakuhongannenbutsushū
Senchakuhongannenbutsushū > > Senjakuhongannenbutsushū

Senjakuhongannenbutsushū 選択本願念仏集
　　Selected Passages on the Nenbutsu of the Original Vow (by Hōnen)
　　[Short form: Senjakushū, pronounced Senchakushū in Jōdo-shū contexts]

Senjakushū > Senjakuhongannenbutsushū

Senjakushūmitsuyōketsu 選択集密要決
　　Essential Commentary on the Senjakushū (by Shōkū)

Senjūshō 選集抄
　　Notes on Selected Essentials (probably by Saigyō)

Settled Mind and Determined Mind in Summary > Anjinketsujōshō
Shídì lùn > Jutchikyōron

Shijūhachigan'yōshakushō 四十八願要釈抄
　　Notes on the Forty-eight vows of Amida (by Shōkū)

Shikantaii 止觀大意 (止観大意)　Zhǐguān dàyì
　　The Essential Meaning of Meditation (by Zhànrán)

Shinjikangyō > Daijōhonjōshinjikangyō

Shinjinmei 信心銘　Xìnxīnmíng
　　Inscription on the Mind of Faith (attributed to Sēngcàn)

Shōdaijōron 攝大乘論 (摂大乗論) Shèdàshèng lùn
　　Treatise on the Essentials of the Great Vehicle
　　Mahāyānasaṃgraha (by Asaṅga)

Shōdaijōronshaku 攝大乘論釋 (摂大乗論釈) Shèdàshènglùn shì
　　Commentary on the Treatise on the Essentials of the Great Vehicle (by Vasubandhu)

Shōdōka 證道歌 (証道歌) Zhèngdàogē
　　Song on the Realization of the Way (by Yǒngjiā)

Shōgonki > Zaijarinshōgonki

Shōzōmatsuwasan 正像末和讃
　　Hymns on the Ages of Dharma (by Shinran)
　　[Hymns on the Three Periods after Buddha's Demise]

SYNOPTIC LIST OF TEXT TITLES

Shōshinge 正信偈
   Verses on True Faith (by Shinran)
   [Widely used abbreviation for Shōshinnenbutsuge]

Shōshingetaii 正信偈大意
   The Cardinal Meaning of [Shinran's] Verses on True Faith (by Rennyo)

Shōshinnembutsuge > Shōshinnenbutsuge

Shōshinnenbutsuge 正信念仏偈
   (by Shinran)
   Verses on True Faith in the Nenbutsu
   [See also Shōshinge]

Shugyōyōketsu 修行要決
   Essential Commentary on Practice (by Shōku)

Shūjishō 執持抄
   Steadfast Holding [to the Name] (by Kakunyo)

Shōzōmatsuwasan 正像末和讃
   Hymns on the Three Dharma-Ages (by Shinran)
   [Hymns on the Last Age]

Shuryōgonkyō 首楞嚴經 (首楞厳経) Shǒuléngyáng jīng
   Śūraṃgama Sūtra
   [Abbreviated title: Ryōgonkyō]

Smaller Sukhāvatīvyūha-sūtra > Amidakyō
Song of the Genuine Faith in Nembutsu > Shōshinnenbutsuge

Songōmeimon 尊号銘文
   Inscriptions for the Revered Name (by Shinran)
   [Abbreviation for Songōshinzōmeimon]

Songōshinzōmeimon 尊号真像銘文
   Inscriptions for the Revered Name and the Portraits (by Shinran)
   [Notes on the Inscriptions on Sacred Scrolls]
   [Inscriptions]

Śrīmālā > Śrīmālādevīsiṃhanāda-sūtra

Śrīmālādevīsiṃhanāda-sūtra

Sukhāvatīvyūha-sūtra > Daimuryōjukyō
Śūraṃgama-sūtra > Shuryōgonkyō
Sūtra of Bodhisattva Precepts > Bosatsukaikyō
Sūtra of Eternal Life > Daimuryōjukyō

APPENDIX 1

Sūtra of Meditation on Amida > Kanmuryōjukyō
Sūtra on Meditation on the Buddha of Eternal Life > Kanmuryōjukyō
Sūtra on the Meditation on Amitāyus > Kanmuryōjukyō
Sūtra of Meditation on Amida > Kanmuryōjukyō
Sūtra on the Great Infinite One > Daimuryōjukyō
Sūtra on the Land of Bliss > Daimuryōjukyō
Sūtra on Humanity > Daimuryōjukyō
Sūtra on Itineration > Yugyōkyō
Suvarṇaprabhāsa-sūtra > Konkōmyōkyō

Tahitsushō 他筆鈔
    Notes Penned by Another (by a disciple of Shōkū)
    [Cf. Jihitsushō]

Tánjīng > Hōbōdankyō

Tannishō 歎異抄
    Notes Lamenting Differences [Recording Sayings of Shinran] (by Yuien-bō)
    [Tract on Deploring Heterodoxies]

Theragātha (P)

Tract on Deploring Heterodoxies > Tannishō
Treatise on Being Born in the Pure Land > Jōdoron
Treatise on the Pure Land > Jōdoron
Treatise on the Explanation of the Ten Stages > Jūjūbibasharon
Treatise on the Sūtra of Buddha Realms > Butchikyōron
Treatise on the Wheel Following Various Schools > Ibushūrinron
Triṃśikā > Yuishikisanjūju
Tsūroki > Kegongokyōshōtsūroki
Vajracchedikā-sūtra > Kongōkyō
Vimalakīrti-nirdeśa > Yuimagyō
Vimalakīrti-sūtra > Yuimagyō

Vimansaka-sutta (P)

Vinaya-piṭaka (P)

Wagotōroku 和語灯録 (和語燈録)
    Records of the Light in the Japanese Language (by Hōnen)
    [Collected Sayings of Hōnen]
    [A Record of the Light]
    [Collection of Hōnen's Preachings]

Wasan 和讚
    Songs in Japanese
    [Sometimes short for Jōdowasan, but at the same time a generic term for the
        genre which also includes Kōsōwasan and Shōzōmatsuwasan by Shinran]
    [Psalms]

SYNOPTIC LIST OF TEXT TITLES

Wúménguān > Mumonkan
Xìnxīnmíng > Shinjinmei
Yogācārabhūmi > Yugashijiron

Yugashijiron 瑜伽師地論 Yúqié shīdì lùn
    Treatise on the Stages of the Yogācārins (by Asaṅga)
    Yogācārabhūmi

Yugyōkyō 遊行經 Yóuxíng jīng
    Sūtra on Itineration
    [= Mahāparinibbāna-sutta. The Sino-Japanese name refers to the later journeys of the Buddha]

Yuikyōgyō 遺教經 Yíjiào jīng
    Sūtra of the Last Sermons [of the Buddha]

Yuimagyō 維摩經 Wéimó jīng
    The Vimalakīrti Sūtra
    Vimalakīrti-nirdeśa
    [Short for Yuimakitsushosetsukyō]

Yuimakitsushosetsukyō 維摩詰所説經 Wéimójié sǔoshūo jīng
    The Sūtra of the Teaching of Vimalakīrti
    Vimalakīrtinirdeśa-sūtra
    (cf. Yuimagyō)

Yuishikinijūron 唯識二十論 Wéishí èrshílùn
    Twenty Theses on Consciousness Only (by Vasubandhu) Vijñaptimātratāsiddhi
    [Viṃśatikā, Vijñānamātra]
    [Concise Treatise on the Theory of Vijñaptimātratā]

Yuishikisanjūju 唯識三十頌 Wéishí sānshí sòng
    Thirty Verses on Consciousness Only (by Vasubandhu)
    [Triṃśikā Vijñaptimātratā, Vijñānamātra]
    [Triṃśikā Vijñaptimātratāsiddhi, when including the commentary by Sthiramati]
    [Concise Treatise on the Theory of Vijñaptimātratā]

Yuishinshōmon'i 唯信鈔文意
    Explanations of the Yuishinshō (by Shinran)
    Explanations of the Texts of the Commentary on Faith Only
    [Essentials of Faith Alone]
    [Essentials]

Yumenoki 夢之記
    Record of Dreams (by Myōe)

Yúqié shīdì lùn > Yugashijiron

Zaijarin 摧邪輪
    Tract Refuting Heresies (by Myōe)

Zaijarinshōgonki 摧邪輪荘厳記
    Elaboration of Tract Refuting Heresies (by Myōe)

Zhàozhōulù > Jōshūroku
Zhèngdàogē > Shōdōka

Zōagon(kyō) 雑阿含（經）Zá āhán (jīng)
    [Approximate equivalent to Pāli Saṁyutta-nikāya]

Zōitsuagon(kyō) 増一阿含（經）Zēngyī āhán (jīng)
    [Approximate equivalent to Pāli Anguttara-nikāya]

Appendix 2
Character List for Historical Persons

In the essays above there are references to leading Buddhist figures from different countries and periods, and the authors took their own decisions about the use of Indian, Chinese or Japanese forms of their names. Since numerous alternatives in the main text would have been a distraction, the list below may be used for cross-checking. Life dates are given (without guarantee) to assist verification of identity.

Japanese names may be recognized in that they have no alternative pronunciation: e.g. Saigyō 西行 (1118–90). Chinese names follow the pattern, Chinese/characters/Japanese pronunciation, e.g. Tánluán 曇鸞 Donran (476–542). Indian names follow the pattern, Indian/Chinese/characters/Japanese, e.g. Aśvaghoṣa: Mǎmíng 馬鳴 Memyō. Alternative names or titles for the same person are indicated with "also", e.g. Hōnen 法然 (1133–1212); also Genkū 源空 (etc.).

Cross-references are shown from the derivatives back to the original for the main entry:

Chinese to Indian, e.g. Mǎmíng > Aśvaghoṣa
Japanese to Indian, e.g. Memyō > Aśvaghoṣa
Japanese to Chinese, e.g. Zendō > Shàndǎo

Sino-Japanese characters shown in brackets are alternative forms for the same characters. These are *not* alternative names as such. Thus, for Japanese names, significantly different older forms may be given in brackets in case the student meets with them in older literature. Example: Kakunyo 覚如 (覺如).

For Chinese names, on the other hand, simplified forms of characters may be given in brackets in so far as they are used in Japan. Example: Línjì Yìxuán 臨濟義玄 Rinzai Gigen (臨済義玄).

Such alternative forms of characters are only listed in the case of major differences. In variations involving only one or two strokes the twentieth-century Japanese orthographic reforms are given preference. Minor variations are ignored even for Chinese names. For example, in the case of "Shàndǎo 善導 Zendō (613–81)" the character 導 was traditionally printed with the element 辶 in the top left corner, but this is not listed separately. Other examples of modern Japanese orthography are 徳 for 德 and 縁 for 緣. This policy arises because the base language for most of our authors was Japanese and in principle the postwar standard has been adopted here. Note, however, that although *pīnyīn* is the norm for the romanized transcription of Chinese, the modern orthography of mainland China (e.g. 导) is not used here.

Meaning of titles:

-bō 房:	monk
Daishi 大師:	Great Teacher
Kokushi 国師 (國師):	National Teacher
Risshi 律師:	Vinaya Master
Shōnin 上人 or 聖人:	Saint
Zenji 禅師 (禪師):	Zen Master

***

Ānàn/Anan > Ānanda
Ānanda: Ānàn 阿難 Anan
Asaṅga: Wúzhù 無著 (also 無着) Mujaku (fourth–fifth century CE)
Aśvaghoṣa: Mǎmíng 馬鳴 Memyō (first century CE)

Bǎizhàng Huáihǎi 百丈懷海 Hyakujō Ekai (749–814)
Bodhidharma: Pútídámó 菩提達磨 Bodaidaruma (+528); also popularly in Japan as Daruma)

Chisha Daishi > Zhìyǐ
Chishin > Ippen

Daiju > Dàzhū Huìhǎi
Daruma: popular name in Japan for Bodhidharma (Bodaidaruma)
Dàzhū > Dàzhū Huìhǎi
Dàzhū Huìhǎi 大珠慧海 Daiju Ekai (+831)
Dengyō Daishi > Saichō
Déshān Xuānjiàn 德山宣鑑 Tokusan Senkan (782–865)
Déshān Yuánmì 德山緣密 Tokusan Enmitsu (tenth century)

Dōgen 道元 (1200–53)
Donran > Tánluán

Engo > Yuánwù Kèqín

CHARACTER LIST FOR HISTORICAL PERSONS

Engo Kokugon > Yuánwù Kèqín
Enkū 円空 (圓空) (1632–95)
Enō > Huìnéng
Enshō Daishi > Ippen
Eshin > Genshin

Fǎzàng 法藏 Hōzō (643–712)

Genjō > Xuánzàng
Genkū > Hōnen
Genshin 源信 (942–1071); also Eshin 恵心(惠心)
Gijō > Yìjìng
Goso Hōen > Wǔzǔ Fǎyǎn

Hakuin > Hakuin Ekaku
Hakuin Ekaku 白隠慧鶴 (1686–1768)
Hánshān 寒山 Kanzan (eighth century CE)
Hézé Shénhuì 荷澤神會 Kataku Jinne (荷沢神会) (+758)
Hōnen 法然 (1133–1212); also Hōnen Shōnin 法然上人, Genkū 源空, Seishimaru 勢至丸 (as child)
Hōnen Shōnin > Hōnen
Hōzō > Fǎzàng
Huángpò = Huángpò Xīyùn
Huángpò Xīyùn 黄檗希運 Ōbaku Kiun (+850)
Huìnéng 慧能 Enō (638–713)
Hyakujō > Bǎizhàng Huáihǎi
Hyakujō Ekai > Bǎizhàng Huáihǎi

Ippen 一遍 (1239–89); also Chishin 智真 (智眞), Ippen Shōnin 一遍上人, Enshō Daishi 円証大師 (圓證大師), Yugyō Shōnin 遊行上人 (this is also a general term for a wandering saint)

Jiácái 迦才 (c.620–80)
Jiāxiáng 嘉祥 Kajō/Kashō (嘉祥) (posthumous name for Jízàng)
Jinne > Hézé Shénhuì
Jittoku > Shídí
Jízàng 吉藏 Kichizō (549–623); also Jiāxiáng 嘉祥(嘉祥)
Jōshū > Zhàozhōu Cóngshěn

Kakunyo 覚如 (覺如) (1270–1351); also Kakunyo Shōnin 覚如上人
Kanchi Kokushi > Shōkū
Kanmu Tennō 桓武天皇 Emperor Kanmu (r. 781–806)
Kataku Jinne > Hézé Shénhuì
Kichizō > Jízàng
Kōbō Daishi > Kūkai
Kūkai 空海 (774–835); also Kōbō Daishi 弘法大師

APPENDIX 2

Línjì Yìxuán 臨濟義玄 Rinzai Gigen (臨済義玄) (+867)
Lóngshù > Nāgārjuna

Mǎmíng > Aśvaghoṣa
Mǎzǔ > Mǎzǔ Daòyī
Mǎzǔ Daòyī 馬祖道一 Baso Dōitsu (馬祖道一) (707–86)
Memyō > Aśvaghoṣa
Mokujiki 木喰 (1718–1810)
Mujaku > Asaṅga
Mumon > Wúmén Huìkāi

Nāgārjuna: Lóngshù 龍樹（竜樹）Ryūju (second–third century CE)
Nichiren 日蓮 (1222–82); also Nichiren Shōnin 日蓮聖人

Rennyo 蓮如 (1415–99); also Rennyo Shōnin 蓮如上人
Rinzai > Línjì Yìxuán
Ryūju > Nāgārjuna

Saichō 最澄 (767–822); also Dengyō Daishi 伝教大師 (傳教大師)
Saigyō 西行 (1118–90)
Śākyamuni (the historical Buddha)
Seishimaru > Hōnen
Sēngcàn 僧璨 Sōsan (+606)
Seshin > Vasubandhu
Setchō Jūken > Xuědoù Chóngxián
Shàndǎo 善導 Zendō (613–81)
Shénhuì > Hézé Shénhuì
Shídí 拾得 Jittoku (eighth–ninth century CE)
Shidō Bunan (Zenji) 至道無難 (禅師) (1603–76)
Shinran 親鸞 (1173–1262); also Shinran Shōnin 親鸞聖人
Shinzui 信瑞 (+1279); also Kyōsai-bō Shinzui 敬西房信瑞
Shìqīn > Vasubandhu
Shōkū 証空 (證空) (1177–1247); also Zenne-bō Shōkū 善慧房証空, Kanchi Kokushi 鑑智国師
Shūbun 周文 (fifteenth century CE); also Tenshō Shūbun 天章周文

Tánluán 曇鸞 Donran (476–542)
Tendai Daishi > Zhìyǐ
Tenshō Shūbun > Shūbun 周文
Tiāntái Dàshī > Zhìyǐ
Tokusan Enmitsu > Déshān Yuánmì
Tokusan Senkan > Déshān Xuānjiàn

Unmon > Yúnmén

Vasubandhu: Shìqīn 世親 Seshin (fourth–fifth century CE)

CHARACTER LIST FOR HISTORICAL PERSONS

Wúmén > Wúmén Huìkāi
Wúmén Huìkāi 無門慧開 Mumon Ekai (1185–1260)
Wúzhù > Asaṅga
Wǔzǔ Fǎyǎn 五祖法演（五祖法演）Goso Hōen (+1104)

Xuědoù Chóngxián 雪竇重顯 Setchō Jūken (980–1052)
Xuánzàng 玄奘 Genjō (602–64)

Yìjìng 義淨（義浄）Gijō (635–713)
Yōka Genkaku > Yǒngjiā Xuánjué
Yōmei Enju > Yǒngmíng Yánshoù
Yǒngjiā Xuánjué 永嘉玄覺（玄覚）Yōka Genkaku (665–713)
Yǒngjiā dàshī 永嘉大師 Yōka Taishi (665–713); also Yǒngjiā Xuánjué
Yuánwù Kèqín 圜悟克勤 Engo Kokugon (1063 – 1135)
Yugyō Shōnin > Ippen
Yúnmén 雲門 Unmon (+966)

Zendō > Shàndǎo
Zhàozhōu > Zhàozhōu Cóngshěn
Zhàozhōu Cóngshěn 趙州從諗（趙州従諗）Jōshū Jūshin (778–897); also Zhàozhōu Zhēnjì 趙州眞際 Jōshū Shinsai (趙州真際)
Zhìyǐ 智顗 Chigi (538–97); also Zhìzhě dáshī 智者大師 Chisha Daishi, Tiāntái dàshī 天臺大師 Tendai Daishi (天台大師)
Zonkaku 存覚（存覺）(1290–1373)

Appendix 3
Original Publication Details

If the title of the article has been edited for the present volume, the original title is given immediately below the other publication details.

Abe, Masao: Zen and Compassion
 The Eastern Buddhist 2.1 (1967), 54–68

Bandō, Shōjun: D.T. Suzuki and Pure Land Buddhism
 The Eastern Buddhist New Series 14.2 (1981), 132–6

Conze, Edward: A Personal Tribute
 The Eastern Buddhist New Series 2.1 (1967), 84–5
 (In Memoriam Daisetz Teitarō Suzuki 1870–1966)

Fromm, Erich: Memories of Dr. D.T. Suzuki
 The Eastern Buddhist New Series 2.1 (1967), 86–9
 (In Memoriam Daisetz Teitarō Suzuki 1870–1966)

Heidegger, Martin: Home: The Seven-Hundredth Anniversary of the Town of Messkirch
 The Eastern Buddhist New Series 1 (1966), 59–67
 Original title: Two Essays by Martin Heidegger; Part I. Ansprache zum Heimatabend, am 22, 7, 1961, anläßlich des 700-jährigen Jubiläums der Stadt Meßkirch. Cf. Nishitani Keiji: Introducing Martin Heidegger

Hisamatsu, Shin'ichi: Zen: Its Meaning for Modern Civilization
 The Eastern Buddhist New Series 1.1 (1965), 22–47
 (Part 2) *The Eastern Buddhist* New Series 31.2 (1998), 209–18

Kaneko, Daiei: The Concept of the Pure Land
 The Eastern Buddhist New Series 28.1 (1995), 127–38
 (Japanese original, 1925; cf. annotation)

Kiba, Ryōhon: Buddhism and Moral World Order
 The Eastern Buddhist 3 (1924), 206–12

Kobori, Sōhaku The Enlightened Thought
The Eastern Buddhist New Series 2.1 (1967), 99–109
(In Memoriam Daisetz Teitarō Suzuki 1870–1966)

Kondō, Akihisa: The Stone Bridge of Jōshū
The Eastern Buddhist New Series 2.1 (1967), 90–98
(In Memoriam Daisetz Teitarō Suzuki 1870–1966)

Nishitani, Keiji: The Awakening of Self in Buddhism
The Eastern Buddhist New Series 1.2 (1966), 1–11
(N.B. also in F. Franck [ed.) *The Buddha Eye. An Anthology of the Kyoto School* [New York: Crossroad, 1982])

Nishitani, Keiji: Introducing Martin Heidegger
The Eastern Buddhist New Series 1.1 (1966), 48–59
Original title: Two Essays by Martin Heidegger (introduction)

Otto, Rudolf: On Zen Buddhism
The Eastern Buddhist 3.2 (1924), 117–25
Original title: Professor Rudolf Otto on Zen Buddhism

Petzold, Bruno: Dengyō Daishi and German Theology
The Eastern Buddhist 2.6 (1923), 348–57

Pratt, James Bissett: The Unity of Buddhism
The Eastern Buddhist 4.2 (1927), 122–44

Soga, Ryōjin: Shinran's Concept of Buddhist History
The Eastern Buddhist New Series 28.1 (1995), 139–54
(Japanese original, 1935; cf. annotation)

Ueda Yoshifumi: Zen and Philology: On Ui Hakuju and Suzuki Daisetsu
The Eastern Buddhist New Series 13.2 (1985), 114–30
(Japanese original, 1982; cf. annotation)

Watts, Alan: The "Mind-less" Scholar
The Eastern Buddhist New Series 2.1 (1967), 124–7
(In Memoriam Daisetz Teitarō Suzuki 1870–1966)

Yanagi, Sōetsu: The Pure Land of Beauty
The Eastern Buddhist New Series 9.1 (1976), 18–41
(Japanese original, 1962; cf. annotation)

Appendix 4

A Note on The Eastern Buddhist

In 1921 a group of leading Buddhists in Kyōto founded the Eastern Buddhist Society in order to propagate the spirit of Buddhism in the modern world.[1] The leaders of this group were Suzuki Daisetsu (D.T. Suzuki), Sasaki Gesshō, Akanuma Chizen and Yamabe Shūgaku. Suzuki's wife Beatrice Lane Suzuki and Yokogawa Kenshō also played a significant role. These writers were variously interested in Zen Buddhism and Shin Buddhism, and in the relations between these two and earlier forms of Buddhism. They were also concerned with the question of how best to express Buddhist teaching in a world which was becoming increasingly internationalized. The well-known journal *The Eastern Buddhist* was also founded in 1921, being edited in the first instance by Suzuki Daisetsu and Beatrice Lane Suzuki. In the Foreword to the first issue of the journal, Suzuki wrote as follows: "The Society has for its objects the study of Buddhism, the publication of the result of such study, and the propagation of the true spirit of Buddhism." These objectives have found ample expression in the pages of the journal over some ninety years so far. In their fulfilment, the journal carries articles on all aspects of Buddhism as well as English translations of classical texts and writings by modern Buddhist thinkers.

While the society became most widely known for *The Eastern Buddhist* it has also encouraged many other projects such as the translation of Buddhist texts and the arrangement of seminars and lectures. Its main office is housed in Ōtani University, Kyōto, and its researchers benefit from the fine library holdings which are easily accessible there. There is also a close connection with the Higashi Honganji and the leading branch of Shin Buddhism (Ōtani-ha) which is based there. At the same time the approaches of both the society and

---

1. This note was first published in the first volume of this series. However, some errors have been corrected relating to the launch of the New Series in the mid-1960s.

of the journal have always been open to, and widely appreciative of, various aspects of the Buddhist tradition. It is well known that Suzuki Daisetsu himself was devoted to the Zen tradition, while the traditions and texts of other branches of Mahāyāna Buddhism have frequently been presented as well.

The publication of the journal was interrupted by the Second World War. It was picked up again in 1949, under the editorship of Suzuki Daisetsu and Sugihira Shizutoshi, but the difficulties of the times led to irregularity of appearance and a new pause in 1958. *The Eastern Buddhist* was relaunched as a "New Series" in 1965, vol. 1.1 appearing in September of that year and 1.2 one year later in September 1966. Shortly before the second issue appeared however, on 12 July 1966, Suzuki Daisetsu had passed away aged 96. Volume 2.1 was therefore designed as a memorial issue to him and appeared in 1967. The general editorship then passed through various hands, notably those of Nishitani Keiji (1900–90), Abe Masao (1915–2006) and Nagao Gajin (1907–2005). Indeed, quite apart from the editorship, writings by some of the best-known names in modern Japanese Buddhist thought may be found in its pages. Increasingly, non-Japanese advisors with excellent reputations in Indian, Japanese and Buddhist studies played supporting roles.

While there has often been a strong interest in Zen, matching the expectations of an international public at particular periods, the presentation of Shin Buddhism has also been actively pursued in the journal. Moreover, Japanese contributors have increasingly been joined by foreigners who have offered translations of texts as well as matters for discussion. If we consider the overall trajectory over many years, it may be said that the balance has shifted from the straightforward presentation of substance in the early years to an emphasis on interaction and dialogue later on. This movement is reflected and celebrated in volumes 1 to 3 of the present series of collected papers. At the same time, the original objectives of the Eastern Buddhist Society have by no means been forgotten, and the overall approach, integrating Buddhist scholarship and thought, is continued by the present editors under the leadership of Yasutomi Shin'ya.

The Eastern Buddhist now looks back on a history of nearly a century and with some interruptions has flourished in an excellent manner. The publication of selections in Eastern Buddhist Voices is a collaborative project designed to celebrate the 90th anniversary of the foundation of the Eastern Buddhist Society. Congratulations!

INDEX

Since they can easily be searched in their own right, the contents pages, the conventions on names, title and scripts, the synoptic list of text titles, the character list for historical persons and the details of original publication are excluded from this index.

Abe, Masao 3–4, 109, 237
ābhāsa 153
abhāva 155
abiding 71, 106, 198
aborigines 85
Abraham a Santa Clara 3, 91, 97, 99–100
absolute 4, 12–13, 15–16, 26–7, 34, 38, 41–3, 64, 67–8, 84–5, 98–9, 104, 142, 191
  compassion 185
  nothingness 156
  subjectivity 113–15
abstract 56, 73–4, 76, 111–12, 186
abstraction/s 73–4, 113
accommodation 44
Aciravatā 84
acitta 155
adaptation 44–7, 50, 173, 183
adoration 33
adults 147, 196
aesthetic 6, 140, 184
  aesthetics 7, 80–81, 192
agapē 87
aggregates 162
aggressiveness 39–40
agriculture 29, 103
ahiṃsā 39–40, 167
Akanuma Chizen 236
Akao 166
Akṣobhya (Buddha/Tathāgata) 51
alienation 106, 108, 128, 133
  alienated 77–8, 128, 133, 139

allegory 13, 96
alms 74, 88
altar 139
alumni 91
ambiguity 20
ambivalence 136
America 5, 76
American/s 34, 87, 143
Amida 24, 120, 167, 174
  Buddha 5, 7, 14, 17, 51, 67, 70, 96, 168–9
Amidakyō 13–14
Amitābha 58
Amitāyus 13–14
Amitayussutropadesa 13
Ānanda 165
anatta 38
ancestors 56–7, 85, 176
angel 28, 41
anger 86
animals 39, 74, 85, 120, 135
annihilation 25, 33
anniversary 24, 91, 102
Ansprache 91, 102
antagonist 13
anthropocentric 79
anthropology 151
anthropomorphic 34
antithesis 191, 200
antithetical 34
antonym 191–2
anxiety 11, 38, 126, 130–31, 198

239

INDEX

aporia 93
appropriate 28, 36, 64, 72, 77–8, 166
apsara 142
arable 29
arch 89
Archbishop Gröber 107
architecture 76
Arhat 33, 37, 67
arising 51, 69, 151
aristocracy 6, 89, 190, 199
artefacts 193
arts 6, 58, 93, 186
Aryan 85
Asahara Saichi 166
Asaṅga 157, 160
ascetics 84
Ashikaga 6
assistance 130
Association of Religious Humanity 2, 11–12, 17
astronomy 25
Asura 169
Aśvaghoṣa 85–6, 88, 127
atheism 25, 43, 90, 169
ātmaka 156
ātman 26
atom/ic 35, 83, 104
attachment/s 84, 89, 95, 119, 130, 179, 195–7
attainment/s 33, 37, 56, 133, 169
　of Buddhahood 63, 65, 75
　of Enlightenment 125–6
　of Nirvana 70
　of Repose 96
　of transcendental/supreme wisdom 138
Augustine 25
authentic 2, 64, 84, 96, 107, 169
　authenticity 85
authority 32, 34, 64, 67, 71, 89, 139, 146
autobiographical 5, 149
Avalokiteśvara 162
Avataṃsaka
　Samādhi 59
　School 64
　Sūtra 58–9, 64, 74
　teaching 79
avijñapti 157
awakened 71–2, 75, 80–81, 95–6, 135–6, 138, 178, 185
　awakened one/s 65, 71, 96, 133
　self-awakened 72, 79
awakening 3, 49, 53, 58, 63, 65–6, 71–5, 80–82, 84–5, 96, 103, 125–19, 131, 135–8, 196
　Awakening of Faith 5, 127, 158, 207
　awakening to self 173–6, 179, 181–2
　self-awakening 73, 75, 79

awareness 71, 112, 116
　self-awareness 152

Báiyǘn Shǒuduān 140
Bǎizhàng Huáihǎi 17, 130
Bandō Shōjun 5, 90, 165
Baroque 99
baskets, three 51
Baso Dōitsu 68, 111
beasts, realm of 85
beauty 6–7, 20, 50, 76–7, 107, 183–8, 190–99, 201
　formless beauty 80–81
　Heaven of Beauty 7, 190–99
　Pure Land of Beauty 7, 190–99
begging 21, 74
　begging bowl 88–9
being (various senses) 19–20, 25, 53, 56, 65, 67, 72–4, 78, 82, 84–7, 98, 99–100, 108, 114, 126, 127–31, 134, 136–9, 180, 182, 196
beings (human, sentient) 14–15, 19, 35, 40, 44, 53–6, 65, 68, 70, 85, 89, 97–8, 118, 120–21, 126, 134–5, 137–40, 162, 165, 167, 169, 181–2, 194, 196, 200, 204
belief/s 4, 27, 33, 34, 37, 39, 41, 43–6, 51, 54, 114, 129, 174, 176, 180
believer/s 28, 34, 37, 51
bell 23, 71
Benedict 18
Benedictines 18
Berdyaev, Nikolai 83
Berlin 11
bhāvanā 162
Bible 25, 64
　biblical 114
birth/s 14, 48, 51, 68, 73
　birth and death 50, 73, 95
　desire for 175–7, 181
　rebirth 70, 126, 129, 131
Bìyán lù 74, 135
blessing/s 47, 167, 192, 202
blind/ed 12, 22, 69, 128
bliss/ful 14–15, 20–21, 138, 152
　Eternal Bliss 31
　Land of Bliss 14, 51, 174
blood 69, 85–6, 98
Blum, Mark 7
Blyth, R. H. 130
Bodensee 91
bodhi 67–8
　Supreme Bodhi 14
Bodhidharma 17–18, 21, 63, 65, 68, 73, 111, 154
bodhisattva/s 13–14, 27–8, 32–3, 37, 40, 45, 57–8, 126, 138, 149, 153, 156, 160–63, 168–9

240

INDEX

body 35, 75, 80, 85, 97–8, 130, 139–40, 184–5, 199
  bodies 97–8
  body/bodies of a Buddha 69, 70–71, 169
  body of believers 34
  body of emptiness/nothingness 70, 98
  Dharma-body 169
  recompense body 70–71
  response body 70–71
  transformation body 70–71
Böhme, Jakob 21, 25–6
bondage 69, 84, 126, 197–8, 204
  Buddha-bondage 69
  Dharma-bondage 69
bones 97–8
Bonhoeffer, Dietrich 94
Bonmō Sūtra, Bonmōkyō 28, 30
Bosatsu, bosatsu 28, 40
Boston 130
bourgeois 89
bowl 117, 205
  alms-bowl 88
  begging owl 88–9
  rice-bowl 190
  tea-bowl 190, 205
Brahmajāla Sūtra 28
Brahmanism 84–5
Brahmans 84–5
Brahman-nirvana 20
Brahmin/s 85–6, 88–9
Britain 149
British 183
  British Museum 149
brotherhood 84
brothers and sisters 38, 181
brushwork 187
Bùdài 20
Buddha 2, 5, 7, 12–23, 25, 27, 33–4, 40–41, 49–56, 58–9, 65–73, 80, 84, 88–9, 95–6, 98, 120, 128–9, 131, 136, 138, 140, 149–52, 154, 165, 168–9, 173–82, 185, 192, 196–8
  Buddha's existence 179–80
  Buddha fields 149
  Buddha-heart 18, 25
  Buddhahood 15, 27, 53, 55, 63, 65, 75
  Buddha-images 22, 80
  Buddha-mārga 49–50, 53, 51–9
  Buddha-mind 65, 154, 198
  Buddha-nature 27, 71–2, 98, 128–9, 131, 178, 196–7
  Buddha-sphere 20
  Gautama Buddha 12–13
  Self-Buddha 68
  Supreme Buddha 70
  True-Buddha/true Buddha 68, 70–72, 79–80
  see also Amida Buddha, Gautama Buddha, etc.
buddhas/Buddhas 19, 23, 32–3, 37, 40, 44, 47, 54–7, 58, 68–70, 174, 178
Buddhism/Buddhist passim
bukkyō 47, 118, 151, 160
bukkyōgaku 151
Bürgermeister 107
Burma 32
busshō 27
Busshōron 178
butsu/s 40

Cakravarti-rāja 88
cakravarti 88
calling in life 104, 196
Caṇḍālas 88
Candrakīrti 152
canonical writings 12, 32, 55
canon/s
  Brahmanical 85
  Buddhist 55–6, 207
  Chinese 207, 209
  Mahāyāna 175
  Theravāda 58, 207
capitalism 83, 89
caste/s 84–6, 88–9
categories 56, 72, 100
category 20, 108, 204
caterpillar 59
cathartic fire 96
Catholic 34, 97
Catholicism 24
catholicity 44
causal
  chain, links 12
  path 53
causation 12–13, 58
cause/s (in Buddhist thought) 11–12, 15, 50, 73, 155–6, 179–80, 194–5, 199–200
cave 136
cavern 21
celestial eye 19
celibacy 30
cemetery 106
centennial 3, 102, 104
ceramics 6
ceremonial
  law 29
  meals 80
ceremony/ies 17, 30, 48
  tea 6
Ceylon 37
chain, causal 12
change (thought) 35–6, 45, 103–7
Chaos 132, 135
characteristics 3, 42

241

INDEX

five 86
kingly 88-9
of Buddhism 35-7
of free beauty 199
of modern art 76
charismatic 150
charitable institutions 42
charity (of a Bodhisattva) 14
Chassid/ic 146
Chéngwéshí lùn 157
child/ren 58, 77, 89, 147, 165, 168-9, 173, 187, 194, 196-7, 231
  childhood 147
  childlike 144, 147, 188
  of God 31
  Suzuki as a child 165
China 32-4, 40, 45, 50, 63-4, 111, 127, 157, 165, 187
Chinese 17, 20, 24-7, 29-30, 32-3, 40, 65, 67, 73, 109, 111, 127, 130, 137, 143, 153, 160, 187, 196, 199
  Buddhism 17, 29, 33, 73, 75
  Pure Land 165
  Taoism 142
  Tiāntái/Tendai 2, 24-5, 30
  Zen 65, 67, 78, 98
Chisha Daishi 25, 30
Chóngxián 137
Christ 25, 27-8, 34, 119
Christendom 42
Christian/s 24-7, 33-4, 37, 40-42, 45-6, 97, 99, 103, 114, 166
  missions 44, 46
  mysticism 25-7, 166
  theology 1, 3, 24, 34
Christianity 2, 4, 25, 34-6, 40-42, 46, 64, 67, 82, 87, 90, 92-3, 96, 101, 114, 169, 185
chronology (of Kojiki) 58
Chuang-Tze (Zhuāngzǐ) 132
church/es 25, 34, 40, 76, 103
Chūron 26
citta 153
cittadharmatā 154
Cízhōu 187
cleric 40
  clerical gown 71
clinging ego 199
cogitation 135
cognition 71
Columbia University 146
commandments
  Buddhist 30
  of God 30
Communism 83
community 52, 167
  Buddhist 84

moral 28, 138
comparison 5, 36, 91, 114
compassion 4, 14-15, 86, 109, 119-20, 126, 131, 136-9, 142, 166-8, 174
  Absolute Compassion 185
  Compassionate Heart 185
  Great Compassion 119-20, 137, 139, 166, 168
conceit 89, 126, 143
concept 5, 47-55, 80, 85, 89, 96, 130, 152, 160, 169, 173-4, 175-84, 186, 192, 197, 201
concepts 18, 92, 98, 152, 160
conception 21, 25, 28, 34, 41, 44-5, 138
conceptual 22, 111, 132
conceptualism 114
conceptualized 161, 163
concrete 55, 74, 112-13, 115, 117, 126, 186
concretely 56
concreteness 74, 112, 115
conditioned 81, 130
conditions 12, 41-2, 45-6, 115-16, 155-6, 201
conduct 12, 17, 19, 29, 37, 86, 131
confession 175-6
Confucian/ist 82, 166
Confucius 40
congregation (Buddhist) 29, 57, 174
conqueror 96
consciousness 3, 6, 11-12, 22, 40, 43, 75, 80-81, 86, 112-13, 116-17, 127-8, 135-6, 140, 162, 168-9
Constance 107
construct 70, 133, 184
construction 73, 199
contemplation 25, 30, 71, 86, 162
contemplative practice 162
contingency 53
contradiction 97, 100, 163
  self-contradiction 154, 157, 159-61
contrivance/s 77, 97, 126, 188, 197
convenience 194
conventional 51, 64, 7, 88, 178, 188, 190
conversion 13, 29
converts 13, 96
Conze, Edward 5, 89, 149, 162
Coptic weaving 192
copying of sūtras 73
corpses 98
cosmic 12, 113, 115-16, 128-30, 134-8, 140
council
  of church 34
  of USSR 83
crafts 186
craftsman 196
craving 86

242

created 78–9, 87, 185
creation 43, 81, 114–15, 132
creative 18, 64, 78, 99, 113, 116, 133, 139, 190–91
creativity 7
creator 43, 139, 185
creature/s 19, 26–8, 85, 120
credal 35, 46
  credal bonds 44
creed/s 11, 34–5, 44, 46, 92
crematorium 140
critical 6, 87, 128, 143
Cuernavaca 145–6
cult 11, 34, 44–6, 77
  of tea 6, 199
culture 6–7, 11, 38, 43, 86, 94, 113–14, 126–7, 130, 133, 160, 196
cypress tree 74

Daichidoron 26
Daie 198
daijō bukkyō (Mahāyāna Buddhism) 151
Daijōkishinron 5
Daiju 65
Daishi 2, 24–31
Daoist 33, 45
dàorén 111
Daòyī 111
dàshī 115
Dàxióng, Mount 130
Dàzhìdù lùn 27
Dàzhū 65
death 24, 28, 33, 43, 50, 59, 69, 95, 97, 99, 119, 128–31, 150
deities (Daoist, Shintō) 33, 45
deliverance 96, 167, 185
delusion/s 13, 56, 138, 167, 179
DeMartino, Richard 81, 130
demon 18
demythologization 6
Dengyō Daishi 2, 24–31
denpō 28–9
Denshinhōyō 68
deśanā 152
deśayāmāsa 152
Déshān 115, 118
desire/s 38, 40, 51–2, 76, 131, 138, 146, 196, 199, 204
  for Birth 174–7, 182
  for the Pure Land 175, 181–2, 196, 204
Deutsch (*Theologia*) 24
deva 27
Devadatta 13
device/s 119, 173
devil/s 136, 199
devotees (of the Nenbutsu) 165, 167, 205
devotion 14–16, 165–6

Dharma 45, 48, 50, 53, 68, 70, 72, 74, 89, 112–13, 115–16, 152, 168–9
dharma/s 65–6, 68–9, 72, 84, 140, 151–2, 155–6, 158, 160, 162–3
Dharmākara 58
dharmakāya/Dharmakāya 70, 169
Dharmapāla 157
dharmatā 156
dhyāna 14, 17, 30, 86, 111
dialectic 37, 200
dialectical 27, 75
dialectics 92
dialects 77
dialogue 1, 7, 75, 92, 135, 237
Diamond Needle Tract 85, 88
Dìng shàngzuò 136
disciple/s 20–23, 28, 30, 37, 51, 84, 95, 136
discipline/s 140, 151
discrimination 130, 137, 152–3, 155–9, 163, 186, 188, 196, 199–200
discriminative 113, 152, 154–7, 159, 163
disease 77, 79, 131
divine 25, 30
doctor 131
doctrine 12–13, 18, 27–8, 38, 43–5, 82, 84, 129, 150, 162
doctrines 19, 25, 34, 44
Dōgen 48
dogma 19, 21, 25, 92–4, 9
dogmatics 92–4, 96
dogmatism 65
Dōitsu 111
dokuzadaiyūhō 130
dōnin 111
Donran 15
Dōshū 166
doubt 50–51, 54, 58–9, 137, 139, 168, 177, 184, 188, 190, 197
Dravidians 85
dream 57, 127, 186, 192
dreamers 147
dualism 4, 114, 185, 196, 199–200
dualistic 73, 114, 158, 168, 185–6, 191, 199, 200
duality 67, 69, 74, 98, 114–15, 121, 155, 157, 167, 169, 180, 184, 191, 191, 199–200
  non-duality 67, 74, 155, 157, 160, 163, 167, 169, 184, 191, 199
Dumoulin, Heinrich 114

earthenware 69
East 2, 39–40, 42, 91–4, 96, 101, 110, 121, 126–7, 129–30, 133–4, 192, 200
  East Asia 2, 127
Eastern 1, 3–4, 6–7, 11, 17, 42, 63, 91, 101, 114, 133, 135, 149, 166, 175, 183, 236–7

243

INDEX

Eastern Buddhist Society 6, 236–7
Eckhart (Master, Meister) 24, 129
economics 89
ecstasy 25
education 103, 127, 196
effects 20–21
effortlessness 198
Egidio, Saint 20
egoism 13
egos 137
eight noes 26
Eightfold Path 3, 33, 38, 142
eighth 231–2
eighty thousand 50
Einstein 134
Ekai 17, 130
Ekayāna 56
elders 166
emancipation 18–19, 68–9, 74, 78–80, 84, 94–5
embodiment 38, 40, 64, 98, 166, 170
emperor 24, 57–8, 73
empirical 53, 55–6, 59
emptiness 70, 72–6, 78, 97–8, 114–16, 129, 152, 155–6, 158, 160–64
empty 73–4, 106, 153–6, 160, 162–3
enamel 190–91
encounter of religions, cultures 2, 92–4, 101
encounter/ing a Buddha, a person 22, 58, 67–8, 94, 130
England 34
English 3, 7, 17, 34, 37, 91, 102, 109, 113, 127, 131, 140, 142, 158, 183
Englishman 150
Engo, Kokugon 22, 136
Enlightened 132, 235
enlightened 33, 44, 89, 120, 126, 129, 133–6, 138–9, 146, 151–2
enlightenment 4, 13–14, 21, 30, 33, 43, 53–4, 84, 115, 125–6, 131, 135–7, 138–40, 146, 151–2, 160
ennui 78, 105–6
epistemological 157, 160
equality 33, 39, 53–4, 87, 89, 139, 190
esoteric 127
essays 4, 54
  Essays in Zen Buddhism 141, 149
essence 2, 38, 89, 104, 119–20, 135–6, 156, 168–9
essentialism 2
essentials 12, 184
eternal 4, 26, 50, 72, 81, 93, 114, 137, 140–41, 185
eternally 78, 85
eternity 13, 27, 115
ethical 30, 112

ethics 30, 166
etiquette 48
etoku 175
Europe 5, 76, 105, 158
European 25
evidence/s 186, 191, 196
evil 12–13, 19–20, 27–28, 31, 40–41, 69, 150, 178–81
evolution 55, 88
evolutionary development 56
exegesis 75
existence 36, 55, 57, 68, 115–17, 119, 134, 160–62, 197
  of (the) Buddha 176, 180
  of Buddha-nature 128
  of God 185
  of humanity 86, 94–6, 104–6, 110, 113, 117, 128, 139, 174
  individual 115–16
  of Jesus 34
  of (the) Pure Land 174, 181, 184–5, 197
  of self, soul, etc. 19, 26, 35, 86–7, 155
  self-awakened 72
  six realms 68
  of subjective mind 155–6
  of world 12, 19
existential/ist 4–5, 108, 115, 128–9
existentially 98, 117
exorcist 18
expediency 174
experience 138, 161, 179–82, 193
  Buddhist 13, 40, 49, 53, 57, 181
  Christian 25, 129
  grace 19
  life 5, 146–7, 157, 179, 200–201
  religious 120, 164, 166, 185
  Zen 4–5, 18–21, 125–6, 128–31, 134–5, 137, 158, 161
extinction
  of Buddhism 52
  of discriminative discourse 152
extinguishment (of fire, passions, etc.) 84, 86, 140
eyebrows 75, 142
eyes 18, 65, 71, 75, 98, 100, 142, 178

Fǎbǎotánjīng 68
face/s 157
  original face 65, 70–73, 129, 196
  facial gates 110, 112, 116
faculty/ies 158, 166, 178, 200
faith 17, 33, 43–4, 50–51, 87, 95, 103, 131, 141, 149, 169, 173–4, 205
  awakening of 5, 127, 158
  faith/dogma 93
  faith/doubt 51
  faith/insight 92–3

244

faith/mind 69
faith/reason 4, 114
nenbutsu 165–6
original 147
saddhā 95
faiths 92
　Eastern 3
　Indian 36
　World Congress of 143
Făyăn 22
feeling/s 11–12, 19, 39–40, 78, 92–3, 126,
　　153, 162, 167, 175, 188, 190
　self-feeling 38–9
festival 104–5, 107
feudal/ism 166, 190, 193
Feuerbach, Ludwig 87
folk
　art 6–7, 188–90
　folkcraft/s 190–91, 201
　songs 77
followers 17, 22, 48, 111, 162–3
form/s 70–76, 79, 80–81, 95, 97, 114–15,
　　132, 140, 153, 158–63, 169, 179, 193
formless 70, 72–4, 78, 80–81, 160–61
founder 3, 17, 25, 29–31, 33–4, 37–40, 42,
　　48, 51–2, 55, 64, 70
four
　castes 84–5, 89
　comprehensive deeds 15
　dimensions 134
　modes of birth 68
　noble truths 33, 38
fourfold
　Dharma-world 74
　vow 19
fourth
　noble truth 142
　step 121
foxes, their holes 94
Francis, Saint 20
Franckforter 24
Frankfurt/er 24, 27–8, 31
Frankfurt 24
fraternité 87
freedom 7, 37–8, 69, 72, 76, 87, 98, 146,
　　190, 196–204
French Revolution 87
Freud, Sigmund 127–9
Friedhof 106
Fromm, Erich 5, 130, 133, 145
Fujinami 174
fujōshō 27
funbetsu 199
function/s 82, 88, 126, 130, 163
　function/substance 73
functioning 80, 125, 131, 155
　functioning self 73

funerals 37
fūryū 140
future 13, 69, 81, 95, 103, 105, 107–8,
　　110, 128, 138, 164, 166, 169
　Buddha 51
　life/lives 43

Gaṅgā 84
Ganges 120
Ganshōge 175
garden/s 6, 71, 106, 141, 143, 145–6, 169
Garza, Francisco 145
gate 41, 49–50
　Dharma-gate 74
　facial gates 110, 112, 116
　Gateless Gate 68, 74
　Original Gate 58
Gautama 12–13
gentleness 39–40
genius 186–7, 196, 204
German 2–3, 11, 18, 24–25, 27, 29, 31,
　　34, 37, 91, 108, 149–50
Germanica *see* Theologica
Germany 1–3, 17, 91
Gewesene, das 108
ghosts (hungry) 179
Gigen 22, 109, 136
gihō 50
gnostic 5
goal 16, 19, 37–8, 41, 53, 56, 125
goats/sheep 41
Goddess of Mercy 34, 40
Godenshō 56
gods 45, 132
goshō 27
Goso 22
Gottesacker 106
grace 17, 19, 33
grasping 154–6
Great Vehicle 1
Greeks 4, 114, 132
Gröber, Archbishop 107
Gūanwúliangshòu 165
guru 141

Hakuin 21, 136
Hakuun 140
Hamada, Shōji 183
handicrafts 79
handwork 196
Hannyakyō 164
Hannyashingyō 69
Hánshān 20
happiness 14, 150, 168, 175–7, 181–2,
　　198
Hawaii 168
Hearn, Lafcadio 149

INDEX

heart 18, 39, 51, 73, 74, 93, 97, 131, 136, 138, 140, 147, 162, 164, 169, 174, 176–7, 179, 185, 199, 201
hearts 34, 127, 147, 177, 196
heaven 7, 23, 119, 133, 139, 183–6, 188, 190–93, 199
heavens 41, 144
Hegel 200
Hegelian 37, 108
Heian 24
Heidegger, Martin 3–4, 91, 94–102, 108
Heidelberg 149
Heilige, das 17–18
Heimat 94–6, 98, 102, 107
Heimatabend 91, 102
Heimatlosigkeit 95
Heimische, das 95, 107–8
Heimkehr 107
Hekiganroku 135–6
Hekiganshū 125
hell/s 41, 119, 143, 173, 179, 185
hemp 29
heresy 44
Herkommen 108
Herkunft 108
Hibbert Journal 36
Hiei, Mount 24, 28, 56
Higashi Honganji 236
Himalayas 36
Hīnayāna 26, 30, 32–4, 37–8, 41, 56–7, 162–3
Hinduism 34–6, 43
Hirota, Dennis 50, 164
Hisamatsu, Shin'ichi 3, 6, 63
history 3, 35, 37, 42, 47–52, 55–9, 71, 74, 78–9, 82–3, 86, 93, 104, 111, 114, 125, 139, 143, 151, 157, 165, 184–5, 200
  historic 56
  historical 1–2, 35, 44, 49, 52, 56–8, 64, 79, 84–5, 93, 104, 200
  historicist 3
  historicity 3
hōben 44, 70, 169
Hōbōdankyō 68
Hōen 22
hōhōron 151
Hokekyō 27–8, 64
Hokkekyō 27
holistic 130
holocaust 139
holy 17, 19, 51, 56
home 84, 94–6, 102–8, 196
homeland 105–6
homeless/ness 84, 94–6, 105
homesickness 95, 105–6
hometown 107
honbun 196

Hōnen 1, 48–50
hongu 196
honrai 196
honshō 196
Horney, Karen 130
horse/s 100, 125–6
hospital 139
hospitality 45
hosshin 70, 169
Hossō 24, 27
Huángbò 67–68, 79
Huánzhuànxīnfǎyào 68
Huáyán 158
Huìnéng 68, 78, 111, 114
humanism 71, 79
humanity 2, 11–12, 17, 87, 89, 112, 147, 165
humankind 53
humanlike 180
humanly 197
humans 65, 85
humble 7, 55, 143, 146, 184, 186, 190–92
humility 19, 38, 176, 179, 199
humorous 97
humour 142
Humphreys, Christmas 169
Húntún 132
Hu Shih 143
Hyakujō 17–18, 130
hypotheses 40, 46

ichimui 111
iconography 6
ideal/s 12, 19, 33, 69, 79, 143, 177–8, 193
idealism 34, 157
idealistic/realistic 33
identity 35–36, 100, 159–60
  of buddhas 24
  of thrift and beauty 193–4
  see also self-identity
ideology 57, 83–4, 89, 134
idols 70
ignorance 12, 29, 86, 126, 128–9, 131, 133, 200–201
ikon-worshiper 34, 37
illusion/s 72, 79, 128–9, 147
immanence 79, 114, 181
immeasurable 19, 140
immediacy 185
immortality 33
immovable 14
impediments 179
imperialism 83
inanimate 27
Inca 192
incense 32, 37, 80, 139
inclusiveness 44, 46
incomprehensibility 119

INDEX

inconceivability 19
independence (in Zen) 67–8
India 1, 20, 36, 50, 72–3, 85, 193
Indian 2, 29, 44, 75, 151, 154, 160
indigo 193–4
individuality 11, 137
individuation 129
Indology 5
Indra 85
industrial 42, 93, 104
ineffability 19, 20–21, 23
infallible 40
infantilism 128–9
infinite 51, 58, 137
   cosmic unconscious 135
   life 58–9
   light 14
   the 25, 72, 141, 161
   void 161–3
Inju 118
injustice 28
innate 36, 138, 196, 198
inner (life, man, peace etc.) 11, 15, 18, 20, 22, 25, 30, 37–9, 41–3, 66, 78–9, 82–3, 92, 115, 146, 164
Innerlichkeit 37, 41–2
innocence 147
innocent 188, 197, 201
innumerable 19, 33–5, 42, 45, 69, 71, 73–4, 84, 139, 169
insight 4, 12, 14, 27, 92, 107, 114, 117, 120–21, 136, 178, 180
   into history 49–50
intellect 113, 138, 154, 157, 164, 184, 196, 200–201
intellection 126
intellectual 1, 4, 6, 15, 19, 25, 31, 33, 40, 50, 59, 126–7, 135, 141, 143, 196
intellectualism/-ization 112–13, 144
intelligence 7, 126, 133, 197
interaction 1, 3–5, 237
interdependence 161
interpretation 45, 66, 89, 97–9, 110, 127, 150, 154, 157, 161–3
interreligious 2
introspection 54
intuition 21, 25, 130, 158
intuitive 49, 182
inventive/ness 45, 91
invincible 167
invisible 168
invocatory 181
inwardness 22, 37, 40, 43
Ippen 7
irrational 20, 22, 146
irreligious 87
Ishikawa Prefecture 165

Islam 46

Jainism 39
James, William 42
jānāti 153
Japan 1–2, 5–7, 17, 20, 24, 28, 32–4, 37, 40, 42–5, 57–8, 76, 130, 143, 145, 151, 153–4, 157, 165–6, 190–91, 193–4
Japanese 2–3, 5–7, 12, 17, 31, 33, 37, 40, 44–6, 57, 65, 67–9, 76–7, 82, 99, 109–11, 113–14, 125–7, 130, 140, 142, 144–5, 152, 166, 183, 188, 193–4, 237
Jātaka 58–9
Jesus 94
jewels 118
jiànxīng 111
Jichin 50
jikaku 158
   reiseiteki 113
Jinenhōnishō 70
Jinmu (Emperor) 57–8
Jinne 111
jiriki 56, 141
jishō 56
Jízàng 162
Jizō 40
jñāna 156
Jōdo 13, 173, 183–6, 199
   School 185
   Shinshū 49–51, 67, 120
jōdokei shisō 166
Jōdoron 13, 175
Jōshū 4, 98, 109, 118–20, 125–6, 131
Jōshūroku 109, 228
Jōshūzenjigoroku 110
Jōza 136–7
Judaism 40
Jūken 137
Jùlíng 137
Jung, C. G. 129–30

Ka, Mount/mountains 137
Kaga 165
Kagawa Prefecture 166
Kamakura 5, 110, 140, 142
Kaneko Daiei 3, 6–7, 47, 173, 178
Kanmu (emperor) 24
Kantian 180
Kapleau, P. 130
karma 12–13, 43, 156–7, 178
karmic 47, 88, 179
karuṇā 119, 126, 131, 139
kasuri 193
Kataku 111
katsu 75, 112, 118, 140
kāyas 22
Kechimyakuron 68

Kegon 168
Kegongyō 64
Kelman, Harold 130
kenchūshi 121
kenshō 111
Kèqín 22, 136
kernel 94
Kern 95
Kiba, Ryōhon 2, 11, 17
Kierkegaard, S. 128
king/ly 88-9
kingdom 39
kinship 31
Kita Kamakura 140
Kiyozawa, Manshi 54
kleśa 120
knowable 176
knower 96, 153
knowing 111, 114, 153, 155, 157-60, 163, 199
knowledge 14, 44, 85, 133, 139, 188, 196
kōan 75, 98, 136
Kōbō Daishi 24
Kobori, Sōhaku 4, 132, 146
Kojiki 58
kokoro 158, 161
kokubunji 29
kokuhō 28
Kokushi 28
Kokuyō 28
Kondō Akihisa 4-5, 125, 146
Kongōshinron 85
konton 132
Korea 33
Korean 188-90, 197
Korei 137
Kōshi 28-9
kosoku (kōan) 74
Kotsu 132
Kreutzer, Conradin 107
kṣatriyas 85
Kūkai 231
Kumārajīva 66
Kusunoki 166
kwatz 140; *see also katsu*
kyakkanteki 175
Kyōgyōshinshō 49-50, 70, 169, 175
Kyōto 1, 3, 5-6, 11, 20, 29, 47, 179
  School 1, 3
  University 3
Kyūshū 48

LaFleur, William R. 4
Lagerqvist, Per 168
Lamenting (differences) 178
andscape/s 23, 188
Langeweile 95

language 77, 105-106, 126
  of cities 77
  honorific 48
  rational 143
Laṅkāvatāra Sūtra 5, 138, 143, 158
lantern 71, 145-6
Lǎozǐ 142
Larger Sūtra of Eternal Life 70
Larger Sūtra of Infinite Life 58-9
laws
  of matter 43
  moral 41, 44
  of spirit 43
layman/men 29, 32, 40, 141
Leach, Bernard 7, 183, 193, 201
Leben 24
legend/s 58-9
legendary 57, 137
Leiber 97
leisure 15, 76-7
Lessing, Gotthold Ephraim 45
letters 63, 112
Leyden jar 18
Liáng dynasty 73
liberality 40, 44-5
liberals 34
liberate 13, 116, 126, 128
liberation 67, 73, 76, 114, 119, 129, 141, 169, 197
liberty 87
libidinal 128-9
light 114-15, 180, 182, 185
  and darkness 13, 136, 138
  infinite 14
  inner 115, 139, 148
  unimpeded 175-6, 180-81
lineage 54, 68, 72, 86
língjué 115
Línjì 22, 67, 71, 79-80, 109-18, 136
Línjì lù 109, 112, 117
Lion's Invincible Charge 167
literal inspiration 40
logic (beyond) 4, 114
London 109, 115, 118, 138, 143
  London Buddhist Society 169
Lóngtán 71
lord (feudal) 166
Lord of Heaven 23
lotus 37, 165
Lotus of the Good Law 41
Lotus Sūtra 57-8, 96
love 15, 26-8, 40, 87, 119, 133, 137, 139-40, 146-7
Luther, Martin 2, 24-5, 28, 30-31

machines 139
Madhyamakakārikā 26

INDEX

Madhyamika 26
Madhyamikaśāstra 26
Madhyāntavibhāga 156
Madonna 34
magic (*sūtra*-magic) 65
Mahamati 138
Mahāprajñāpāramitā Sūtra 66
Mahāprajñāpāramitāśāstra 26
Mahāyāna
   Buddhism 1, 5–7, 17, 20, 25–6, 28, 51, 55, 57, 96–7, 149–50, 160, 164
   doctrine, thought 28, 32–3, 38, 40, 53, 97, 127, 138, 156, 161–2, 168–9, 175
   /Hinayāna 30, 32–3, 37–8, 41, 58
   texts 5, 58–9, 174–5, 182
Mahāyānasaṃgraha 153, 157–8
Mahī (river) 84
maibotsu 159
Maitreya 51, 156
Makashikan 25
Malenkov 83
manas 153
Marburg 1–2, 17
mārga 7, 49, 52, 56; see also Buddha-*mārga*
Marx 128
Marxism 89, 108
materialism 43, 52, 54–5, 59, 128
Matsubara, Yūzen 47
māyā 72
mayoi 167
Mǎzǔ 68, 111
McDougall 38
meaning 3, 63, 15, 30, 69, 71–3, 95–9, 105, 107, 127, 131, 134, 139, 161, 163, 177–8, 188, 194
   of enlightenment 125–6
   of life 19
   original 66
   of Pure Land 174–5
   of Pure Land of Beauty 184–6, 188, 194
   of subjectivity 154–8
   of Zen 129
means, *see* skilful means, *upāya*
mediaeval 2–3, 24, 45
mediation 158–9
meditation 1, 25, 102, 107, 111, 136, 142, 147, 150, 165
Megerle, Ulrich 91
Meiji Period 51, 54
   Restoration 193
mendicant 88
mercy 34, 39, 40
merit/s 19, 29–30, 43, 73
   no-merit 73
Messkirch 3, 91, 97, 102–3, 105–7
metaphors 100
metaphysical 32–4, 112, 134, 142, 149–50

metaphysics 37
method/s 23, 34, 46, 53, 56, 71, 74, 136, 152–4, 188
methodology 55, 57, 151–4, 157, 161
Mexican 145–146
   Mexican Psychoanalytic Society 146
Mexico 130
Middle Stanzas 26
militarist 57
mind 143, 153–6, 175–7, 181–2, 185–6, 195, 198–9, 203–4
   in Zen 63, 65–71, 73–5, 79, 111, 114, 116, 125, 136, 155–63
modern 1, 3, 5–7, 11, 24, 41, 51, 57, 63–4, 76–9, 83, 86–7, 89, 94–5, 104–6, 111, 118, 127, 130, 133, 139, 151–3, 166, 196, 200, 234, 236–7
modernity 3, 7
modernization 76, 127
mingei 6
miracle (of beauty) 183, 186–7, 191–3
miraculous 21, 191–2
missionaries 42, 44–6
Mohammedanism 33–4, 40, 82
molecules 56
monasteries 73–4
monastic
   life 56
   name 91
monasticism 28
mondō 75–6, 117–20
monk/s (Buddhist) 17, 22, 32, 37, 39–41, 98, 110–11, 115, 117–18, 120, 125, 136–7, 142, 144
   Christian 91
   way of life 39, 73–4, 88
Monodane, Kichibei 166
moon, finger pointing to 146
moral/s 12–13, 15, 25, 27–8, 30, 33, 38, 41, 43–4, 55, 141
   Moral World Order 2, 11–15, 30
morality 30, 33, 41–2, 85, 93
Mori, Hina 166
motivation 5, 86, 91, 136
mountains 137
   a thousand 100
mudrā 80
Mūlamadhyamakakārikā 151–2
multiplicity 77–8
Mumon 68
Mumonkan 68, 113
mundane world 199
murder/ers 13, 143
museum 2, 17, 149, 188
mushin 144
mushinron 154
myōkōnin/s 164–9

mysterious
  east 127
  realm 135
mystery 19
mystic/al 1–2, 19–20, 24–5, 30, 55, 84, 126, 129, 161, 166
  mystic/s 17–18, 25, 29, 31, 129
  mysticism 20, 25–7, 166
myth 6, 17
mythological figures 85

Nabeshima porcelain 190–91
Nagao Gajin 237
Nāgārjuna 26, 160
naikan 54
naivety, abandonment of 6
nāma 167
name 26, 32, 34, 48, 58, 84, 132, 191
Nánquán 71
Nara 6, 24, 27, 29
narcissism 147
Nathan der Weise 45
national 44, 148, 150, 188, 190
nationality 11, 126, 148
native 108
  beliefs 45
  place 94, 196
natural
  mind 198
  order 194
  science/s 56, 134
  world 74
naturalness 198
nature (natural, true, real, own, of the Buddha, etc) 4, 7, 13–14, 22–3, 27, 34, 38–9, 42–3, 46, 53–4, 56, 63, 65–7, 70–72, 74–5, 77, 84, 104, 111, 113–14, 126–9, 133–5, 137–9, 151, 153, 155–7, 166, 169, 178, 181, 185, 191, 194–201
  natures, five 27, 156
  see also Buddha-nature, original nature, self-nature
negation 64, 68, 72, 74, 84, 100, 136, 156, 159–60, 163, 191
negations, eight 26
nenbutsu/Nembutsu 49–50, 164–7, 173, 198
Nichiren 48, 64
Nichts 97
Nietzsche 4, 93, 128
nihilism 26
nihonteki 166
nippon seishin 57
nirvana/Nirvana 18–20, 23, 70, 79, 84, 95–6
Nishida Kitarō 3
Nishitani, Keiji 3–4, 7, 82, 91–2, 159

Nobel Prize 168
noetic 121, 126–7
non-abiding mind 198
nondifference 160
  nondifferent 156
nondiscriminated 158
  nondiscrimination 137, 155–8, 163
nondual 156, 160
  nondualistic 156
  nonduality (non-duality) 67, 74, 155, 157, 160, 163, 167, 169, 184, 191, 199
nonexistence 154–7, 160
  nonexistent 155–7
  nonexisting 155
nontheistic 169
nopalabdhi 156
norm/s 33, 64–5, 93–4
north 5, 32, 38, 40, 132, 165
northern 32–4, 37–8, 43, 132
nōsho 53
nostalgia 196
nothing/Nothing 26, 89, 107, 112, 160
nothingness/Nothingness 11, 78, 89, 97–9, 155–6, 161
nucleus of Zen 110–11
numberless 23, 169
numinous 17–18
Nyorai 24

Ōbaku 67, 140
objectifying 158–9
objective 37, 70–71, 80–81, 134, 175
objectively 65, 77, 133, 157
objectivity 93, 113
obscurantism 143
Occident 79
ocean 77, 84, 119, 135–7, 144
offerings 33, 73, 118
Okamura, Mihoko 130, 142, 147
Okinawa 192
Oldenberg, H. 84
Old Testament 34
oneness 73, 77–9, 100, 111, 116, 120, 134, 151
ontological 108, 155, 157, 160
opposites 141, 188
opposition/s 7, 13, 15, 30, 112, 158, 185, 188, 190, 200
ordained 22, 48
order 132, 161, 190–91, 194, 200
Order, Moral World 2, 11–15, 30
ordination of monks 73
organism/s 35–6
Oriental/s 23, 25–6, 42, 78–9
orientalism 4
origin/s 26, 36, 50, 57, 77, 73, 103–8, 114
  common 11

250

humble 191
of world 12, 149
original 12, 26, 38-9, 42, 91-2, 111
  beauty 196
  being 74, 196
  doctrine 150
  face 65, 70-71, 73, 129, 196
  faith 147
  gate 58
  ignorance 12
  meaning 66
  nature 63-7, 84, 135, 185, 195-7, 200-201
  sin
  subject 78
  true self 71
  vow 5, 7, 49-50, 199-20
  way of life 66, 71
originally not a single thing 72
origination, co-dependent 151-2, 161, 163
orthodox/Orthodox 34
Ōtani University 11, 48, 236
Ōtani-ha 47, 56
other-dependent 156-7
Otherness 100
Otto, Rudolf 1-2, 11-12, 17-18
Oxford 150
oyasama 169

pagan 13
pain 200
pains 126, 131
painter/s 20-21, 188
painting/s 6, 17-18, 23, 76, 188-9, 196-7
Pāli 32
pantheon 17, 33, 45, 113
parable 41
Paradise 37, 142
paradisiacal 181
paradox 89, 145, 157
paradoxical 22-4
Paramārtha 153-4, 157
paramārtha 156, 160
pāramitā 138
paratantra 155
parāvṛtti 113
parent 169
parikalpita 155
pariniṣpanna 156
Patriarch 22, 67-9, 72, 78, 111, 165
  patriarchs 47, 68, 72, 143
  patriarchal 48-9, 52
patronage 6
Paul, St. 31
peace 37-9, 106, 134, 138, 175-7, 181-2, 199-201
pedagogic device 173

personality
  of Amida 169
  saintly 50, 119
  split 130
  of Suzuki Daisetsu 143-7
  Zen 142
pessimism 129
Petzold, Bruno 2
phenomena 71, 77, 105
philology 25, 151
  limits of 153-4
philosopher/s 3, 34, 54, 168
philosophic/al 35, 46, 55, 100-101, 107, 108, 113, 141
philosophy 11, 34, 46, 55, 66, 79, 85, 92-3, 151
  Buddhist 46, 137
  Hegelian 200
  Kantian 180
  Kegon 168
  Mahāyāna 32-3, 138, 158
  Tendai 26, 27
  Zen 168
philosophies 40
pilgrim 36
pīnyīn 109, 111
Platform Sūtra 68, 72
plainsong 178
Plotinus 30
poet 85
poetic/al 99, 100
polytheism 33-4
pope 40
popular 3, 34, 127
porcelain 190
Porcu, Elisabetta 7
pottery 145
power 11, 27, 39, 42, 46, 67, 103-7, 127, 131, 139, 166-7, 201, 200
practice 34, 38, 49, 50, 54-6, 85-6, 125-6, 153, 161-3
  practices 177
praise 15, 47, 185, 198
prajñā 4, 17, 30, 86, 111, 113, 119, 125-6, 128-9, 131, 137-9, 156, 158, 160, 163-4
prajñāpāramitā 149-50, 158, 160-63
Prajñāpāramitā 5, 59, 149, 156, 161-2
Prajñāpāramitāhṛdaya (sūtra) 69, 75
praṇidhāna 119-20
prapañca 152
pratibhāsa 153
pratītyasamutpāda 152
Pratt, James Bissett 2, 32
pratyekabuddha 27
Pravda 83
praxis 55, 176-7, 179-80
pray 70, 175, 181-2

INDEX

preach/ed 39, 41, 84, 95, 152
preacher 97, 99
preaching 48
precepts 30
  precepts 30, 37, 41
priest/s 24, 27–30, 48
priesthood 28
propagation 236
Protestant 1, 34, 42
Protestantism 31
provisional 28, 32, 169, 191
Psalms 226
psychiatrists 129
psychoanalysis 109, 127–8, 130, 133, 146
psychoanalyst/s 5, 121, 130, 133, 146, 149
psychological 30, 84, 112
psychology 5, 37, 79, 151
psychotherapy 129
puṇḍarīka 165
pure 13–15, 27, 30, 74, 99–100, 153, 169, 180–81, 196
Pure Land 5–7, 13–14, 49, 51, 64, 70, 96, 167, 173–7, 182, 184–6, 188–9, 190–92, 194, 196–202, 204–6
  Buddhism 1–2, 7, 34, 50–51, 79, 96, 120, 131, 165, 168–9, 174
  of Beauty 184–6, 189, 191–2, 197–9, 204–6
  sūtras 70
púsà 32, 40

Quaker 150
quarters, ten 116, 175
Quixote, Don 147

rāja 89
rajñā 137
ratibhāsā 159
rationalistic
  atheism 25
  culture 127–8
rationality
  in Buddhism 133, 154
realism
  in Buddhism 129, 133
reality 4, 14, 37, 40, 43, 79, 100, 114, 129, 132, 134, 136, 140, 142, 147, 153, 156, 160, 163, 169, 179, 182, 185–6, 190
realization 50, 53–4, 56, 79, 83, 86–90, 93, 111, 113–14, 120, 131, 153, 158–9, 169
realm 22, 53, 80, 85, 114, 128, 135, 163, 181–2, 197
realms 81, 103
  six 68
reason/ing 4, 22, 40, 55, 86, 87, 99, 114, 127–9, 200

rebirth 41, 70, 126, 129, 131
recompense 19, 43
  body 70–71
reform
  of Buddhism 45
  of society 41
reformation
  German 24, 31
  Japanese 31
  religious 85
reformer
  Dengyō Daishi 24
  Shinran 15
reikaku 115
reisei 166
reiseiteki jikaku 113
religion 6, 30, 32, 33–4, 37–9, 42, 44–6, 52–3, 55, 57, 64, 66–7, 79, 84, 87–9, 92–4, 112, 120, 128–9, 151, 174, 176, 179
  state 29
religions 32–6, 38, 40, 42, 45–6, 64, 67, 92, 94, 96, 133, 179
  history of 3
  Indian 2
  musem of 2, 17
  study of 1–2
Religionskundliche Sammlung 2, 17
Religiöser Menschheitsbund 2, 11–12, 17
religiosity 7
religious (orientation, etc.) 1–3, 6, 17, 27, 48–50, 57, 70, 82, 85–9, 92, 94, 101, 129, 133, 136, 141, 149, 173–4
  anti-religious, irreligious 68–9, 87
  experience 120, 164, 185
  naivety 6
  philosopher 54
  religiousness 79
  union 17
religiously neutral 2
religiousness 79
Rennyo 1, 174
renunciation 14, 19
revelation 49, 53, 58
revivalism 51, 82
revolution 85, 88
  French 87
  industrial 42
  social 82–3, 90
revolutionary 65, 83–4, 86, 89
Rinzai 20, 22, 67, 96, 109–12, 136–7, 140
Rinzairoku 109, 117
rōshi 141
rūpa 153, 159
Russian 34
Ruysbroeck, John 129
Ryūmin Akizuki 110

INDEX

sabi 140
sacerdotalism 28
sacred
  texts 21
  tortoise 165
saddhā 95
Saddharmapuṇḍarīka Sūtra 27, 64, 74
Sages, Path of 167
Saichō 2
Śākya, house 84
Śākyamuni 24, 33, 44, 51–5, 57–9, 64, 66, 72, 179
salvation 13, 16–17, 19, 21, 30, 33–4, 41, 44, 51, 58, 118–19, 184, 192
Salvation Army 46
samādhi 59, 68, 167–8
samgha 84
saṃsāra 18–19, 20, 23, 73
saṃskṛta 156
samurai 6
Śaṅkara 20
Sānlùn 162
Sanskrit 17, 26–7, 65, 70
Sanuki 166
Sarabhū (river) 84
Sasaki, Gesshō 56, 236
śāstra 26–7, 29
satori 4, 74, 98–9, 114, 125–6, 129, 135–6, 158, 161, 167
Schühle, Siegfried 91
scriptures (Buddhist) 13, 32, 63–5, 74
sculpture 18, 76
sect/s (Buddhist) 24–5, 29–30, 33–4, 37, 41, 48
secular/ization 56, 86–7, 94
seeker/s 51, 175, 178–9
seer 114–15, 155–60
Sein 108
seishin 57
self 3, 18–19, 33, 35, 38–9, 42–3, 51, 63, 66–9, 70–75, 78–82, 84–9, 93, 96, 103–4, 111–14, 117–19, 126, 128–30, 138–9, 144, 156–64, 166–8, 174–6, 178–82, 194, 197, 199–200
  self-Buddha 68, 72
  self-discipline 19, 37
  self-existent 20
  self-identity 35–6, 46, 158–9
  self-interest 14, 38
  self-mind 68, 72
  self-nature 65, 70–72, 111, 156
  self-power 166
  self-sacrificing 15
  self-will 30
Sēngcàn 69
senses 25, 80, 86
  five 116

sentient beings 19, 39–40, 43–4, 53, 126, 139, 167, 178, 181–2, 200
sermon/s 22, 38, 91, 110–12, 165
Setchō 137
seven 102
  Brahmanic items 85
  holes of a being 132
  seventh centennial 3, 102
  seventh month 29
seventeenth century 97, 99
Shàndǎo 165
shàngzuò 136
shari 186
Sheehan, Thomas 3, 102, 107
sheep/goats 41
Shénhuì 111
Shia (Muslims) 34
shibui 142
shibusa 198
Shichiri, Gōjun 166
Shídé 20
Shidō Bunan 99
shiki 153
Shikoku 166
Shin (Buddhism) 1, 3, 5–7, 15, 48, 53–4, 56, 67, 70, 120, 164–6, 173, 175, 236–7
  Jōdo Shinshū 49–51, 67
  Shin-shū/Shinshū 17, 37, 42, 47–51, 56, 120
  Shinshū Ōtani Daigaku 48
shin (mind) 111
Shingon 6, 25
shinjun 50
shinnin 111
Shinran (Shōnin) 1, 3, 15, 31, 47–53, 56, 70, 131, 169, 178–9, 198
Shinshinmei 69
Shintō 33, 45, 82
Shōdaijōron 153–4
Shōdōka 68, 115
shōgun/s 6, 166
Shogunate (Tokugawa) 82
Shōju 21
shōken 142
Shōkokuji 20
Shōma (*myōkōnin*) 166
shōmon 30
Shōnin, the (Shinran) 48; for other *shōnin* see Hōnen, Ippen, Nichiren
Shōtoku Taishi 29
Shǒushān 71
Shūbun 20
Shuku 132
shūkyō 164
Shutan 140
Siam 32, 43
sign/s 89, 103, 106–7, 201

253

INDEX

śīla 30
silence 18, 75, 107, 142, 168
sinner/s 41, 143, 185
sinologists 143
sins 40, 184
   five deadly 69
sisters (and brothers) 38, 181
sixfold (sense perception) 80
sixth
   century 63, 73
   patriarch 68, 72, 78, 111
sixty blows 140
skilful
   knowledge 188
   means 44, 169
skilfulness 188, 195
skill, technical 188-9, 197, 199
society 41, 82-3, 89, 166-7, 174
sociology 151
Socrates 20
Sōen Shaku 140
Soga, Ryōjin 3, 6-7, 47, 49, 53-4, 56-7
sokkon 186
solipsism 13
solitude 116, 139
Sòng (Dynasty) 138, 140, 187-8
song (of Yǒngjiā) 68, 115
songs, folk 77
sorrow/s 12, 19, 126, 178-81
Sōsan 69
soul/s 15, 21-2, 25-7, 30-31, 33, 37, 58, 63, 174, 179
Southern (Buddhism, School) 32-4, 38, 43
Soviet Union 83
space
   age 104
   and time 72, 79-80, 115, 135, 180, 192
spaceless worlds 37
Spain 149
   Spanish 34
speculation 33, 101
speech 21, 23
spirit 43, 55, 119, 180, 191
   of affirmation 99-100
   of Buddhism 37, 49-50, 52
   combative 42
   enlightened 133-5, 139
   of God 31
   of individual 30, 38-9, 43-4, 137
   of Japan 57-8
   of service 87
   of Zen 110, 125-7, 143-4
spiritual 5, 7, 15, 20, 24, 35-9, 43-4, 49-50, 56, 58, 92-3, 113, 126, 129, 133, 140-41, 143, 166-7, 175-6, 199
spiritualism 54
spirituality 7, 54, 113, 134, 166

śrāvaka 27, 30
Stalinism 149
Sthiramati 154-7
subject 78-80
subjectivity 37, 51, 57, 113, 115, 153-60, 163-4, 175, 180
suchness 6, 70, 153-8, 160, 163, 169
Sudhana 58
Śūdra/s 84-6, 88-9
suffering/s 12, 14-15, 39, 77, 95, 118-19, 126-8, 131, 138, 167-8, 179-80, 183, 200
Sugihira, Shizutoshi 237
sumie 76
Sunday School 46
Sunnis 34
śūnyatā 97-8, 152
supernatural/ly 43-4, 135
superstition 44-5, 77
Suso 24
sūtra/s 21, 29, 63-9, 72-5, 162, 165, 174, 182
   specific sūtras 5, 13, 14, 27, 28, 30, 57-9, 64, 66, 68-70, 72, 74-5, 80, 96-7, 138, 143, 156, 158, 162, 164-5, 191
   see names of sutras in this index
Suzuki Daisetsu (also Daisetz, or D.T.) 2, 4-7, 17, 21, 56, 63, 109-15, 117-21, 123, 125-30, 132-9, 141, 147, 149-52, 154-5, 157-70, 175, 236-7
Suzuki, Beatrice Lane 236
Swankolok 194-5
swordsmanship 6
symbolic truth 45-6

Takakusu, Junjirō 143
Takasago 201
Tamba 194-5
Táng Dynast 136
Tánluán 15, 169, 175, 181
Tannishō 16
Taoism 133, 142
tariki 56, 141, 166
Tathāgata/ tathāgata 30, 50, 75, 80
   Akṣobhya 51
   Amitābha 58, 174-7, 181-2
tathatā 156, 164
Tauler 24
Tendai 1-2, 6, 24-30, 50, 64
Tenri/kyō 179
tetsugaku 164
Teutonic Order 24
textile/s 192-4, 197
text/s 21, 151-4, 158, 164
   Mahāyāna 5, 21
   Pure Land 13, 131
   Zen 74-5, 110

INDEX

Thailand 194-5
Thank Amida 167
theism 71, 169
theocentric 79, 90
Theologia Deutsch 24
Theologia Germanica 2, 24, 26-7, 29-30
theology 1-3, 24-5, 27, 29, 31, 33-5, 53, 175
theonomy 79
therapy 129-30
Theravāda 2, 51, 56-8
thousand mountains 100
three
  baskets 51; *see also* three *kāyas*
  gods 132
  impure worlds 14-15
  kāyas 22; *see also* three baskets
  natures 156
  principles 175-7
  sūtras (Pure Land) 12, 64
thusness 154, 156, 164
Tiāntái 2, 64
Tillich, Paul 4
time 95, 102-6
  and eternity 115
  and place 71, 74-5, 78, 80, 102, 204
  and space 72, 79-80, 115, 134-5, 180, 192
Tokiwa, Gishin 81
Tokugawa 82
tolerance 40, 44-5
tortoise, sacred 165
Tōyō no kokoro 158, 161
training 21, 38-9, 121, 136, 144, 152
transcendence 25, 30, 71-2, 80-81, 96, 114, 116, 138, 142, 180-81
transformation 83-4, 90, 129, 168
  body 70-71
transitoriness 95-6, 100
transmigration 39, 44, 59
transmission 2, 18, 21, 63, 68, 79, 89, 111, 125, 129, 130, 150
transplantation 44-5
treasure (national, state) 28, 190
Triṃśikā 154-7
Tripiṭaka 32, 51, 85
triple world 116
twelve causal links 12

Ueda, Shizuteru 160
Ueda, Yoshifumi 5, 151
Ui, Hakuju 5, 151-62
Umheimliche, das 107
unawakened 53-6, 74-5
unconscious, the 127-30, 135
unconscious/ness, cosmic 113, 115-16, 128, 130-38, 140
Unheimische, das 94-5, 107-8

Unheimliche, das 95, 108
unhindered 69, 177
unimpeded 175-6, 180-81
unio mystica 25, 30
Unitarianism 34
United States 76, 127, 146
universality 28, 39-40, 43, 85, 94-5, 130, 137, 100
universe/s 27, 41, 43-4, 104, 114, 132, 134-5, 175, 177, 181
university
  Columbia 146
  Hawaii 168
  Kyōto 3
  Marburg 1, 17, 146
  Ōtani 11, 48, 236
unlimited 70, 161
Unmon 22-3
unobstructed 198
unskilfulness 195, 197
Unvergängliche, das 100
upalabdhi 155-6
Upaniṣads 95
upāya 44, 70, 119, 126, 169
USSR 83
Utopia of Beauty 184

Vairocana 19
Vaiśya/s 84-5
Vajracchedikā Sūtra 74-5, 80
Vanitas vanitatum 99
vassa 29
Vasubandhu 13, 15, 153-5, 157, 160, 175, 177-9
Veda 85
Vedānta 20
vehicles 41
verse/s 80, 139-40
  of Hakuun 140
  of Nāgārjuna 26, 151-2, 154
  of Sēngcàn 69
  of Setchō 137
  of Sixth Patriarch 72
  of Vasubandhu 154
vijñāna 126, 153
vijñapti 153, 159
vijñaptimātratā 153
vikalpa 155
Vimalakīrti 72, 74, 119
Vimalakīrtinirdeśa 79
Viṃśatikā 153
vinaya 30
virtue/s 11, 13-14, 28, 42-3, 86-9
void 114-16, 132, 161; *see also* emptiness
wabi 140
waka 99
Watts, Alan 5, 130, 141

way/s
  of salvation 41
  of thinking 4, 6, 127, 137
  of weaving 193
weaving/s 192–3, 197, 201
weft 193, 197
Weltbejahung 99
Weltgestaltung 99
West 4, 7, 32, 39, 42, 79, 83, 86–7, 89–94, 96, 101, 110, 121, 126–30, 133–4, 137, 192, 200
Western
  mind, world, etc. 1–5, 7, 25, 39, 42, 45, 66, 76, 86, 101, 114, 127–9, 132–3, 136, 139, 158, 169
  Paradise, Pure Land 37, 51, 142
Westerners 4, 121, 132, 169
wheel (turner) 88–9, 140
Whitehead (Alfred North) 4
whiteness 99–100
will 14–15, 33, 39, 140
  of God 86
  self-will 30
wisdom 4, 13, 20, 25, 30, 46, 73, 127, 133, 146, 160, 188
  of the Buddha 14, 21
  great wisdom 119–20, 137–9, 196
  non-discriminative 154–60, 163–4
  perfection of 5, 86, 111, 138, 149, 160, 162–3
women (woman) 105, 118–19, 121, 166
work/ing 58, 80–81, 99, 104, 111–13, 115, 121, 138, 191–2, 196, 199, 201, 205
works (religious) 28–30, 73, 99, 144
World Congress of Faiths 143
world/s (erring, real, etc) 7, 11–15, 17, 19–20, 23, 37, 40–46, 49–51, 56, 59, 74, 77, 79, 83–85, 88–9, 94–6, 99–100, 104–6, 112, 114, 116, 121, 129, 131, 133–4, 136–40, 142–3, 157, 164, 175, 177–9, 167–8, 181–2, 184–6, 191–2, 197, 199–200, 205, 236
  order 2, 11, 15
  pure/impure 13–15, 184–5, 199, 204
  religions 92–3
  worldly 84, 126, 191

worlds 83, 185
worldview 40
World Congress of Faiths 143
worship/er 17, 33–4, 40, 70, 80
Wúménguān 68, 74, 113
wúyī 112
Wǔzǔ 223

Xīnfǎyào 68
Xìnxīnmíng 69
Xuánzàng 157
Xuědòu 137
Xuèmàimòlúnlùn 68

ya-fūryū 140
Yajñadatta 71
Yakushi 24
Yamabe, Shūgaku 236
yamatodamashii 57
Yamunā 84
Yanagi Sōetsu 6–7, 183
Yasutomi Shin'ya 237
Yellow River 137
Yìxúan
Yìxuán 22, 109, 136
Yogācāra 153, 156–9
Yōka (Taishi) 68, 115
yōkigurashi 179
Yokogawa Kenshō 236
Yokoyama, Wayne S. 3, 6, 47, 59, 173, 182
yòng 111
Yǒngjiā 68, 78, 115
Yoshikawa, Kōjirō 160
Yuánwù 22, 136
Yuishinshōmon 70
Yúnmén 22, 71

zazen 42
zentaisei 158
Zhàozhōu 4, 71, 109–10, 117–21, 125
Zhèngdaò 115
Zhēnjì 109
Zhíyǐ 2
Zhōng 26
Zhuāngzǐ (Chuang-Tze) 132
Zukunft 108

www.ingramcontent.com/pod-product-compliance
Lightning Source LLC
Chambersburg PA
CBHW070322240426
43671CB00013BA/2332